Muslims and Sarkar-i-Khalsa

Sikh Warrior
'The Awakening'

Narindar Singh Dhesi

Published by

The Naval & Military Press Ltd
Unit 5 Riverside, Brambleside
Bellbrook Industrial Estate
Uckfield, East Sussex
TN22 1QQ England

Tel: +44 (0) 1825 749494

www.naval-military-press.com
www.nmarchive.com

© Copyright Narinda Singh Dhesi

Baba Sain Mir Mohammed Sahib (Mian Mir),
Who laid the foundation of the Harmandire Sahib.

Contents

Sikh Warrior 1
Baba Sain Mir Mohammed Sahib (Mian Mir) 2
Contents 3
Forward 4
Introduction 5
Dedication 6
Punjab 7
The Early Years 8
Islamic invasions 15
The Sikh Gurus 19
Banda Singh Bahadur 38
Sikh Jathas 40
Dal Khalsa 42
Misldars 43
Sikh Jathas 51
Sikhs and Mughals 52
Sikhs and Afghans 54
Sikh Confederacy 55
Ancestry of Ranjit Singh 62
Sardar Ranjit Singh 68
Sarkar-i-Khalsa 74
First Anglo-Sikh war 158
Second Anglo-Sikh war 200
Post-Maharajah Ranjit Singh period 228
Appendix 235
Sources 251
Index 252

Foreword

The history of India in the eighteenth century is mainly a record of anarchy and confusion, selfishness, cowardice and treachery, unpatriotic betrayals and horrible reigns of terror, the tyranny of the strong, the agony of the weak and the futility of isolated attempts. The depth of this gloom is, however, relieved by the story of the rise of Sikh political power, as a result of the collective endeavour of a united people. Guru Gobind Singh first made the Sikhs a militant nation. He inspired the proverbial sparrow to turn around and put to rout the pursuing hawk. He placed his faith in the collective wisdom of the community and not in the devotion of a favourite disciple. The rise of Sikh power in Punjab, in the early nineteenth century and its precipitous decline after the death of Maharajah Ranjit Singh has been touched on by several authors in noteworthy efforts. After writing a number of books on various aspects of Sikh history which have been very well received, Narindar Dhesi in his present book has taken on the period of Maharajah Ranjit Singh and its immediate aftermath. He analytically brings out how Maharajah Ranjit Singh in a very short time span not only expanded his empire in all directions, but more importantly, was able to win over the loyalty of Muslims, Afghans and Kashmiris. His successors faltered amidst their own machinations and the Sikh Empire, which was considered undefeatable, was demolished? A period is to be judged by its results and not by its episodes. In the Sikh annals we do not read of great battles or prolonged sieges, brilliant strategy or novel tactics. A nation was up in arms against its enemies and it is the collective efforts of the masses rather than individual achievements that ultimately made the Sikh Empire a success. Naturally enough, the story is of great things and small; but, when all is said, blunders effaced the readiness for self-sacrifice displayed by the whole people. It is the peculiar tragedy of Sikh history that the very success of the collective struggle had in it the germs of its failure. The "theocratic confederate feudalism" succeeded where a centralized monarchy would have failed. But in its very success were concealed the germs of dissolution.

Narinder Dhesi, in simple and lucid language, illuminates how and why this happened. It is a well-researched effort and I commend it to the readers.

Chandigarh   Lieutenant General B S Dhaliwal (Retd)

Introduction

It is a book about the Sikh Gurus and their amicable relations with the Muslims. It continues with the repression of the tiny community by the Mughals and the Afghans. After much bloodletting, Sikhs became sovereign of the Punjab, led by Maharajah Ranjit Singh. He rose from the status of a petty chieftain of a few villages and by welding together the rude Barons of the Sikh Confederacy became a King of an Empire extending from Tibet to the deserts of Sindh and from the Khyber Pass to the Satluj. He died in 1839. Yet within a few years of his death, all the hard-earned and cherished victories of the 'Lion of the Punjab' were wasted by his unscrupulous successors, and subsequently the Sikh kingdom fell to the British. 'The Sikh monarchy founded by Ranjit Singh was 'Napoleonic in the suddenness of its rise, the brilliancy of its success and the completeness of its overthrow'. His foresight and his fair conduct earned him the allegiance and loyalty of the Muslim majority in the Punjab. Despite the Muslim repression in the rich history of the Sikhs, he skilfully handled the relationship between Sikhs and Muslims. At his death the British East India Company cunningly exploited this opportunity and waged wars against the Sikhs to realize their long-held dream of taking over the Punjab. The British and their Dogra allies were successful in capitalizing on the situation and were able to capture and merge the Punjab into the British Raj. An attempt has been made in this book to in how some Muslim states reacted to the declining Sikh rule in the Punjab and their policies. It is ironic as some of the Muslim soldiers paid the ultimate price in the defence of the Punjab, while the Sikh royalty and Dogras were in league with the enemy to shatter the Punjabi army!

Thanks very much to Lieutenant General B S Dhaliwal (Retd), for writing the foreword to this book.

Narindar Singh Dhesi

Dedication

for

Emperor Ranjit Singh

and

My darling Grandchildren:

Laurie Michael Singh Dhesi
Clara Rosalind Kaur Dhesi

Emperor Ranjit Singh

Punjab

The Punjab

Sikh homeland, the Punjab, is a very fertile region in the Northwest of India. The word Punjab is a compound of two Persian words, *Panj* ("five") and *ab* ("water"), thus signifying the land of five waters, or rivers. Punjab spans three physiographic regions, the smallest being the Siwalik Range in the northeast, where elevations reach about 3,000 feet. Farther south, the narrow, undulating foothill region is dissected by closely spaced seasonal torrents, locally known as *Chos*, several of which terminate in the plain below without joining any stream. To the south and west of the foothills lies the broad flat tract, with low-lying floodplains separated by slightly elevated uplands. This region, with its fertile alluvial soils, slopes gently from an elevation of about 900 feet in the northeast to about 550 feet in the southwest. The south-western part of the plains, formerly strewn with sand dunes, has mostly been levelled off with the expansion of irrigation projects. Punjab has an inland subtropical location, and its climate is continental, being semiarid to sub humid. Summers are very hot. In June, the warmest month, daily temperatures in Ludhiana usually reach about 100 °F from a low in the upper 70s F. In January, the coolest month, daily temperatures normally rise from the mid-40s into the mid-60s F. and lowest in the southwest, which may receive less than 12 inches state-wide average annual precipitation is roughly 16 inches. Most of the annual rainfall occurs from July to September, the months of the southwest monsoon. Winter rains from the western cyclones, occurring from December to March, account for less than one-fourth of the total rainfall.

The Punjab, being the main gateway into India, was fated to be the perpetual field of battle and the first home of all the conquerors. Few Nin their conquered domains acquired local women. Thus the blood of many conquering races came to mingle, and many alien languages came to be spoken in the land. Out of the mixture of blood and speech were born the Punjabi people and their language. By the end of 15TH century, the different races that had come together in the Punjab had lost the nostalgic memories of the lands of their birth and began to develop an attachment to the land of their adoption. The chief factor in the growth of Punjabi consciousness was the evolution of one common tongue from Babel of languages. Although the Punjabis were divided into Hindus and Muslims, attempts had been made to bring about a rapprochement between the two faiths and certain desire to live and let live had grown among the people. It was left to Sikh Gurus to harness the spirit of tolerance among the Punjabis.

The Early Years

Stone Age, (70000 BC–3 300 BC)
One of the earliest Stone Age cultures of South Asia was nourished in the Punjab. Oldest Homo sapiens lived here from 5–2 million years ago. Many articles of Stone Age are found from different Archaeological sites and are displayed at different museums of Pakistan.

Mehrgarh Culture, (7000 BC–2600 BC)
Mehrgarh, one of the most important Neolithic sites in archaeology, lies on the Western edge of the Indus valley, where a large urban civilization emerged at the same time as those of Mesopotamia and the ancient Egyptian Empire. Early Mehrgarh residents lived in mud brick houses, stored their grain in granaries, fashioned tools with local copper ore and lined their large basket containers with bitumen. They cultivated six-row barley, einkorn and emmer wheat, jujubes and dates, and herded sheep, goats and cattle. The site was occupied continuously until about 2600 BC. Mehrgarh is now seen as a precursor to the Indus Valley Civilization.

Indus Valley Civilization, (3300 BC–1500 BC)
The Indus Valley civilization, flourished from about 3300 B.C. to about 1500 B.C. At its height, its geographical reach exceeded that of Egypt or Mesopotamia. The chief cities of the Indus civilization had large complex hill citadels, housing palaces, granaries and baths. Houses, often two-storied and spacious, lined the town streets; they had drainage systems that led into brick-lined sewers. The economy of the Indus Civilization was based on a highly organized agriculture, supplemented by an active commerce, probably connected to that of the ancient civilizations of Mesopotamia. The origin, rise and decline of the Indus valley civilization remain a mystery, but it seems most probable that the civilization fell (1500 B.C.) to invading Aryans.

The Aryans, (1500 BC)
The Indo–Europeans, emerging from the Russian steppes in the region of the Caspian Sea, started spreading to Greece, Europe, and Asia Minor in search of pasture. By this time, they were known as Aryans. By 1500 B.C., a wave of them pushed through the passes of the Hindu Kush Mountains to the Punjab, where they destroyed an advanced Indus Valley Civilization. 'The coming of the Aryans was a backward step, since the Harappa culture had been far more advanced than that of the Aryans who were yet pre-urban.'(Khushwant Singh). The next thousand years' history of the Punjab is dominated by the Aryans.

The Early Years

The Aryans, (Contd)

The primitive Aryans were not allowed to settle in the Punjab unmolested as long and bloody struggles were maintained in the wild. The life of the Aryans in the Punjab was martial and manly. Their warlike character developed and they adapted themselves to the conditions of tropical climate, very different to their cold, northern home. The Aryans spoke Sanskrit, which became the common language of the people. It was in the Punjab that Vedic Hinduism was evolved and the four Vedas, the oldest living scriptures in the world, composed around 1500-1700 BC, supplies evidence concerning the life of the Aryans who settled in the Punjab. The Aryans were a spirit-drinking race and indulged freely in drinking beer, wine and spirit. Sages and saints drank alcohol and offered the fermented juice to the gods. The Aryans were tall and fair, and the people they subjugated were darker and of alien culture, of whom the Aryans were contemptuous. As they wanted to maintain the purity of their race, they developed a system of social exclusiveness, by breaking the society into separate Units: The Caste System. The caste system was enforced as law throughout the subcontinent until the adoption of the Indian Constitution in 1949, which outlawed the caste system. However, it remains a deeply ingrained social structure, particularly in rural India. There are four main castes into which everyone was categorized. At the very top were the Brahmins – (priests), scholars, and philosophers. The second highest caste was the Kshatriyas. These were the warriors, rulers, and those concerned with the defence and administration of the village or state. Third the Vaishyas, who were traders, merchants, and people involved in agricultural production. The lowest caste was the Shudras - the labourers and servants for the other castes. Each caste included many hierarchical sub castes divided by occupation. Below the Shudras were the Untouchables. These people had no caste at all. They performed the most menial of jobs, such as dealing with dead bodies and cleaning toilets. Higher-caste people believed that if they touched one of the casteless, they would be contaminated and would need to go through cleansing rituals. Caste was determined by birth - you fell into the same caste as your parents, and there was almost no way to change it. The caste system dictated your occupation, choice of spouse and many other aspects of your life. If you did something outside your caste, you could be excommunicated from your caste.

The Early Years

The Persians, (516 – 485 BC)

The foundation of classical Persian culture was the Achaemenid Empire. Created in 550 BC, Achaemenid Empire was one of the largest land empires in the world at that time. The location of the Punjab was on the outskirts of the Great Persian Empire. Indian emissaries were present at the courts of Cyrus the Great. It is also believed that when Cyrus was threatened by Croesus of Lydia, he received military assistance from at least one Indian king. Under Darius, parts of India became the 24TH province of the Persian Empire. Under Xerxes I, the successor of Darius, Indians fought alongside the Persian Army against the Greeks in the battlefields of Plataea and Marathon. The Persian Empire under the Achaemenid dynasty came to an end when Alexander defeated Darius in the battle of Arebala and paved the way for Alexander to penetrate the Punjab.

King Porus

When Alexander occupied Gandhara, (Afghanistan) the Indian kingdoms had already regained their independence. While many clans and their chiefs were busy carving out principalities for themselves in the Punjab and the Northwest of India, a chief of the Paurava tribe, called King Porus also set up an independent kingdom between the Jhelum and the Chenab. While the Persians influenced secularist and central theory of government, under the shadow of Achaemenid institutions at Taxila, the elements of anarchy, isolation and tribalism in the Punjab were being fought by King Porus. At the same time, a scion of the Ambha family, who was called Ambhi, established himself at Taxila. Naturally, the relations between King Porus and Ambhi were strained, for being neighbours they had a conflict of interests. Porus not only struck East and South but also exerted relentless pressure in the North and the West with the result that his next-door neighbour Ambhi was seriously menaced and profoundly perturbed by him. Hence, to cope with the menace, he had trained most of the husbandmen of his kingdom into soldiers. While these preparations were going on, Alexander appeared on the horizon. Ambhi took the occasion by the forelock and hastened to befriend him to secure his assistance against King Porus and his ally.

The Early Years

Alexander of Macedon, (326 BC)
In 336 BC when Alexander succeeded to the Macedon throne. In 334 BC he invaded Persian-ruled Asia Minor, and began a series of campaigns lasting ten years. He broke the power of Persia in a series of battles, most notably the decisive battle of Gaugamela where the Punjabis had fought alongside the Persians. Subsequently he overthrew the Persian king Darius III; this left him to campaign to the furthest limits of the Achaemenid Empire. Porus, the King of the Punjab, had come to the aid of Darius, but when he heard that Darius was slain, he returned to his country together with his troops. The fame of the might of Porus, his help to Darius with dispatch of his elephant corps and the view that it was not desirable to let a powerful king live and flourish across the frontier of an empire, compelled Alexander to gather his armies together, and command his soldiers to march against Porus. Alexander crossed the mountains at Attock and proceeded to Taxila, where he partook of the hospitality of its King Ambhi. From Taxila, he invited all the local rulers of the Punjab to submit to his authority. Some of the rulers did the same, but the ruler of the kingdom between the rivers Hydaspes (Jehlum) and Akesines (Chenab), the legendary king Porus, refused to submit to his authority. As a result, fierce battle took place. Both sides suffered heavy casualties. Porus lost his sons and got injured. In the end Alexander's forces took over the Punjab and they brought Porus to Alexander's court. Here the legendary conversation took place. Alexander asked Porus "How should I treat you?". Porus shot back "In the same way as a king treats another king". Alexander was struck by his genius and bravery. He not only returned the kingdom back to Porus but added to his original territory another of still greater extent. The battle of Jhelum ended in a treaty of peace between Porus and Alexander and the joint endeavour of both of them in reducing the independent tribes of the Punjab. The Greeks were involved in some very had fought battles across the five rivers of the Punjab. The resistance and fighting was so fierce that Alexander's soldiers mutinied, laid down their arms and refused to advance any further. Alexander, leaving garrisons and governors in the Punjab, marched away with the remnants of his armies in 326 BC to Persia and Susa. Alexander had conquered the whole of the then known world. He died in his palace in Babylon on June 10^{Tth} or 11TH, 323 B.C., in the 32ND year of his age. Within a few years of his death his vast empire divided among his generals, so that nothing remained of him but his name. Porus was recognised as the undisputed master of the Punjab to the East of Jhelum.

The Early Years

The Maurya Empire, (322 BC –185 BC)
Under Chandragupta, the Maurya Empire liberated the Trans-Indus, which was under Macedonian occupation. The Maurya dynasty was the largest and most powerful political and military empire of ancient India. At its greatest extent, the empire stretched to the North along the natural boundaries of the Himalayas, and to the East stretching into what is now Assam. To the West, it conquered beyond modern Pakistan, annexing Baluchistan, South Eastern parts of Iran and much of what is now Afghanistan, including the modern Herat and Kandahar provinces. Chandragupta's grandson Ashoka ruled 273-232 BC. When he personally witnessed the devastation and destruction of war, Ashoka embraced the teachings of Gautama Buddha, and renounced war and violence. Ashoka sponsored the spreading of Buddhist ideals into Sri Lanka, South East Asia, West Asia and Mediterranean Europe. The reign of Ashoka was followed for 50 years by a succession of weaker kings. Brhadrata, the last ruler of the Maurya dynasty, ruled territories that had shrunk considerably from the time of emperor Ashoka, but he was still upholding the Buddhist faith. He was assassinated in 185 B.C. during a military parade by the commander-in-chief of his guard. The fall of the Maurya Empire left the Khyber Pass unguarded, and waves of foreign invasions followed. The Greco-Bactrian king, Demetrius, capitalized on the break-up, conquered Southern Afghanistan and the Punjab around 180 BC, forming the Indo-Greek Kingdom

Indo-Bactrian kingdom, (189 BC)
The kingdom was founded when the Graeco-Bactrian king Demetrius invaded India early in the 2ND century BC. The Greeks in India were eventually divided from the Graeco-Bactrians centred in Bactria. The most famous Indo-Greek ruler was Menander (Milinda). He had his capital at Sakala (modern Sialkot) in the Punjab, modern Pakistan, and he successfully invaded the Ganges-Yamuna Doab. During the two centuries of their rule, the Indo-Greek kings combined the Greek and Indian languages and symbols, as seen on their coins, and blended ancient Greek, Hindu and Buddhist religious practices, as seen in the archaeological remains of their cities and in the indications of their support of Buddhism, pointing to a rich fusion of Indian and Hellenistic influences. The Indo-Greeks ultimately disappeared as a political entity following the invasions of the Indo-Scythians. The kingdom of the last Indo-Greek king Strato was taken over by the Scythian ruler Rajuvula around 10 AD.

The Early Years

Scythians, (80 BC)
Scythians had their own kingdom north of the Black Sea. They had proved dangerous opponents for Persians, Macedonians and Bactrians. The Scythian tribes had poured into Persia. The Persians had fought desperately but were finally defeated. The Scythian hordes then continued their march towards India. They forced the Bolan Pass to conquer Sindh, and then swept up the Indus and occupied Taxila and Gandhara. The Scythian king Maues and his successor Azes in the process had destroyed any remaining Greek power in the Punjab. After the death of Azes, the rule of the Scythians in North-western India was shattered with the rise of the Parthian ruler Gondophares in the last years of the 1ST century BC.

Parthian Empire
After the death of Gondophares I, the Parthian empire started to fragment. The name or title Gondophares was adopted by Sarpedones, who become Gondophares II. The most important successor was Abdagases, Gondophares' nephew, who ruled in the Punjab. There were other minor kings but the Indo-Parthians never regained the position of Gondophares I, and from the middle of the 1ST century AD the Kushans under Kujula Khadphides began absorbing the Northern Indian part of the kingdom that was now expanding into India to create a Kushan Empire.

Kushan Empire
Their traditional raids into the Chinese empire were denied to them by the construction of the great wall. The Kushans cleared the Scythians from the lands surrounding the Aral Sea and occupied Bactria. The leading chief Kujula Khadphides then led them to the Punjab, destroying the Scythian kingdom of Gondophares. He also established himself in Kashmir by defeating the military governor Hermaues. When Kanishka ascended the throne, his empire consisted of Afghanistan, Sind, Punjab, Kashmir, and most of the Genetic valley. He annexed three provinces of the Chinese empire, namely, Tashkent, Khotan and Yarkhand. Kanishka's immediate successor was Vashiska who was then succeeded by Huvishka. Mathura became the centre of the Kushans. Many monuments were erected during Huvishka's reign. The last great king of the Kushans was Vasudev I. The Kushans were overthrown by the Sassanians of Persia in the Northwest and the Guptas in the North.

The Early Years

Gupta Dynasty, (320 AD)
The Gupta Empire was one of the largest political and military empires in the world and covered most of Northern India. The time of the Gupta Empire is referred to as the Golden Age of India. Historians place the Gupta dynasty alongside the Han Dynasty, Tang Dynasty and Roman Empire as a model of a classical civilization. The Gupta dynasty was founded by a man known as Chandra Gupta I. During his reign Chandra Gupta extended his empire and controlled a substantial area of North India. There was renewed enthusiasm in religions like Hinduism and the world's first universities were established. The Guptas were able to check further invasions from central Asia for a considerable time, but the Huns overran the empire by 500 AD.

The Huns, (480 AD)
The Hephthalites, also known as the White Huns, were a nomadic confederation in Central Asia. A branch of them stormed upon Europe and devastated the Roman Empire. In Northern India, the Guptas put up fierce resistance to keep the Huns out. Eventually they broke through. The Hun king Tormana created an independent kingdom in Northern and central India. The Guptas continued to resist the Huns, and allied with the rulers of the neighboring Indian states. The Huns suffered a defeat by Yasodharman of Malwa in 528 AD, and by 542 AD Tormana's successor Mihirakula had been driven off the plains of Northern India, taking refuge in Kashmir, and he is thought to have died soon after. Mihirakula is remembered in contemporary Indian and Chinese histories for his cruelty and his destruction of temples and monasteries, with particular hostility towards Buddhism. After the end of the sixth century little is recorded in India about the Huns, and what happened to them is unclear; some historians surmise that the remaining Huns were assimilated into the South Indian population.

King Vardhana, (606 AD)
Harsha Vardhana was an Indian emperor who ruled Northern India from 606 to 647. King Harsha blocked the mountain passes against future invasions. He was tolerant towards all other religions and supported them fully. At Harsha's death, apparently without any heirs, his empire died with him. The kingdom disintegrated rapidly into small states as the invaders once again forced open the Hindu Kush passes and poured into Northern India.

The Early Years

The Delhi Sultanate, (1206-1526 AD)
Prince Mohammad of the Ghur dynasty invaded the Punjab in 1206. Taking Peshawar and Lahore and crossing the Satluj, he captured Bhatinda. He defeated and killed the rajah of Delhi at the battle of Tarain. He went on to conquer Delhi and establish the Sultanate. The Delhi Sultanate is a term used to cover five short-lived dynasties. The sultanates ruled from Delhi between 1206 and 1526, when the last was replaced by the Mughal dynasty. The Delhi Sultanate was founded in 1206 and lasted for 320 years.

Genghis Khan
From the establishment of Delhi Sultanate, the Punjab bore the brunt of foreign attacks. In this painful process, the Punjab's population and prosperity diminished and its entire life was crippled. Despite the strenuous efforts of the Delhi Sultans to secure the Northern frontiers, Genghis Khan, through a series of battering raids between 1229 and 1241, took control of the Punjab. The Mongols remained in the Punjab until about 1270.

Tamerlane, (1398)
In 1398 came the visitation of Tamerlane, the Mongol descendant of Genghis Khan. With one of his grandsons taking Lahore and the other Multan, he fell on the plains and the cities. All the towns and cities were raised to the ground and one hundred thousand people were put to the sword. The same fate awaited the people of Delhi, where he created more carnage and devastation. He is described as having been pleased that he had penetrated India more deeply than had Alexander the Great or Genghis Khan. Leaving behind famine and decades of anarchy, he finally re-crossed the mountains and returned with Indian artists, craftsmen, and booty.

Islamic Invasions

Sindh
During the Caliphate of Muawiyah, six expeditions were lead by the Arabs to that Makran or Baluchistan was finally subjugated. Muhammad captured Sindh including Multan after a year in 713. At this stage Muhammad was recalled and there was again a revival of Hindu power and the Arabs were able to retain only a toehold of land along the coastal strip. In 718, Junaid the then Governor of Sindh again defeated Dahir's son and pressed forward into Gujarat and Kashmir, where their advances were checked and thus the Arabs were confined only to Sindh.

Islamic Invasions

Afghanistan

Afghanistan, as late as the seventh century, formed part of India both politically and culturally and constituted the borders of India. Immediately after the fall of Persia, the Muslims turned their attention to it. After initial attacks which were repulsed, the province of Seistan was annexed in 653. They lost it for a while in 683. Attempts to annex the rest of the kingdom were made repeatedly but Ranbal; the ruler repulsed them with bravery. Ultimately, by deceit both kingdoms were captured by the Turk Yakub in 870 AD thus ending the glorious resistance of this border state against mighty hordes for over two hundred years. Even then the kingdom was not fully subjugated and the Shahis continued to rule Kabul until the ruler of Ghazni, Sabuktigin, finally conquered Kabul in 987.

Mahmud of Ghazni

Mahmud of Ghazni was the first sultan of the Ghaznavid dynasty in Afghanistan. He plundered wealthy India and used the booty to patronize culture in Ghazni, making it the centre of Perso-Islamic civilization. Born on November 2ND, 971, eldest son of Emir Sabuktigin, Mahmud helped his father gain a kingdom from the Samanids through successful campaigns against Turkish nobles of Samarkand and Bukhara. Mahmud was confirmed as sultan of Ghazni by Caliph al-Kadir. Mahmud repulsed all attempts against his territories. Mahmud is chiefly remembered as the plunderer of India. Between 1000 and 1026 he mounted at least 17 raids against India with the aim of extirpating idol-worshiping Hindu infidels and destroying Hindu temples, which were great repositories of wealth. His most important expedition was against the temple of Somnath in 1025. It is estimated that Mahmud took from India jewels, gold, and silver in excess of 3 billion dinars, in addition to hundreds of thousands of slaves. His only territorial acquisition in India was the Punjab (1021). Fanatical, cruel to Hindus as well as to Moslem heretics, fickle, and uncertain in temper, Mahmud was extremely greedy of wealth. When Mahmud was about to die, he ordered all his hoards to be placed before his eyes. He grieved over his impending separation from his wealth but refused to give the smallest amount to charity. Yet though he loved money passionately, he also spent it lavishly. To his court came scholars like al-Biruni; Utbi, the historian; Farabi, the philosopher; and Baihaki, the diarist. Mahmud became the hero of many legends, many of them entering on his relationship with his favourite slave, Ayaz. He died on April 30TH, 1030, and his tomb at Ghazni has survived.

Islamic Invasions

Mohammad Ghori

Meanwhile the Ghori replaced the Ghazni's in Kabul. He fortified Multan and attacked Gujarat but his army was routed. He therefore captured southern Sindh and Lahore. Ghori attacked the Bhatinda fort in 1189 and captured it because of lax defence. Prithviraj with a large army laid a siege in 1191. In the fierce battle that ensued Mohammad Ghori's army was completely routed and he had to flee. Several more attacks were made but they were repulsed. He asked for truce until he received his brother's instructions. Prithviraj fell for the ruse and spent the night in revelry. The same night Mohammad Ghori made a surprise attack from the rear. In the Fierce battle that ensued, Prithviraj lost his life and Delhi fell into the hands of the Muslims. Mohammad Ghori appointed Kutbuddin Aibak, his Turkish slave as his representative in India. In 1197, Kanauj, Janupur and Mirzapur came under his control. Mohammad Ghori was murdered in 1206. Muhammad's death left his generals in control of the whole of North India. He was succeeded by Qutb-ud-din Aybak, who had started off by sacking Ajodhya in 1193. Then served as Muhammad's governor in India. He was Sultan until 1210, claiming the title "Sultan of Delhi. His established the Ghulam Dynasty, which ruled until 1290.

Iltutmish

After a brief rule by his son, his son-in-law, Iltutmish seized power and ruled until 1235. During his reign the dreaded Chengiz Khan the Mongol (Mongols or Hoons as we called them were from the Central Asian steppes and were nominally Buddhists then), after destroying the Islamic kingdoms elsewhere came upto Indus in 1221 in pursuit of a Muslim king and caused a scare. Iltutmish put down a number of rebellious governors and also was the first Muslim ruler to be recognised as a Sultan by the Caliph of Baghdad. He expanded his territory by annexing Gwalior and Malwa. The famous Mahakal temple of Ujjain was destroyed. A number of his descendants including his well known daughter Razia ruled until 1266. In 1266, Balban, a Turk and a powerful Wazir of the last Sultan killed him and ruled during 1266-87.

Alauddin

In 1296, Alauddin, subdued the Yadava king, Ramdeo and overran Gujarat and plundered many temples including Somnath. The impregnable fort of Ranthambhor was captured. He next turned his eyes towards Chitor which was captured in 1303. Gradually Mandi, Dhar, Ujjain and Chandri were also taken and Alauddin became the emperor of North India. Now Alauddin turned his attention to the south.

Islamic Invasions

Alauddin (Contd)

He defeated Ramdeo again but treated him honourably and married his daughter so that he had a Hindu ally in South. He now sent his able general, Malik Kafur, further south; Kafur attacked and made successful treaties with the kings of Warangal and Hoysala. The Pandyan territory was attacked next and Kafur returned to Delhi in 1311 with a large booty. Ramdeo died in 1312, and his son resisted the Muslims. Again Kafur raided the south and killed him and installed another king. These raids did not annex the south politically but facilitated establishment of small Muslim kingdoms in the south. Alauddin died in 1316 and thus ended the career of the 'most ruthless empire builder and conqueror in the world history'.

Ghiyasuddin Tughlaq

Ghazi Malik Tughlaq of Turkish blood ultimately crowned himself Sultan under the title Ghiyasuddin Tughlaq. Rebellions took place all over but were crushed. Tughlaq's policy of replacing local Hindu chieftains with Muslim governors enabled the establishment of many local Muslim kingdoms and hence Muslims effectively ruled a large portion of India during this period.

Lodhi

The Lodhi dynasty was an Afghan dynasty that ruled the Delhi Sultanate from 1451 to 1526. It was the last dynasty of the Delhi Sultanate, and was founded by Bahlul Khan Lodi when he replaced the Sayyid dynasty. Daulat Khan Lodhi, who was the Subedar of Punjab, invited Babar, the then king of Kabul and Kandahar, and a descendent of Chengiz Khan and Timur. Babar had already attempted unsuccessfully to penetrate India. But now he descended with full force and in the first battle of Panipat in 1526 defeated Ibrahim Lodhi and became the ruler and started a new epoch in Indian history of the Mughal Rule.

The Mughals

Zahiruddin Babbar made his first advance upon India in 1519 and reached Bhera in the Punjab. The fort of Birhala, with all its treasures, fell into his hands. In 1520, he again marched into India and captured Sialkot and Syadpur, and massacred the inhabitants or carried them to slavery. In 1525, he plundered Lahore and defeated the Sultan's Army with great slaughter. As he advanced on Delhi, Sultan Ibrahim Lodhi offered him battle at Panipat. With his seasoned soldiers and strong Artillery, Babbar defeated and killed Ibrahim Lodhi and went on to lay the foundation of the Mughal Empire.

Sikh Gurus

Guru Nanak Dev

Guru Nanak Dev was born about 40 miles from Lahore in 1469. His family were Hindus, but Guru Nanak Dev soon showed an advanced interest in religion and studied Islam and Hinduism extensively. At that time the Ulema controlled the religious and social life of the Muslim society. They generally supported the rulers in their policy of intolerance towards the majority population in the country. Zia-ud-din Barani, the famous historian and scholar, admitted that they wrongly interpret the Holy Quran to meet the wishes of the rulers. The Ulema did not lead the Muslim society for piety and virtue. The Hindu society was engaged in meaningless ritual, Idol worship and practiced the Caste System. As a child Guru Nanak Dev demonstrated great ability as a poet and philosopher. He worked for a while as an accountant but while still quite young decided to devote himself to spiritual matters. He was inspired by a powerful spiritual experience that gave him a vision of the true nature of God, and confirmed his idea that the way to spiritual growth was through meditation and through living in a way that reflected the presence of the divine within each human being. In 1496, Guru Nanak Dev set out on a set of spiritual journeys through India, Tibet and Arabia that lasted nearly 30 years. Bhai Mardana accompanied Guru Nanak Dev on his journeys across India and Asia. He studied and debated with the learned men he met along the way and as his ideas took shape he began to teach a new route to spiritual fulfilment and the good life. The last part of his life was spent at Kartarpur in the Punjab, where he was joined by many disciples attracted by his teachings. The most famous teachings attributed to Guru Nanak Dev are that there is only one God, and that all human beings can have direct access to God with no need of rituals or priests. His most radical social teachings denounced the caste system and taught that everyone is equal, regardless of caste or gender. Guru Nanak Dev was one of the greatest religious innovators of all time and the founder of the Sikh religion. It is part of Sikh religious belief that the spirit of Guru Nanak's sanctity, divinity and religious authority descended upon each of the nine subsequent Gurus when the Guruship was devolved on to them. Guru Nanak Dev appointed Bhai Lehna as the successor Guru. Guru Nanak said that every individual has a right to food regardless of social status, religion, background and beliefs. We are blessed to be part of a principle started by the Guru Nanak and followed by proceeding Gurus. Guru Nanak Dev died on 22ND September 1539 in Kartarpur, at the age of 70.

Sikh Gurus

Bhai Mardana

Bhai Mardana was the first Sikh and long time companion of Guru Nanak Dev, first in the line of gurus noted as Sikh. Bhai Mardana accompanied Guru Nanak Dev on his journeys across India and Asia. He was born in a Muslim family, to a Mirasi couple, Badra and Lakkho, of Rai Bhoi di Talwandi, now Nankana Sahib of Pakistan. Bhai Mardana first contacted Guru Nanak Dev to seek help as many people in his family were dying at a young age. Guru Nanak Dev approached the family and had seen that Mardana's mother was crying because she felt her son will die. Mardana's mother told Guru Ji that the reason she was crying is because all her children were dying. Following this, Guru Ji asked what her son's name was, to which she responded "MarJana" meaning "He will die". Guru Nanak Dev kindly asked the mother if she is willing to give him her son so that she will not have to bear the burden of her child's death. The mother accepted this and gave her son to Guru Nanak Dev to take care of. As a result of this, Guru Nanak Dev gave Bhai Mardana the assurance that henceforth people in his clan will not die early. It is said that Mar-Da-Na means 'Does not die'. Guru Nanak Dev and Mardana were brought up in the same village. Bhai Mardana was ten years elder to Guru Nanak Dev and was his companion since his childhood days. Bhai Mardana sang hymns written by Kabir, Trilochan, Ravidas, Dhana and Bern. When Guru Nanak Dev took charge of the granaries and stores of the Nawab of Sultanpur Lodhi, he became known for his generosity. Mardana was by then married and had two sons and a daughter, Mardana went to meet Guru Nanak as Guru Nanak's father wanted news of his son, Bhai Mardana never went back from his trip and was with Guru Nanak Dev from then on. He used to play the Rabab or rebeck as Guru Nanak Dev spoke/sang his words about God. When Guru Nanak planned to travel the world to spread his message, he wanted Mardana to accompany him, Mardana wanted to marry off his daughter before doing so, Bhai Baghirath a disciple of Guru Nanak helped Bhai Mardana materially to enable the daughter's marriage and allow Mardana to accompany Guru Nanak. The chronicles of their travels use Mardana to show worldly doubts and bring forth Guru Nanak Ji's message, in many situations Bhai Mardana is portrayed as doubtful and wanting clarifications in every situation. The Puratan Janam Sakhi tells of these situations. In 1534, Bhai Mardana fell ill at Baghdad, where Baba Nanak Ji buried him near today's Baghdad Railway Station. Bhai Mardana also wrote poetry. One of his compositions appears in the Guru Granth Sahib in Bihagadre ki Var.

Sikh Gurus

Rai Bular

Rai Bular, a Muhammadan noble of the Bhatti clan, was the chief of Talwandi Rai Bhoi, the village where Guru Nanak Dev was born in 1469. Rai Bular perceived the Divine in Guru Nanak and became a devotee. Once young Guru Nanak Dev was arraigned before him for having allowed the cattle herd he was tending to damage a farmer's crop. The Rai sent for Baba Kalu, the Guru's father, and directed him to compensate the farmer for the damage. But footmen sent to estimate the loss reported that they had seen no damage whatsoever. Rai Bular was as much surprised as the complainant himself, who insisted that he had seen with his own eyes the whole crop ruined and the buffaloes. On another occasion, Guru Nanak Dev, while out with his herd, lay down to rest under a tree in the summer afternoon and fell asleep. After a while, Rai Bular along with his servants happened to pass by. He was surprised to see a strange phenomenon. The shadows of other trees had travelled round with the sun, but not of the tree under which Nanak slept. Returning to the town, the Rai called Father Kalu and said to him, "Your son is a great man. He is the honour of my town. Kalu, thou hast become exalted and I too am exalted in whose town such a one has been born." Guru Nanak Dev reciprocated the honour and affection extended to him by Rai Bular and never failed in between his long travels to visit him, who always felt blessed to see him. Even when he lay dying in 1515 circa, the Guru was by his bedside.

Qazi Ruknuddin

Qazi Ruknuddin, supposed to be a shrine caretaker, chanced to meet Guru Nanak Dev during his visit to Mecca. The Purdtan Janam Sakhi narrates the story: "It had been inscribed in books beforehand that Guru Nanak Dev, a dervish, would come. Then water would rise in the wells of Mecca. The Guru entered the holy precincts. He lay down in the colonnade to rest. Then he fell asleep. His feet were stretched out towards the Ka'ba. Qazi Ruknuddin came to say his namaz. When he is held him lying in this posture, he spoke out, `0 thou, man of God, see!' Thou street chest thy feet towards the House of God, the Ka'ba, Dost thou not see?` The Guru answered, `Where the House of God is not, turn my feet to that direction.` Then Qazi Ruknuddin dragged his feet round. In whatever direction he turned his feet to that direction the Ka'ba was also turning. Qazi Ruknuddin became astonished and kissed his feet, 'He said, `Marvellous, Marvellous! Today I have seen a true Faqir of God'.

Sikh Gurus

Guru Angad Dev

Guru Angad Dev was born on March 31ST, 1504. He succeeded Guru Nanak Devin 1539. Guru Angad Dev committed to writing much about his predecessor and also recorded the results of his own devotional observations which became the nucleus of the sacred writing of the Sikhs. (Adi Granth). Angad also created Gurumukhi, the Punjabi script which gave the Sikhs a written language distinct from the written language of the Hindus or the Muslims and thus fostered a sense of their being a separate people. The second Mughal Emperor of India Humayun visited Guru Angad at around 1540 after Humayun lost the Battle of Kannauj, and thereby the Mughal throne to Sher Shah Suri. Guru Angad is said to have blessed the emperor, and reassured him that someday he will regain the throne. The Guru attached no importance to the incident, and ignored it altogether. Guru Angad Dev passed away in 1552.

Guru Amar Das

Guru Amar Das acceded to the Guruship in 1552. He introduced the Anand Karaj, the Sikh marriage ceremony that is not merely a legal contract but a fusion of souls. He abolished among the Sikhs the Hindu requirement for a married woman to immolate herself on her husband's funeral pyre and encouraged the re-marriage of Hindu widows. He made Langar an integral institution of the Sikh Church by insisting that anyone who wanted to see him had first to accept his hospitality by eating with the disciples, He met the Mughal Emperor Akbar. According to the Sikh legend, he neither received Akbar nor was Akbar directly ushered to him, rather the Guru suggested that Akbar like everyone sit on the floor and eat in the langar with everyone before their first meeting. Akbar, who sought to encourage tolerance and acceptance across religious lines, readily accepted the suggestion. The Sikh hagiographies mention that Guru Amar Das persuaded Akbar to repeal the tax on Hindu pilgrims going to Hardwar, which he did. Akbar also had made up his mind to do something for the house of Nanak. He presented the land of Amritsar to Bhani the daughter of Guru Amar Das as gift in her marriage. He founded centres of Sikh pilgrimage, and picked the site for the Golden Temple. Guru Amar Das remained the leader of the Sikhs till age 95, and named his son-in-law Bhai Jetha later remembered by the name Guru Ram Das as his successor. Guru Amar Das died in Goindwal, on May 14TH, 1574.

Sikh Gurus

Shah Husain

Shah Husain, a Muslim recluse said to have possessed high spiritual powers, was an admirer of Guru Amar Das. He once miraculously cured a genetic lameness of a devoted Sikh whom Guru Amar Das had directed to him. When the Sikh fell at his feet to express his gratefulness, Shah Husain would not take the credit and ascribed the miracle to the Guru. He said 'Guru Amar Das, the benign lord, has helped you. He himself does all, but bestows fame on us. Go, fall at his feet and pay him my respects'.

Allayar

Allayar, a wealthy Muslim horse dealer of Delhi, who turned a preacher of Sikhism, first came to Guru Amar Das at Goindwal escorted by Bhai Paro, a prominent Sikh of Dalla, and a village in present day Kapurthala district of the Punjab. It is said that returning from Kabul once with 500 newly purchased horses, he was held up near Goindwal owing to the River Beas being in spate. He had not been there long before he saw someone tearing across the swollen river on horseback from the opposite bank. This was Bhai Paro coming to make his daily obeisance to Guru Amar Das. Allayar was still wondering at the man's daring when Bhai Paro was again seen emerging from Goindwal and preparing to plunge into the river on his way back. Allayar beckoned him to come near him and asked him what made him run such a great risk. Bhai Paro replied that he had his Guru's protection and felt no risk of any kind. The intrigued merchant begged him to take him to the Guru who inspired such faith and confidence in the heart of his disciple. He was led into the Guru's presence and was converted at first sight. Guru Amar Das remarked to him: "It is difficult to become a Yar (friend) of Allah (God), but I shall make God thy Master and thee His servant." Allayar became a disciple. He left his trade to his son, and devoted himself whole heartedly to the Guru's service. Guru Amar Das appointed him head of a manji or diocese to preach the word of Guru Nanak. In later life, Allayar came to reside near his friend Bhai Paro, at village Dalla, where a shrine in honour of his memory still exists.

A Manji is a Sikh religious administrative unit. Manji refers to each zone of religious administration with an appointed chief called Sangatia, with officially appointed representatives known as Masnad. It has been conceptually similar in its aims to the diocese system in Christianity, and has been similarly important in Sikh missionary activity. The word Manji or Manji literally means a cot (taken as the seat of authority in this context).

Sikh Gurus

Guru Ram Das

Guru Ram Das was born on 24TH September 1534 in Lahore. At age 12, Bhai Jetha moved to Goindwal, where they met Guru Amar Das. The daughter of Guru Amar Das got married to Bhai Jetha. Guru Amar Das chose Bhai Jetha as his successor and renamed him as Ram Das or "servant or slave of god ". Ram Das became the Guru in 1574 and founded the city of Amritsar and started the construction of Harmandir Sahib (Golden Temple) and had tank dug at the site granted to his wife by Emperor Akbar. He composed the Lawan, a four-stanza hymn around which the Anand Karaj is centred. Guru Ram Das composed 638 hymns, or about ten percent of hymns in the Guru Granth Sahib. Guru Ram Das died in March, 1581.

Sheikh Bhikhan

Sheikh Bhikhan was a medieval Muslim saint two of whose hymns are included in the Guru Granth Sahib. He lived a very simple life, and was held in high repute for his piety and learning. Sheikh Bhikhan breathed his last in 1631, at the time when Guru Ram Das occupied the spiritual throne of Guru Nanak.

Guru Arjan Dev

He was born in Goindwal, in the Punjab, the youngest son of Bhai Jetha, who later became Guru Ram Das, and Mata Bhani, the daughter of Guru Amar Das. He was the first Guru in Sikhism to be born into a Sikh family. Guru Arjan Dev acceded to the Guruship in 1581. He was responsible for the construction of many tanks and buildings. In 1588, he planned to build a temple in the centre of the holy tank called Amritsar or the pool of nectar. As the temple was to be thrown open to people of all castes, creeds and climes, he invited Mian Mir to lay the foundation stone of the Harmandir Sahib. He came to the city of Amritsar wearing a religious mendicant's long cloak made up of patches of coarse wool and a cone-shaped cap, with a rose flower on top. Mian Mir was given one of the warm welcomes for which Guru Arjan was famous. The two holy men embraced each other in sincere love and regard. The purpose of the temple was disclosed to the Sufi saint. Mian Mir was delighted at the fine objectives the Guru had in mind. Guru Arjan Dev and Hazrat Mian Mir were divine figures of their respective religions, had mutual respect for each other and also had a similar notion: respect for humanity. On these grounds Mian Mir laid the foundation of a worship place of a nascent religion. Hymns were sung in praise of God and sweets were distributed among the audience. Harmandir Sahib also marked as a Gurdwara — literally meaning Lord's door or the door of the Guru.

Sikh Gurus

Guru Arjan Dev (Contd)

He finalised the Adi Granth in 1604. With the installation of the Granth Sahib in the Harmandir, Amritsar became the central attraction of the town and a site for pilgrimage, so that people of any religion and Caste would have a door or direction through which all worshippers could enter. The rear of the Harmandir Sahib faces the rising Sun and the Guru Granth Sahib is also seated in that direction, but the Granthi reading the Bani faces the West. Amritsar became the most important place of pilgrimage to the Sikhs. Emperor Akbar was impressed by the Guru's work, for it echoed some of the beliefs he held sacred. On one occasion he stopped at Goindwal for the express purpose of meeting the Guru. The Emperor's admiration was an important factor in building Sikh fortunes. During the seven years between the Emperor's first visit to Goindwal and his death in 1606, the number of Sikhs increased and trade thrived in the four towns Arjan had built. The death of Akbar brought a sudden reversal in the policy of the state towards the Sikhs. The new Emperor Jehangir disapproved of the growing popularity of Guru Arjan Dev. Within few months of his accession, Khusrau rebelled against his father and sought the Guru's assistance and blessing. Guru Arjan received the Prince, and he did not give Khusrao and assistance beyond wishing him well. However the war of succession which followed was won by Jahangir. The rebellion had been suppressed and Khusrao apprehended. Jehangir wreaked terrible vengeance on the people he suspected of having helped his son. Guru Arjan Dev was arrested. Jahangir was convinced of Guru Arjan's treason against the imperial authority. Eventually the Guru was thrown in prison and tortured; he died of heat apoplexy in prison. Guru Arjan's killing made him the first Sikh martyr. The assassination of Guru Arjan was the beginning of series of atrocities which forced the religious and reformist community to become a martial tribe. The death of Guru Arjan Dev was a turning point in the history of the Punjab. He was embodiment of many things that Guru Nanak Dev had preached and stood for. He had brought the Hindu and Muslims together in creating a Scripture where both were represented and in raising a temple whose foundation was laid by a Muslim and the superstructure built by Hindus and Sikhs. He was a builder of cities and a merchant-prince who brought prosperity to all communities. Guru Arjan Dev's blood became the seed of the Sikh Church as well as the Sikh resistance to the intolerance in the Punjab.

Sikh Guru

Mian Jamal

Mian Jamal a pious Muslim was an admirer of Guru Arjan. The Guru exhorts Jamal to sec what beauty emerges from humility. In the mud in the low pit grows the handsome lotus. Likewise, says the line, a truly humble heart gives birth to noble action. Jamal formally embraced the Sikh faith and received spiritual instruction from Guru Hargobind. He died in 1650.

Balvand Rai

Balvand Rai was a poet mystic and rebeck player in the court of Guru Arjan. He was a Muslim belonging to the Mirasi community who embraced Sikh thought during the time of Guru Arjan. His three hymns are included in Guru Granth Sahib in Ramkali measure at Amritsar. He co-composed this Ballad of Ramkali with his rebeck player brother, Satta Doom, which includes a total of six hymns. He is said to have died in Lahore during the time of Guru Hargobind and was buried on the bank of the River Ravi.

Mian Mir

On hearing the news of Guru Arjan's tortures Mian Mir came to see him. At the sight of the Guru, the Muslim saint shed tears of blood. He cursed the government for these atrocities on an innocent man of God. In his agony he began to cry. He said he would pray for the destruction of such a cruel government. The Guru though writhing in pain calmed Mian Mir. He said this was will of God, and no man should try to obstruct the working of his Will. He expressed satisfaction at the saint's visit. He said it had brought him cooling breeze in the burning heat. Sorrow had given place of joy. Whatever was happening, it must be taken for one's good and must be cheerfully accepted. The Guru forbade the saint to do anything against government. Mian Mir prayed and left the Guru with a heavy heart.

Death of Guru Arjan Dev

The Guru suffered from heat apoplexy. Sewing up political prisoners in fresh hides of animals seems to be a general practice in those days. Same punishment was now proposed for the Guru. Same punishment was now proposed for the Guru. When a new raw hide of a cow was brought before him, the Guru asked permission to bath in the Ravi as he did not want to die unclean. The swift current owing to the melting of snow carried his weak body. This took place on 30TH May, 1606. The Guru was only 43 years old.

Sikh Gurus

Guru Hargobind

Guru Hargobind acceded to the Guruship in 1606, when Guru Arjan was cruelly put to death by the Mughal governor of Lahore. 'This act of tyranny changed the Sikhs from inoffensive quietists into fanatical warriors. They took up arms under Hargobind, the son of their martyred pontiff, who inspired them with his own spirit of revenge and hatred to their oppressors. This became the turning point of the Sikh history, and developed the struggle which changed the whole character of the reformatory movement.' (Dr. Elphinstone). He established a small army and was the first Guru to take up arms to defend the faith. In due course from an inherited body guard of 52 soldiers, he came to possess three hundred horsemen and 60 gunners. Five hundred young men from Majha were recruited as infantry. He built a fort at Amritsar called Lohgarh or fortress of steel. He had his own flag and a big drum which was beaten at sunrise and sunset. The Guru created a government of his own like that of Mughals. All of his disciples formed a separate and independent entity, and had nothing to do with the agencies of the day. Thus the Sikhs came to occupy a kind of a separate state within the Mughal State. Jahangir discovered the circumstances and felt Guru Hargobind was harmless, so he ordered his release. 52 Rajas who were imprisoned in the fort as hostages for opposing the Mughal Empire were dismayed as they were losing a spiritual mentor. Guru Hargobind requested the Rajas to be freed along with him as well and stood surety for their loyal behaviour. Jahangir ordered their release as well. Guru Hargobind got a special gown stitched which had 52 hems. As Guru Hargobind left the fort, the captive kings caught the hems of the cloak and came out along with him. After his release, Guru Hargobind more discreetly strengthened the Sikh army and reconsolidated the Sikh community. During the reign of Shah Jahan that started in 1627, relations became bitter again. Guru Hargobind fought six defensive battles against the Mughals. With his slender resources he could not maintain a constant struggle against the Mughal government. The Guru anticipated the return of a larger Mughal force, so retreated into Shivalik Hills to strengthen his defences and army. He nominally accepted Jehan's authority but resisted the Islamic persecution, fighting four wars against Shah Jehan's armies, and was defeated by the Sikhs. Guru Hargobind breathed his last, peacefully, at Kiratpur Rup Nagar, Punjab, on 19TH March 1644. After this says Cunningham: 'the Sikhs were in little danger of relapsing into the limited merit or utility of monks and mendicants.'

Sikh Gurus

Painda Khan

His parents died while he was still very young, and he was brought up by his maternal uncle, Ismail Khan. Ismail Khan along with his 16 year old nephew and some other Pathans of his village once accompanied a Sikh sangat proceeding to Amritsar to see Guru Hargobind. The Guru, pleased with Painda Khan, engaged him to be trained as a soldier. Painda Khan grew up into a brave, hefty warrior and showed his mettle fighting against the imperial troops at Amritsar. Guru Hargobind always treated him with special consideration. The Guru would take him out for the chase, and shower him with praise and gifts. After the death of Mata Damodari there in November that year, he was told to escort the family back to Kartarpur, while the Guru himself set out on a journey across the Malwa tract to meet the Sangat. As the Guru arrived at Kartarpur after the battle of Mehraj in December 1634, Painda Khan presented himself and spoke boastfully: "Had I been there I would not have let the Guru go forward and expose himself to danger, nor would have Bhai Jetha died." f. On the occasion of the next Baisakhi, 29TH March 1635, Sikhs from far and near came with presents to pay homage to the Guru. Chitra Sain, a rich merchant, presented a beautiful horse, a white hawk, a costly dress and a khand or dual-edged sword. Guru Hargobind gave the hawk to Baba Gurditta, his eldest son, and bestowed the horse, the dress and the sword upon Painda Khan. As the latter went home, elated at having been so honoured by the Guru, his son-in-law, Asman Khan, claimed the gifts which Painda Khan reluctantly passed on to him. Asman Khan, donning the dress and sword, went out hunting the following day riding the horse. Baba Gurditta, with his newly acquired white hawk, also happened to be sporting in the same area. The hawk fell into the hands of Asman Khan, who took it home. Painda Khan who turned up without wearing the dress gifted to him, denied before the Guru that the gifts had changed hands or that the hawk was in the possession of his son-in-law. Guru Hargobind sent a Sikh, Bhai Bidhi Chand, to Chhota Mir, and the gifts along with the hawk were recovered from Asman Khan. Chagrined at the exposure of his perjury, Painda Khan openly turned against his patron. With the help of the faujdar of Jalandhar, he attacked the Guru but was worsted in the battle which, according to Bhatt Vahi Multani Sindhi, raged for three days, from 26 to 28TH April 1635. Painda Khan fell to Guru Hargobind's sword on the final day. As Painda lay dying, the Guru told him to recite the kalmia, the Muhammadan confession of faith, shading with his shield his face from the scorching sun.

Sikh Gurus

Abdulla Bhai

Abdul according to some Sikh chroniclers was a Muslim minstrel who recited heroic balladry at Sikh congregations in the time of Guru Hargobind. Abdul was born in the village of Sursingh, now in Amritsar district of the Punjab. He first came to Amritsar in 1606 at the time of the installation ceremony for Guru Hargobind at the Akal Takht. According to Gurbilas Chhevin Patshahi, he and his companion, Bhai Nattha, sang the stanza on the occasion: The Throne everlasting has by the Holy Guru's presence become haloed, Indescribable is its splendour, and how may I sing its glory! Seeing the Guru, Both the sun and the moon were shamed. So sat on the throne the Holy Guru to the remembrance of the Lord God attached. Abdul and Nattha have composed verse to sing his praise. Both Abdul and Nattha remained at Amritsar thereafter and recited poetry extolling chivalrous deeds of past heroes. As Baba Gurditta, Guru Hargobind's eldest son, got married, he was taken round by the Guru to Akal Takht and Harmandir Sahib to make obeisance. The Guru then invited Abdul to recite a panegyric. Abdul and Nattha, as reports Gurbilas Chhevin Patshahi, accompanied Guru Hargobind when he left Amritsar for Kiratpur in the Sivalik hills. As his time came, Guru Hargobind asked them to return to their native Sursingh.

Kattu Shah

Kattu Shah, a Muslim resident of Kashmir who converted a Sikh, was known for his piety and devotion. Journeying through Kashmir once, Guru Hargobind put up with him in his house for a night. He was received with great respect Crowds of Kashmiris both from Srinagar and the surrounding villages paid homage and many embraced Sikhism. A group of Sikhs, carrying a jar of honey as their offering to Guru Hargobind, and Kattu Shah who requested them to let him have some honey to taste. They refused saying that they could not do so before the Guru had partaken of it. When the Sikhs reached the Guru, the honey was found rotten and full of worms. The Guru remarked, "This is the result of not having given to my Sikh in who is the spirit of the Guru." He ordered them to return and satisfy Kattu Shah. It is said that the honey became fresh and sweet when they returned to Kattu Shah. 'Hungry mouth is Guru's treasure.' The Sikh begged for enlightenment. Guru Ji told him by pointing towards Bhai Kattu, the poor Sikh, who was hungry and was refused when requested for the honey while accompanying the Sangat. Guru Sahib further enlightened him, saying, "Gharib Da Muh - Guru Ki Golak." (Feeding the poor is actual feeding the Guru).

Sikh Gurus

Babak
Babak a Muslim rababi or musician kept Guru Hargobind Company and recited the sacred hymns at divans morning and evening. The word Babak, from Persian, means faithful. As says the Gurbilas Chhevin Patshahi, Babak was, at the death of Satta and Balvand, who used to recite sacred hymns for the Guru, asked to perform the obsequies for them under their (Muslim) rites. Babak, it is said, dug the graves for the deceased on the bank of the River Ravi and after the burial service, performed the kirtan on the site where sat Guru Hargobind. To quote the Gurbilas again, he took part in the battle of Amritsar in 1629 during which he assisted in the evacuation of the Guru's family to Jhabal. Going by the Gurbilas account, Guru Hargobind, before he departed the world, asked Babak to return to Amritsar. As bidden by the Guru, Babak retired to Amritsar where he died in 1642.

Guru Har Rai
Guru Har Rai guided the Sikhs for about seventeen years, till his death at age 31. He is notable for maintaining the large army of Sikh soldiers that the sixth Sikh Guru had amassed, yet avoiding military conflict. He supported the moderate Sufi influenced Dara Shikoh instead of conservative Sunni influenced Aurangzeb as the two brothers entered into a war of succession to the Mughal Empire throne. Aurangzeb won the succession war in 1658. Guru Hai Rai spent most of his time in devotional meditation and preaching the teachings of Nanak. Guru Har Rai passed away on 6TH October 1661.

Guru Har Krishan
Guru Har Krishan became the youngest Guru in Sikhism at the age of five, on 7TH October 1661, succeeding his father, Guru Har Rai. Despite his young age, Guru Sahib used to delight the hearts of his disciples by his commentaries on the passages from the Holy Scripture, the Guru Granth Sahib. He reminded people to cherish the One God alone, asking them to discard passions and learn the virtues of patience, charity and love. During the year 1663, when Guru Har Krishan Sahib was in Delhi, a swear epidemic of cholera and smallpox broke out. The seven year old Guru attended to and served the suffering people with complete devotion. By his grace, the lake at Bangla Sahib provided a cure for thousands of peoples. In the process of serving the diseased, the Guru was himself seized by high fever and an attack of smallpox, eventually passing away on 30TH March 1664, aged just eight years.

Sikh Gurus

Guru Tegh Bahadur

The Sikh movement was rapidly growing in the rural Malwa region of Punjab, and the Guru Tegh Bahadur was openly encouraging Sikhs to be fearless in their pursuit of just society: he who holds none in fear, nor is afraid of anyone, is acknowledged as a man of true wisdom. He built a fort near the Sutlej, and there established his ecclesiastical and military headquarters, and continued the fitful life of the struggle with the Mughal Empire. After having been approached by the Kashmiri Pandits, Guru Tegh Bahadur resisted their forced conversions to Islam. He was imprisoned in a cage, tortured and publicly beheaded in 1675 on the orders of Mughal Emperor Aurangzeb in Delhi, for refusing to convert to Islam.

Abdulla Khwaja

Abdulla Khwaja, a Muslim native of Mani Majra, near present day Chandigarh, was the keeper of the jail at Chandni Chowk kotwali in Delhi, where Guru Tegh Bahadur, was detained under the Imperial Warrant. He was a pious man and truly reverenced the holy detune. He tried to mitigate the rigour of his incarnation as far his official position permitted. After Tegh Bahadur's execution, he resigned his post and went to live at Anandpur, where he served Guru Gobind Singh as a physician. His son Ghulam Abbas served under Nawab Kapur Singh as a physician during Misl times.

Shaikh Farid

Shaikh Farid, Sufi mystic and teacher, who is also known to be the first recorded poet in the Punjabi language. The main theme of Shaikh Farid's banis what in the Indian critical terminology would be called vairagya that is dispassion towards the world and its false attractions. In Sufi terminology this is called tauba or turning away. Guru Nanak, Guru Amar Das and Guru Arjan have continued the theme of some of Farid's couplets. These continuations appear in the body of Farid's Bani. Guru Nanak has left a sabads in measure Suhi as a corrective to Farid's beautiful lyric in the same measure, which, however, appeared to view the future of the human soul in a rather pessimistic light. The Gurus gave Farid's Bani the place of honour the most revered Muslim Sufi of the Punjab. The high level of poetry, the sheer genius which has created it would make lay claim of a lesser man than Shaikh Farid to authorship insupportable. History does not know of any other man as famous as Farid, the name used in the verses included in the Guru Granth Sahib.

Sikh Gurus

Guru Gobind Singh

At the martyrdom of Tegh Bahadur, his son Gobind succeeded to the Guruship. To save the faith and the infant community from annihilation, he decided to transform the Sikhs into a fierce military brotherhood. In 1699, he created the Order of the Khalsa (the pure). He summoned the Sikhs to the city of Anandpur and baptised them to the fold of the Khalsa. Henceforth their profession was to wield the sword in the cause of justice and defending the weak. They formed the nucleus of a fighting fraternity and were given new names with the surname Singh – Lion. They were to observe five Ks, Kesh (unshorn hair), to carry a Kangha (a comb in the hair), to wear Kacha (military pants), to wear a Kara (a steel bracelet) and always carry a Kirpan (a Sabre). The outward symbols of the Singhs were to set them apart, so they could not deny their faith, and to give them the courage to defend it. The orchard of the Sikh faith needed the thorny hedge of armed men for its protection. The Singhs of the Khalsa were the orchard and the hedge rolled into one, ever willing to wield the sword in righteous cause. When Guru Gobind Singh created the Order of the Khalsa, he laid the foundations of the Sikh military might by setting up a tradition of reckless valour, which became the distinguishing feature of Sikh soldiery. They came to believe in the triumph of their cause as an article of faith, and like their Guru asked for no nobler end than a death on the battlefield. Guru Gobind Singh fought many desperate unequal battles against the Mughals. Two of his sons died in the fighting and Nawab Wazir Khan, the Mughal Governor of Sarhind, had executed the two younger ones. Wazir Khan later sent assassins to kill the Guru. They found the Guru in Nanded and attacked him after his evening prayer, stabbing him beneath his heart. Guru Gobind Singh fought and killed his assailant. The wound began to heal but reopened several days later when the Guru attempted to use his bow. Realizing his end had come; Guru Gobind Singh assembled his Sikhs and instructed them that the scripture of the Granth should forever be their irreplaceable Guru and Guide. What Guru Gobind Singh had succeeded in doing was to "Teach the sparrow to hunt the hawk and one man to have the courage to fight a legion." During the course of the Guru's life he met people of calibre and character, many who were Muslims, who loved and respected him. That love was returned in full measure, without regard to religious differences. Sometimes that relationship resulted in great personal sacrifice on the part of the devotee, a price these great men of Islam willingly paid. The Guru died of his wounds on 7TH October 1708. Here are only a few of their stories:

Sikh Gurus

Pir Bhikham Shah

Pir Bhikham Shah, a seventeenth century Sufi saint. Pir Bhikhan Shah, as he learnt through intuition of the birth of Guru Gobind Singh at Patna, made obeisance that day to the east instead of to the west. At this his disciples demurred, for no Muslim should make such respectful gestures except towards the Kaba. The Pir explained that in a city in the east, the Beneficent Lord had revealed Himself through a new born baby, to whom it was that he had bowed and to no ordinary mortal. Bhikhan Shah with his disciples then travelled to Patna to have a glimpse of the infant Gobind Ra. Desiring to know what would be his attitude to the two major religious peoples of India, he placed two small pots in front of the child, one representing in his own mind Hindus and the other Muslims. As the child covered both the pots simultaneously with his tiny hands, Bhikhan Shah felt happy concluding that the new seer would treat both Hindus and Muslims alike and show equal respect to both.

Pir Budhu Shah

Pir Budhu Shah, a Muslim divine whose real name was Badruddin and who was an admirer of Guru Gobind Singh, was born on 13 June 1647 in a prosperous Sayyid family of Sadhaura, in present day Ambala district of Haryana. Because of his simplicity and silent nature during his early childhood he was given the nickname of Budhu (lit. simpleton) which stuck to him permanently. He was married at the age of 18 to a pious lady, Nasirari, who was the sister of Said Khan, later a high ranking officer in the Mughal army. It is not certain how Budhu Shah first became acquainted with Guru Gobind Singh, but it is recorded that he called on him in 1685 at Paonta, on the bank of the Yamuna. At his recommendation, the Guru engaged 500 Pathan soldiers under the command of four leaders, Kale Khan, Bhikhan Khan, Nijabat Khan and Hayat Khan. In 1688, when Guru Gobind Singh was attacked by a combined force of the hill chiefs led by Raja Fateh Shah of Srinagar (Garhwal), all the Pathans with the exception of Kale Khan deserted him and joined the hill monarch. The Guru conveyed the news of the treachery to Pir Budhu Shah, who immediately rushed to Bharigani, the battlefield, with 700 of his followers, including his brother and four sons. Many of the Pir's disciples as well as two of his sons, Ashraf and Muhammad Shah, and his brother, Bhure Shah, fell in the action.

Sikh Gurus

Pir Budhu Shah (Contd)

After the battle Guru Gobind Singh offered rich presents to the Pir which the latter politely declined to accept. However he, as the tradition goes, begged the Guru to bestow upon him the comb from his hair and the turban he was going to tie. The Guru gave him the two articles and a small Kirpan or sword which the Pir and his descendants kept in the family as sacred heirlooms until Maharajah Bharpur Singh of Nabha acquired them in exchange for jagir or land grant. The relics are still preserved in the family's palace at Nabha (in the Punjab). The Rajput chiefs defeated at Bharigani remained hostile towards Guru Gobind Singh, and wished to evict him from Anandpur to where he had returned. To solicit help from the imperial government, they sent to the emperor reports describing the Guru as a dangerous rebel. Complaints also reached the authority against Pir Budhu Shah who had rendered assistance to the Guru. The Faujdar of Sarhind, under whose jurisdiction the parganah of Sadhaura then fell, directed a local official, 'Usman Khan, to chastise the Pir. The latter marched on Sadhaura, arrested Budhu Shah and had him executed on 21 March 1704. Banda Singh Bahadur avenged the Pir's execution in 1709 by storming Sadhaura and killing 'Usman Khan. Pir Budhu Shah's descendants migrated to Pakistan in 1947. Their ancestral house in Sadhaura has since been converted into a Gurdwara named after Pir Budhu Shah.

General Said Beg

Said Khan, a Mughal general, came in February 1703 at the head of a large army to invade Anandpur and force Guru Gobind Singh into submission. Guru Gobind Singh had only 500 warriors with him at the time came out of the town to face the attack. A severe battle followed in which Maimun Khan with his contingent of 100 Muslim retainers who had changed sides some time earlier, fought on the Guru's side with conspicuous courage. While the battle was raging, Guru Gobind Singh, riding his famous charger, made a dash through the ranks and reached where Said Khan was and challenged him. Said Khan had heard many marvellous stories about the Guru's spiritual power and had secretly cherished in his heart a wish to meet him in person. Now that he was face to face with him, Said Khan was so much impressed by the Guru's presence that all intent of war vanished from his heart. Dismounting his horse, he touched the Guru's stirrup to do homage to him. Guru Gobind Singh blessed him and he quietly left the field. He became a recluse and spent the rest of his life in prayer.

Sikh Gurus

Nihang Khan

Nihang Khan was the ruler of a small principality called Kotla Nihang Khan near Ropar. He was a friend and follower of the tenth Sikh Guru, Guru Gobind Singh. The Guru and his associates frequently stayed with Nihang Khan, who often sheltered and provided succour to them in the period when they were facing persecution by Mughal forces. By way of faith and ethnicity, Nihang Khan was a Muslim Pathan. Guru Gobind Singh and Nihang Khan first met on the Amavas of the month of Maghar in Vikram Samvat year 1745. Nihang Khan was so impressed that he declared that he would "dedicate his all in the cause of the Guru."

Mumtaz

Mumtaz was the daughter of Nihang Khan, Muslim chief of Kotla. She served the Sikh warrior Bhai Bachittar Singh who, severely wounded in a skirmish after the evacuation of Anandpur in December 1705, had been brought to her father's house. To throw the pursuers off the scent, Nihang Khan told them that the wounded person in the house was his son-in-law. Even Mumtaz declared Bhai Bachittar Singh to be her husband. The latter, though well looked after by his hosts, did not survive and succumbed to his injuries.

Bhikhan Khan

Bhikhan Khan was a Pathan who had served in the Mughal army before joining Guru Gobind Singh at Paonta Sahib on the recommendation of Pir Budhu Shah of Sadhaura. He had one hundred soldiers under his command, but he crossed over to the hill rajas on the eve of the battle of Bharigani. He suggested that they could save their lives by taking the side of the hill men. They would fight in the rear of the hill armies and would obtain from the hill chiefs permission to plunder the Guru's wealth. The Pathans applauded Bhikhan Khan's advice and joined the hill rajas against Guru Gobind Singh. When Budhu Shah learnt how the Pathan soldiers had reneged, he came forward with his four sons and seven hundred disciples to assist the Guru. Guru Gobind Singh says in his Bachitra Natak that as he saw Shah Sarigram (Sarigo Shah), a cousin of his, fall in the battle of Bharigani, he took up his bow and arrows. With the first arrow, he struck a Khan who fell to the ground. He then drew out another one and aimed at Bhikhan Khan, hitting him in the face. Leaving his horse, the bleeding Khan fled, but was killed by another arrow from the Guru's bow.

Sikh Gurus

Ghani Khan

Ghani Khan and his brother Nabi Khan, Pathan horse dealers of Machhivara in present day Ludhiana district of the Punjab, were admirers of Guru Gobind Singh whom they had visited at Anandpur and to whom they had sold many good animals. When they learnt that, travelling in a lonely state after the battle of Chamkaur (1705), the Guru had come to Machhivara; they at once turned out to meet him and offered their services. They provided him with a blue coloured dress and carried him out of Machhivara in a palanquin disguised as a Muslim divine. They declared him to be Uchch da Pir, the holy man of Uchch, an old seat of Muslim saints in south-west Punjab. They escorted him thus up to Hehrari, a village near Raikot in Ludhiana district, where a group of Sikhs relieved them. The Guru dismissed Ghani Khan and Nabi Khan with his blessings and a Hukamnamas meant to be a letter of commendation which was reverently preserved by their descendants. The family migrated to Pakistan in 1947. Their house in Machhivara is now a Gurdwara known as Gurdwara Uchch da Pir.

Jamshaid Khan

Aurangzeb died in 1707, and immediately a succession struggle began between his sons who attacked each other. The official successor was Bahadur Shah, who invited Guru Gobind Singh with his army to meet him in person in the Deccan region of India, for reconciliation but Bahadur Shah then delayed any discussions for months. Wazir Khan, a Muslim army commander against whose army the Guru had fought several wars, commissioned two Afghans, Jamshed Khan and Wasil Beg, Ruhila Afghans, to follow the Guru's army as it moved for the meeting with Bahadur Shah, and then assassinate the Guru. The two secretly pursued the Guru whose troops were in the Deccan area of India, and entered the camp when the Sikhs had been stationed near river Godavari for months.[1] They gained access to the Guru and Jamshed Khan stabbed him with a fatal wound at Nanded. The Guru fought back and killed the assassin, while the assassin's companion was killed by the Sikh guards as he tried to escape. Guru Gobind Singh survived the attack. However after a few days, as he stretched a powerful bow, the wound opened up again and he bled profusely. He passed away on 1ST October 1708.

Sikh Gurus

Muazzam Bahadur Shah

Muazzam Bahadur Shah also known as Shah Alam I was the Mughal emperor of India from 1707 to 1712. He replaced his father Aurangzeb. In contrast to his father, Bahadur Shah had a friendly relation with Guru Gobind Singh. Jealousy of this growing friendship would ultimately cause a worried Wazir Khan to dispatch Pathan assassins, without the required Paktunwali warning, to kill the Guru. The assassins were killed but the Guru had been stabbed in the side, it is said that the Emperor's European surgeon tended the wound and the Guru's condition improved but the wound later grew infected and Gobind Singh died.

Muazzam was born in Burhanpur, the fourth son of the emperor Aurangzeb in the year 1643. In his father's lifetime, Muazzam was deputed governor of the Northwest Territories by Aurangzeb. His province included those parts of the Punjab where the Sikhs were gaining in power. As governor, Muazzam relaxed the enforcement of Aurangzeb's severe edicts, and an uneasy calm prevailed in the province for a brief time. In fact, he maintained a cordial relationship with the Sikh Guru, Guru Gobind Singh and it is recorded in Sikh history that he received help from the Guru in taking the throne in 1707. Also, he travelled with the Guru from the north to Nanded where they parted company. After Aurangzeb's death, Muazzam Bahadur Shah won the throne. His younger brother, Prince Azam Shah, proclaimed himself emperor and marched towards Delhi, where he fought Bahadur Shah unsuccessfully and lost. Another brother, Muhammad Kam Baksh, was killed in 1709. Aurangzeb had imposed Sharia law within his kingdom through harsh enforcement of strict edicts. This led to increased militancy by many constituencies including the Marathas, the Sikhs and the Rajputs. Thus, rebellion was rife at the time of Aurangzeb's death and Bahadur Shah inherited a very unstable kingdom. A more moderate man than his father, Bahadur Shah sought to improve relations with the militant constituencies of the rapidly crumbling kingdom. However, he could do little to mitigate the enormous damage already done by his father over his long reign. Indeed, Bahadur Shah's shortcomings, his lack of military and leadership qualities, added to the problems of the empire. After his reign of less than five years, the Mughal Empire entered a long decline, attributable both to his ineptness and to his father's geographical overextension and religious bigotry. Historians of his time had recorded about him as a learned man and also add that he possessed a mild temper and was dignified. Muazzam Bahadur Shah died on February 27TH, 1712.

Banda Singh Bahadur

At age 15 he left home to become an ascetic, and was given the name ''Madho Das''. He established a monastery at Nanded, where in September 1708 he was visited by, and became a disciple of, Guru Gobind Singh, who gave him the new name of Banda Singh Bahadur after initiating him into the Khalsa. Armed with the blessing and authority of Guru Gobind Singh, he came to Khanda in Sonepat and assembled a fighting force and led the struggle against the Mughal Empire. Guru Gobind Singh also appointed five Sikhs to assist him. His first major action was the sacking of the Mughal provincial capital, Samana, in November 1709. After establishing his authority in Punjab, Banda Singh Bahadur abolished the zamindari system, and granted property rights to the tillers of the land.

On 14TH April, 1711 it is reported:

"The wretched Nanak-worshipper has his camp in the town of Kalanaur up to the 19th instant. During this period he has promised and proclaimed. 'I do not oppress the Muslims'. Accordingly for any Muslim who approaches him, he fixes a daily allowance and wages, and looks after him. He has permitted them to read khutba and namaz. As such, five thousand Muslims have gathered round him. Having entered into his friendship, they are free to shout their call and say their prayers in the army of the wretched (Sikhs)"

On 20TH May, 1711, it is reported:

"Whosoever from amongst the Hindus and Muslims comes to him for service is looked after and fed. He has granted the right of booty to them. It is decided that if the (Imperial) forces come, he will oppose them; if not, they (Banda & his troops) will move towards Ajmer via Lakhi Jungle and go to Shahjahanabad (Delhi)" The response from Mughal authorities was harsh and severe. Orders were given to kills Sikhs wherever they were found. This did not change Banda's attitude towards Muslims. Banda was clearly able to draw a distinct line between the tyrannical officials and the general mass of the Muslims who were as much the part of the country as Sikhs and Hindus. In March 1715, the army under the rule of Abdus Samad Khan, the Mughal king of Delhi, drove Banda Bahadur and the Sikh forces into the village of Gurdas Nangal, Gurdaspur, Punjab and laid siege to the village. The Sikhs defended the small fort for eight months under conditions of great hardship, but on 7TH December 1715 the Mughals broke into the starving garrison and captured Banda Singh and his companions. Banda Singh Bahadur was put into an iron cage and the remaining Sikhs were chained.

Banda Singh Bahadur (Contd)

The Sikhs were brought to Delhi in a procession with the 780 Sikh prisoners, 2,000 Sikh heads hung on spears, and 700 cartloads of heads of slaughtered Sikhs used to terrorise the population. They were put in the Delhi fort and pressured to give up their faith and become Muslims. The prisoners remained unmoved. On their firm refusal these non-converters were ordered to be executed. Every day a few were brought out of the fort and murdered in public. This continued for approximately seven days. After three months of confinement, on 9 June 1716, Banda Singh's eyes were gouged out, his limbs were severed, his skin removed, and then he was killed.

Nawab Sher Muhammad Khan
Nawab Sher Muhammad Khan, an Afghan feudatory of the Mughals, was the chief of Malerkotla and held a high military position in the Sarkar or division of Sarhind. He had participated in the battle of Chamkaur and was present in the court at Sarhind when Nawab Wazir Khan, the faujdar, pronounced death for Sahibzada Zorawar Singh and Sahibzada Fateh Singh, the younger sons of Guru Gobind Singh, who were 9 and 7 years of age, respectively. Sher Muhammad Khan pleaded against the death sentence on the ground that the boys were too young to be given such a harsh penalty and could not in any case be held responsible for the actions of their father. Wazir Khan, however, overruled the objection and the Sahibzadas were brutally executed.

Wazir Khan gave the two children a choice: Either gives up the Sikh Faith or Die. True to the spirit of their grandfather Guru Tegh Bahadur and their father Guru Gobind Singh, the love for the Sikh faith was so strong that the young children chose death. Mata Gujri ji, the Guru's mother, was informed about her grandchildren's fate in the prison where she died.

It is said that when Guru Gobind Singh came to know about the fate of his younger sons he uprooted a shrub with his arrow and declared that the tyrannical reign of Wazir Khan would be put to any end. This prophecy came true when the Sikh forces under the command of Banda Singh Bahadur, after a fierce fight, defeated the forces of Wazir Khan. Nawab Sher Muhammad Khan at the head of his Malerkotla contingent, formed part of Wazir Khan's army, and died in the conflict. Guru Gobind Singh also ordered the Sikhs to always help and support the people of Malerkotla has fulfilled so far.

Sikh Jathas

Sarbat Khalsa

After the capture and execution of Banda Singh Bahadur in 1716, the terror let loose by the Mughal government upon the Sikhs forced them to leave their homes and hearths and move about in small bands or jathas. For every able-bodied Sikh who had undergone the vows of the Khalsa, it became necessary to join one or the other jathas to fight against the oppressors. Besides skill in the use of arms, he had to be a good horseman, because in guerrilla warfare, such as the Sikhs had to resort to against the superior might of the State, speed and mobility were of paramount importance. The weaponry, in the beginning, ranged from knobbed clubs, spears and battle axes to bow and arrows and matchlocks. A long sword and a dagger were of course carried by every member of the Khalsa. Some of them wore armour, but no helmets. During raids on enemy columns and baggage trains, the booty most valued was good horses and matchlocks so that most of the jathas were gradually equipped with firearms. They got great success in raiding sorties. Whenever they got a chance they would suddenly pounce upon their target and disappear with the spoils. All these fighting Jathas had a single aim to further the cause of the Panth (community) and to strengthen it for waging the struggle. All were followers of the Guru and each one of them considered the defence of the Panth his primary duty. The diverse jathas voluntarily accepted the control of Sarbat Khalsa, the assembly of all the Sikh jathas at Amritsar on the occasions of Baisakhi and Diwali when plans of action were formulated in the form of gurmatas or resolutions adopted in the presence of Guru Granth Sahib. The brief respite provided by a temporary detente with the government during 1733-35 enabled the Sikh jathas to assemble and stay in strength at Amritsar with immunity. Nawab Kapur Singh, their chosen leader, knit the entire force into two dals, i.e. branches or sections—the Buddha Dal (army of the old) and Taruna Dal (army of the young). Taruna Dal was further divided into five jathas each with its own flag. With the end of the detente and the renewal of State persecution with redoubled vigour, the Sikhs had again recourse to smaller and more numerous jathas. Need for co-ordination forced them again to regroup themselves on the Diwali of 1745 into 25 jathas, but the number multiplied again.

Sikh Jathas

Nawab Kapur Singh

Sikh Jathas which came into being during the turbulent period of the second half of the eighteenth century and which became a formidable fighting force of the Sikhs in the north-western part of India. The first Khalsa army formed and led by the creator of the Khalsa, Guru Gobind Singh had broken up at the time of the evacuation of Anandpur in December 1705. Another force, at one time 40,000 strong, raised by Banda Singh Bahadur, was scattered after the capture and execution of its leader. The fierce persecution which overtook the Sikhs made the immediate reformation of a similar force impossible, yet the Sikh warriors in small groups continued to challenge the State's might. Armed with whatever weapons they could lay their hands upon and living off the land, these highly mobile guerrilla-bands or jathas remained active during the worst of times. It was not unusual however for the jathas to join together when the situation so demanded. Ratan Singh Bharigu, Prachin Panth Prakash, records an early instance of the warrior bands of the Ban Doab (land between the Rivers Beas and Ravi) being organized into four squadrons of 200 each, with specified area of operation and provision for mutual assistance in time of need. Moreover, it was customary for most jathas to congregate at Amritsar to celebrate Baisakhi and Diwali. Divan Durbara Singh (d. 1734), an elderly Sikh, acted on such occasions as the common leader of the entire congregation. In 1733, Zakariya Khan, the Mughal governor of Lahore, having failed to suppress the Sikhs by force, planned to make terms with them and offered them jagir or fief, the title of Nawab to their leader and unhindered access to and residence at Amritsar. Kapur Singh, a senior and dedicated warrior, was accepted by Sikhs as their leader and invested with the title of Nawab. Sikh soldiers grouped themselves around their leaders most of whom were stationed at Amritsar. In consideration of administrative convenience, Nawab Kapur Singh divided the entire body of troops into two camps called Buddha Dal (the elderly group) and Taruna Dal (the younger group), respectively. Taruna Dal was further divided into five jathas, each with its own flag and drum. The compact with the government broke down in 1735 and, under pressure of renewed persecution, the Khalsa was again forced to split into smaller groups and seek shelter in hills and forests. Nadir Shah's invasion in 1739 gave a severe blow to the crumbling Mughal empire, and this gave the Sikhs a chance to consolidate themselves.

Dal Khalsa

Sardar Jassa Singh Ahluwalia

The number of jathas multiplied further and by March 1748 there were as many as 65 groups operating independently of each other, although they still acknowledged the pre-eminence of Nawab Kapur Singh. By this time a new claimant to power had appeared on the scene. Ahmad Shah Durrani had launched his first invasion of India and occupied Lahore on 12 January 1748. On the Baisakhi day, 29TH March 1748, when the Sikh jathas gathered at Amritsar, Nawab Kapur Singh impressed upon them the need for solidarity. Through a Gurmata or resolution, the entire Fighting force of the Khalsa was unified into a single body, called the Dal Khalsa, under the supreme command of Sardar Jassa Singh Ahluwalia. The 65 bands were merged into 11 units, Misls, each under a prominent leader and having a separate name and banner. The Dal Khalsa was a kind of loose confederacy, without any strict constitution. All Amrit Dhari Sikhs were considered members of the Dal Khalsa which was mainly a cavalry force. Anyone who was an active horseman and proficient in the use of arms could join any one of the eleven Misls, having the option to change membership whenever desired. The Misls were subject to the control of the Sarbat Khalsa, the biannual assembly of the Panth at Amritsar. Akal Takht was the symbol of the unity of the Dal Khalsa which was in a way the Sikh State in the making. The Dal, with its total estimated strength of 70,000, essentially consisted of cavalry; artillery and infantry elements were almost unknown to it. The Dal Khalsa established its authority over most of the Punjab region in a short time. As early as 1749, the Mughal governor of the Punjab solicited its help in the suppression of a rebellion in Multan. In early 1758, the Dal Khalsa, in collaboration with the Marathas, occupied Sarhind and Lahore. Within three months of the Vadda Ghallughara or the Greater Holocaust of 5TH February 1762, the Dal Khalsa rose to defeat Ahmad Shah's governor at Sarhind in April May 1762 and the Shah himself at Amritsar in October of the same year. Sarhind and its adjoining territories were occupied permanently in January 1764. The Khalsa thenceforward not only had the Punjab in their virtual possession, but also carried their victories right up to Delhi and beyond the Yamuna into the heart of the Gangetic Plain. Although they failed to sustain or consolidate their gains in that direction, they had liberated the Punjab from foreign rule inch by inch and had sealed forever the north-western route for foreign invaders. Themselves victims of the worst kind of religious tyranny, the leaders of the Dal Khalsa established a just and humane rule in the Punjab.

Misldars

Sardar Jassa Singh Ahluwalia (Contd)
After the initial period of predatory raids aimed at undermining the authority of the Mughal government, they established a system of rakhi, protection, to protect the life and property of the people. Rakhi was a levy of a portion, usually one-fifth, of the revenue assessment of a territory as a fee for the guarantee of peace and protection. After the conquest of Sarhind in January 1764 when Sikh Sardars started occupying territory, the Misaldari system came into operation. Peace that returned to the Punjab after half a century of turbulence resulted in increased prosperity of the people. The removal from among its midst by death of the towering personality of Jassa Singh Ahluwalia in 1783, virtually meant the end of the Dal Khalsa.

Battle of Eminabad
About 1745, a large Sikh force assembled near the town of Eminabad (modern Gujranwala district near Lahore) The Subedar of Lahore sent forces under the command of Diwan Jaspat Rai to disperse it. The Sikhs fought with full zeal and fervour forcing the Diwan to get forced in pitch battle. An intrepid Sikh youth climbed the Diwan's elephant by catching hold of its tail, beheaded the Diwan with a stroke of his sword, jumped down and fled. Seeing this, Diwan's army lost ground and fled the field carrying the head of the Diwan. On hearing the killing of Jaspat Rai, his brother's Lakhpat Rai's anger, who was Diwan of Lahore, knew no bounds. He marched against the Sikhs with a massive force. Consequently there was a general massacre of the Sikhs. Many of the fleeing Sikhs were captured and mercilessly butchered at Lahore. The site where the carnage took place is well-known as Shahidganj (Lahore). After the battle of Eminabad a wave of severe persecution was let loose against the Sikhs by the Governor of Lahore. It seemed as if the Sikhs would have to face the same kind of atrocities as they had been subjected during the regime f Abdus Samad Khan. But to their good fortune a dispute rose between Nawab Zakariya Khan's two sons, Yahiya Khan and Shah Nawaz Khan over the governorship of the Punjab. At last Shah Nawaz Khan was able to overpower his elder brother, Yahiya Khan and occupy Lahore and Multan after expelling him from the Punjab. Yahiya Khan went to Delhi to seek help from the Mughal Emperor. At this Shah Nawaz got terrified and entered into negations with Ahmed Shah Abdali, the king of Afghanistan, whom he invited to invade India.

Misldars

Chhota Ghallughara

Chhota Ghallughara, minor holocaust or carnage, as distinguished from Vadda Ghallughara or major massacre, is how Sikh chronicles refer to a bloody action during the severe campaign of persecution launched by the Mughal government at Lahore against the Sikhs in 1746. Early in that year, Jaspat Rai, the faujdar of Eminabad, 55 km north of Lahore, was killed in an encounter with a roving band of Sikhs. Jaspat Rai's brother, Lakhpat Rai, who was a Diwan or revenue minister at Lahore, vowed revenge declaring that he would not put on his head dress nor claim himself to be a Khatri, to which caste he belonged, until he had scourged the entire Sikh Panth out of existence. With the concurrence of the Mughal governor of Lahore, Yahiya Khan, Lakhpat Rai mobilized the Lahore troops, summoned reinforcements from Multan, Bahawalpur and Jalandhar, alerted the feudal hill chiefs, and roused the general population for jihad or crusade against the Sikhs. As an immediate first step, he had the Sikh inhabitants of Lahore rounded up and ordered their execution despite intercession on their behalf by a group of Hindu nobles headed by Diwan Kaura Mall. He ignored the request even of his guru, Sant Jagat Bhagat Gosairi, that the killing should not be carried out on the appointed day which being an amavasya, the last day of the dark half of the lunar month, falling on a Monday was especially sacred to the Hindus. Execution took place as ordered on that very day, 10TH March 1746. Lakhpat Rai then set out at the head of a large force, mostly cavalry supported by cannon, in search of Sikhs who were reported to have concentrated in the swampy forest of Kahnuvan, 15 km south of the present town of Gurdaspur. He surrounded the forest and started a systematic search for his prey. The Sikhs held out for some time striking back whenever they could but, heavily outnumbered and under equipped, they at last decided to make a final sally and escape to the hills in the northeast. They crossed the River Ravi and made for the heights of Basoli in the present Kathie district of Jammu and Kashmir only to find that the Hindu hill men in front were as hostile to them as the Muslim hordes following close upon their heels. Caught in this situation and bereft of provisions, they suffered heavy casualties in the area around Parol and Kathua. Yet making a last desperate bid, the survivors broke through the ring and succeeded in re-crossing the Ravi, though many were carried away in the torrent. With Lakhpat Rai still close behind, they crossed the Beas and the Sutlej to find refuge in their old sanctuary, the Lakhi Jungle, deep into the Malwa region.

Misldars

Chhota Ghallughara (Contd)

An estimated 7,000 Sikhs were killed and 3,000 captured in the action fought on 1 and 2ND May 1746. Lakhpat Rai marched back in triumph to Lahore where he had the captives beheaded in batches in the Nakhas or site of the horse market outside the Delhi gate where, in later times, the Sikhs raised a memorial shrine known as the Shahidganj, the treasure house of martyrs. Lakhpat Rai ordered Sikh places of worship to be destroyed and their holy books burnt. He even decreed that anyone uttering the word guru should be put to death. Considering that the word Gur meaning jaggery sounded like guru, he ordered that jaggery should be called a lump, and not Gur. The nightmarish episode of March May 1746 came to be known among the Sikhs as Ghallughara, later Chhota Ghallughara as compared to a still greater killing that befell those 16 years later, the Vadda Ghallughara of 5TH February 1762. Lakhpat Rai's boast of a total annihilation of the Sikh people, however, was soon falsified. In about six months time, the Sikhs were back on the scene converging upon Amritsar in small groups, and, on 30TH March 1747, the Sarbat Khalsa, congregation representative of the entire Panth, at Amritsar adopted a Gurmata, holy resolution, that a fort, named Ram Rauni be constructed by them at Amritsar as a permanent stronghold.

Ahmed Shah Abdali

Ahmed Shah Abdali at the head of a huge army entered the plains of the Punjab. Shah Nawaz prepared to oppose him. But Abdali was not deterred. A single assault by Abdali tired out Shah Nawaz's army, and he ran towards Delhi. On the other hand, the Mughal armies advanced to face the invader, Abdali. The two armies clashed at Sarhind. In this battle Mir Mannu (Muin-ul-Mulk) the son of the Imperial Prime Minister, fought so bravely that even the enemy praised him. Ahmed Shah Abdali was defeated and had to beat a shameful retreat to Afghanistan. The Mughal Emperor of Delhi pleased with the courage shown by Mir Mannu, appointed him as the governor of Punjab. For the Sikhs the invasion of Ahmed Shah Abdali proved a blessing in disguise. On the one hand they got relief from the atrocities of the Punjab government for some time and on the other hand they got an opportunity to strengthen their position during the prevailing chaotic conditions. They raised a fort at Amritsar which they called Ram Rauni. During the same period, a great Sikh general, Sardar Jassa Singh, sought to cobble together different Sikh Jathas into a single organization and knit them into a united fighting force named Dal Khalsa. This was to be the first Sikh army under the command of one general.

Misldars

Zakariya Khan

Zakariya Khan replaced his father Abd us-Samad Khan as governor of Lahore in 1726. After becoming the governor he launched severe policy against the Sikhs and let loose terror upon them. His moving military columns forced the Sikhs to seek shelter in remote hills and forests. Yet Sikh bands continued harassing the administration attacking government caravans and treasuries. Such was the effect of their depredations that Zakariya Khan was obliged to make terms with Diem. In 1733, he decided to lift the quarantine forced upon the Sikhs and made an offer of a grant. His envoy, Subeg Singh, a Sikh resident of the village of Jambar, near Lahore, who was for the time Kotwal or police inspector of the city under Muslim authority, reached Amritsar where the Sikhs had been allowed to assemble and celebrate the festival of Baisakhi after many years of exile, and offered them on behalf of the government the title of Nawab and of jagir consisting of the Parganahs of Dlpalpur, Karaganda and Jhabal, worth a lakh of rupees in revenue. But the entente soon came to an end, before the harvest of 1735; Zakariya Khan sent a force and occupied the jagir. The Silks were driven away towards the Malwa region by Lakhpat Rai, the Hindu minister at the Mughal court at Lahore. In the clashes that followed many officers of the Lahore army, including Lakhpat Rai's nephew Duni Chand, were killed. Zakariya Khan took the Held himself to re-establish his authority in the region. He had the fortress of Dallewal blown up and ordered village officials to capture Sikhs and hand them over for execution. A graded scale of rewards was laid down a blanket for cutting off Sikh's hair, ten rupees for information about the whereabouts of a Sikh, fifty rupees for a Sikh scalp. Plunder of Sikh homes was made lawful; giving shelter to Silks or withholding information about (heir movements was made a capital offence. Zakariya Khan's police consisting of nearly 20,000 men especially recruited for this purpose, scoured the countryside and brought back hundreds of Sikhs in chains. Prominent Sikhs including the revered Bhai Mani Singh and Bhai Taru Singh were, after the severest of torments, publicly beheaded at the horse market of Lahore, renamed by Sikhs Shahidganj in honour of the martyrs. Yet Zakariya Khan remained unsuccessful in his object of vanquishing the Sikhs. He died at Lahore on 1ST July 1745 a dispirited man, bequeathing to his sons and successors chaos and confusion.

Misldars

Mir Mannu

As governor of the Punjab, Mir Mannu continued the witch hunt of the Sikhs with much greater severity. His first act was to storm the fortress of Ram Rauni, in Amritsar, where 500 Sikhs had taken shelter. This drove the Sikhs to seek refuge in the mountains and jungles. Mannu issued orders to the hill chiefs to seize Sikhs and send them in irons to Lahore. Hundreds of Sikhs were thus brought daily to Lahore and executed at the horse market. As Ahmad Shah entered the Punjab, Mir Mannu, agreed to make over to the invader all territory west of the Indus and the revenue of Char Mahal or the four districts of Sialkot, Aurangabad, Gujrat and Pasrur. By the autumn of 1751 the Punjab was rife with rumours of another Afghan invasion. Mir Mannu had failed to pay the revenue of the four districts ceded to the Durrani and advance units of Afghan army under General Jahan Khan crossed the Indus. Mir Mannu summoned Kaura Mall from Multan and Adina Beg Khan from Jalandhar and made preparations to join battle. In December 1751, he crossed the Ravi to check the Afghans. Ahmad Shah made a detour, and closed in on Lahore from the north-east. Mannu quickly retraced his steps and entrenched himself outside the city walls. Hostilities between the two armies opened on 5 March 1752. Mir Mannu fought as long as he could, and then laid down arms. The Afghans extracted an indemnity of thirty lakh of rupees in cash from Mannu. By the terms of the treaty, Lahore and Multan were ceded to Ahmad Shah Durrani. The Sikhs had taken advantage of the conflict between the Afghans and the Mughals to spread out in the Bari Doab, Jalandhar Doab and across the Sutlej as far as Jind, Thanesar and beyond coming within 50 miles of Delhi. Mannu discovering how Sikhs had occupied large parts of his territory, now resumed his policy of repression. Prices were once again laid on their heads and strict orders were passed against giving refuge to them anywhere. Skirmishes between Sikh bands and Mannu's roving columns took place in different parts of the province. The able-bodied from among them were killed fighting; the non-combatants including women and children were brought in chains to Lahore and slaughtered in the horse market. The fighting and reprisals went on until the death of Mannu on 4TH November 1753 of an accidental fall from his horse. With Mannu's death ended yet another attempt to quash the rising power of the Khalsa. A Punjabi doggerel which became current among Sikhs in those days sums up how light they made of the atrocity Mannu heaped upon them:

"Mannu is our sickle, We the fodder for him to mow, the more he cuts, the more we grow."

Misldars

Lahore

One significant result of Ahmed Shah Abdali's repeated invasion was the Mughal administrative organization in the Punjab broke down. There remained no stable government in Punjab which could restore order. The Sikh Jathedars would not let such rare opportunity slip from their hands. They increased their strength many-fold. Their regular army, Dal Khalsa, had been organized and many well-known generals came to the fore. Prince Taimur proved an ordinary ruler and it was easy for the Sikhs to overpower him. As soon as Taimur attacked the sacred city of the Sikhs, Amritsar, and their fort Ram Rauni, the Sikhs assembled in thousands and shouting slogans of Akal, Akal, fell upon the enemy. Sikhs were adept in techniques of irregular warfare. They avoided giving a pitched battle in an open field. Their technique was to seize their chance, surprise the enemy, plunder goods and disappear immediately in the forests. Sikh horsemen used to have light equipment, swift steeds and they ran to hiding instantly. They put the enemy in a disadvantage position by repeated raids. Prince Taimur had to face such difficulties, and he left the battlefield in disgust. The Sikhs chased the retreating army of the Prince and created such disorder and confusion in his ranks that Taimur left Lahore and halted on the bank of the River Chenab. Sardar Jassa Singh Kalal of the Khalsa occupied Lahore and struck coin in his own name. Although the Sikhs had occupied Lahore and had even struck coin in their name, yet this time they were not powerful enough to retain their supremacy over Lahore for long. Taimur returned to Lahore after reinforcements arrived from Kabul. Thereupon the Sikhs withdrew from Lahore.

Battle of Panipat

Ahmed Shah Abdali set out towards India with a massive army. He knew full well that this time his encounter was not with the weak king of Delhi but with the mighty Martha confederacy. The encounter between the two armies took place in the year 1761 at Panipat. The Marathas were clearly defeated. They lost two hundred thousand soldiers killed and wounded. It was a great blow to the rising Maratha power, and it became hard from to recover from the shock for some time. Delhi lost whatever power it still possessed. The Mughal Emperor bid farewell to the throne of his ancestors, and found refuge at first in Oudh and then in Bengal. Ahmed Shah Abdali did not stay in Delhi for long. He returned to Afghanistan after appointing Zain Khan as Faujdar at Sarhind and Khwaja Obald as the governor of Lahore.

Misldars

Battle of Panipat 1761(Contd)

The Sikhs took full advantage of the battle of Panipat. They plundered Abdali's camp to their hearts content during his return journey. After that, all the Khalsa Sardars assembled at Durbar Sahib Amritsar along with their Jathas. A great council was held in which plans for future expeditions were deliberated upon. Such meetings were held at Amritsar from time to time. The Sikhs called these meetings Gurmata. (Resolution in the name of the Guru).

Vadda Ghallughara

Vadda Ghallughara, major holocaust or carnage, so called to distinguish it from another similar disaster, Chhota (minor). As Ahmad Shah was returning home after his historic victory over the Marathas in the third battle of Panipat in 1761, the Sikhs had harassed him all the way from the Sutlej right up to the Indus. Returning to the Central Punjab, they ravaged the country all around, annihilated the Afghan force in Char Mahal, drove away the faujdar of Jalandhar, plundered Sarhind and Malerkotla, defeated a force, 12,000strong, sent by Ahmad Shah from Afghanistan to punish them and another led personally by the Afghan governor of Lahore, and even captured Lahore, all within a short period, June September 1761. At a general assembly (Sarbat Khalsa) of the Dal at Amritsar convened on the occasion of Diwali, 27TH October 1761, it was resolved to punish the agents, informers and collaborators of the Afghans, beginning with Aqil Das of Jandiala, head of the heretical Niranjania sect and an inveterate enemy of the Sikhs. Aqil Das despatched messengers post-haste to Ahmad Shah Durrani, who had in fact already entered India at the head of a large army. Meanwhile, the Sikhs had besieged Jandiala, 18 km east of Amritsar. Aqil Das's messengers met the Shah at Rohtas. The latter advanced at quick pace but before he reached Jandiala, the Sikhs had lifted the siege and retired beyond the Sutlej with the object of sending their families to the safety of the wastelands of Malwa before confronting the invader. Ahmad Shah, on the other hand, determined to teach the Sikhs a lesson, sent messages to Zain Khan, faujdar of Sarhind, and Bhikham Khan, chief of Malerkotla, directing them immediately to check the Sikhs' advance, while he himself taking a light cavalry force set out at once and, covering a distance of 200 km including two river crossings in fewer than forty-eight hours, caught up with the Sikhs.

Misldars

Vadda Ghallughara (Contd)

Sikhs who were encamped at Kup Rahira, north of Malerkotla, at dawn on the 5TH of February 1762. The Sikh Misls was taken by surprise. The attacks of Zain Khan and Bhikham Khan were easily repulsed, but the main body of Ahmad Shah, much larger and better equipped, soon overtook them. Having to protect the slow moving baggage train including women, children, old men and other non-combatants, the Sikhs could not resort to their usual hit-and-run tactics, and a stationary battle against such superior numbers was inadvisable. Sardar Jassa Singh Ahluwalia, the commander in chief of the Dal, therefore, turning down a suggestion by Sardar Charhat Singh Sukarchakia to form a solid square of four Misls to face the enemy with two Misls each protecting either flank of the vahir and balance in reserve, decided that all the Misls combining to form a single force should make a cordon round the vahir and start moving towards Barnala, 40 km to the southwest, with the agents of the Malwa chiefs acting as guides. Thus "Fighting while moving and moving while fighting and kept the vahir marching, covering it as a hen covers its chickens under its wings." On several occasions, the Shah's troops broke the cordon and butchered the helpless non-combatants, but every time the Sikh warriors reformed and pushed back the attackers. By early afternoon they reached a big pond, the first they had come across since the morning. The fighting stopped automatically as the two forces fell pell-mell, man and animal, upon the water to quench their thirst and relax their tired limbs. The battle was not resumed. The Sikhs marched off towards Barnala and Ahmad Shah thought it prudent not to pursue them in the little known semi desert with an army that had had no rest during the past two days, and had suffered considerable loss of life in the daylong battle. Estimates of the Sikhs` loss of life vary from 20,000 to 50,000. The more credible figures are those of Miskin, a contemporary Muslim chronicler, 25,000, and Ratan Singh Bhangu, 30,000. This could have been. a crippling blow to the Sikhs, but such was the state of their morale that, to quote the Prachm Panth Prakash again, as the Sikhs gathered in the evening that day, a Nihang stood up and proclaimed aloud"... the fake has been shed. The true Khalsa remains intact." The Sikhs rose again within three months to attack Zain Khan of Sarhind, who bought peace by paying them Rs 50,000 in May, and they were ravaging the neighbourhood of Lahore during July-August 1762, Ahmad Shah, who was still in the Punjab, watching helplessly the devastation of the Jalandhar Doab at their hands.

Sikh Jathas

Occupation of Sarhind

Such tremendous loss could prove disastrous for this small community, but the Sikhs did not let the idea of defeat pass their minds. As soon as Ahmed Shah Abdali turned his back, the Sikhs began to regroup their Jathas and marched against Zain Khan, Abdali's faujdar at Sarhind. During December 1763, Zain Khan and his ally, Hangam Khan, Chief of Malerkotla, died fighting, and the Sikhs occupied Sarhind, and later handed over the land to Maharajah Ala Singh of Patiala State.

Occupation of Lahore

No sooner had Ahmed Shah Abdali returned to Afghanistan, than the Sikhs launched a combined attack on Lahore, Abdali's governor Kabuli Mal fled after a brief encounter, and the Sikhs occupied Lahore. Three Commanders of the Dal Khalsa, Gujar Singh, Sobha Singh and Lehna Singh, divided Lahore and its surrounding territories amongst themselves.

Equality

All the members, high or low, of a Jatha were considered equal. All of them were Singhs of the Guru and members of the Khalsa Panth. They fought for the protection of the Panth. Whatever booty fell into their hand during battle was distributed equally amongst them in accordance with the principal of equality. If a territory came under occupation of any Jatha, its villages and towns were also divided approximately, according to the same principal. Each Jatha had one Chief whom all the members of the Jatha accepted as their leader. Any member of the Jatha whenever he desired, could join another Jatha. He enjoyed full freedom to form his own Jatha. There are scores of instances of persons leaving their Jatha and organising their respective new Jathas. Smaller Jathas combined to form bigger ones under the command of Leaders who possessed better qualities to lead. But smaller Jathas did not lose their identity altogether. They maintained their colours even after joining the bigger ones. Thus they continued to have an identity of their own and every unit remained keen to exhibit its distinct role. As members of a Jatha used to divide plunder amongst them, now the Jathas began to divide territories accordingly. Thus different Jathas took possession of different territories. About the year 1764 twelve prominent Jathas of the Sikhs had come to existence, and they had divided among themselves the entire country from Jhelum to Saharanpur. In history books a Jatha has been described as Misl.

Sikhs and Mughals

Sikhs and Mughals

The Janam Sakhis, traditional accounts of the life of Guru Nanak Dev, describe a meeting between him and Babar, founder of the Mughal dynasty, who was impressed by the former's spiritual manner. Four of the Guru's sabads included in the Guru Granth Sahib allude to the havoc and misery Babar's invasion brought in its train. Emperor Humayun, while fleeing to Iran in 1540, waited upon Guru Angad at Khaḍur to seek his blessing. Akbar, liberal in his religious policy, treated Guru Amar Das, Guru Ram Das and Guru Arjan with reverence. His son and successor, Jahangir, was not an open-hearted. He had Guru Arjan executed and Guru Hargobind imprisoned for a time, though later he adopted a friendly attitude towards the latter. Gurū Hargobind gave a martial turn to the career of the Sikh community, and there occurred in his lifetime armed encounters with the imperial troops. Emperor Shah Jehan's eldest son, Dara Shikoh, was known to be an admirer of Gurū Har Rāi. Dara lost to Aurangzeb in the battle of succession. Aurangzeb, emperor from 1658 to 1707, summoned Guru Har Rāi to Delhi probably to explain his alleged support to Dara. The Guru did not go himself but sent his son, Ram Rai, who won the Emperor's favour by deliberately misreading a verse by Guru Nanak to please the king for which he was anathematized by his father. Gurū Har Rai's successor, Gurū Har Krishan, was also summoned by the Emperor to Delhi where he died of smallpox. Gurū Tegh Bahadur, Nānak IX, was executed in Delhi under Aurangzeb's orders. Gurū Gobind Siṅgh was forced to remain in a constant state of warfare owing to the intolerance of the Emperor. He addressed a strong letter of protest and admonition in Persian verse to Aurangzeb who invited him for personal parleys. But the Emperor died before the two could meet. The next Emperor, Bahādur Shah I, displayed friendly respect towards the Guru and relations between the Sikhs and the State would have taken a positive turn but for the sudden death of Gurū Gobind Siṅgh. Gurū Gobind Siṅgh shortly before his death vested the Guruship in the Granth or the Holy Book and the Panth or the community as a whole, ending the line of living Gurūs. On the other hand, the Mughal Empire, following the death of Aurangzeb, started disintegrating. There were rebellions everywhere, and outlying provinces had become virtually independent Emperors at Delhi came and went in quick succession, the throne changing hands eight times between 1707 and 1720.

Sikhs and Mughals

Sikhs and Mughals (Contd)
Sikhs rose in rebellion under the leadership of Banda Singh Bahadur and Emperor Bahādur Shah issued, on 10TH December 1710, a general warrant for the faujdars to "kill the worshippers of Nanak [i.e. Sikhs] wherever found." Persecution of the cruellest kind was let loose upon the Sikhs, who yet rose again and again with redoubled strength until in the late 1760's they became sovereign masters of the country between the Indus and the Yamuna. They took full advantage of the disorder caused by foreign invaders, Nadir Shah and Ahmad Shah Abdali. Shah Alam II was emperor only in name. Following the murder of his father, 'Ālamgīr II, on 29 November 1759, he had fled from Delhi, crowned himself in the camp, and lived at Allahabad up to 1771, returning to Delhi thereafter as a protégé of Mahadji Scindia, the Maratha chief of Gwalior. The Sikhs had established themselves in the Sarhind province up to Karnal and Panipat beyond which laid the crown-lands of the Emperor on both sides of the Yamuna. These territories became a perpetual raiding ground of the Sikhs. Even the imperial capital was not beyond their reach. In January 1774, they sacked Shahdara and in July 1775 they raided Paharganj and Jaisinghpura. Their depredations extended beyond Delhi as far as 'Aligarh and Farrukhabad. The Sikhs entered the Red Fort on 11TH March 1783, the Emperor and his courtiers hiding themselves in their private apartments. At the Emperor's request, Begam Samrū persuaded the Sikhs to retire from Delhi and spare the crown-lands. It was agreed that only Sardar Baghel Siṅgh of the Karorsiṅghīā Misl with 4,000 men would remain in the capital, with Sabzī Maṇḍi as his headquarters. He was allowed to build seven Gurdwaras at places sacred to the Sikhs. To meet the expenses of his troops and of the construction of Gurdwaras, he was permitted to charge six annas in a rupee (37.5 %) of the income from octopi duties in the capital. In 1787, the Sikhs aided Ghulam Qadir Ruhila to capture Delhi. Mahadji Scindia expelled the Ruhila chief from Delhi and reasserted his authority over the Emperor in October 1788. He tried without much success to placate the Sikhs, who had resumed their attacks on the crown-lands, which came to an end only after the Maratha's defeat at the hands of the British and the establishment of British supremacy at Delhi in 1803.

Ahmed Shah Abdali's repeated invasion was the Mughal administrative organization in the Punjab broke down. Consequently the Afghans controlled the fate of the Punjab, but they had to reckon with the Sikhs.

Sikhs and Afghans

Sikh and Afghans

Afghan Sikh Relations go back to the first invasion of India by Ahmad Shah Durrani, although he must have heard of the Sikhs when in 1739 he accompanied Nadir Shah, the Iranian invader, as a young staff officer. As a result of Ahmad Shah Durranis invasions of the Punjab the provinces of Lahore and Multan were annexed to the Afghan empire. This meant that Sikhs had now to contend with Afghans as well as with Mughals. The Sikhs preyed upon him during his own his march while transporting the plundered wealth of the Punjab. During Ahmad Shah`s fifth invasion (October 1759, May 1761), the Sikhs gave a battle to the invader in the neighbourhood of Lahore, in which the Afghans lost as many as 2,000 men, with their general Jahan Khan wounded. The Sikhs emboldened to raid Lahore in November 1760. They stayed there for eleven days and the Afghan deputy appeased them with a present of Rs 30,000 for sacramental karahprasad. In November 1761, they captured Lahore and struck their own coin. Ahmad Shah, on hearing of these developments, hurried to the relief of his deputies. Sikhs retreated as he marched upon them, but were overtaken near Kup and Rahira villages, near Malerkotla, on the morning of 5TH February 1762. About 25,000 Sikhs were killed in the daylong battle known in Sikh annals as Vadda Ghallughara or the great holocaust. On his return he blew up the holy Harmandir at Amritsar with gunpowder. The Sikhs retaliated with attacks on Sarhind in May 1762. They freely roamed around Lahore during July-August 1762 and celebrated Diwali at Amritsar in defiance of the Shah who was still present in the Punjab. After the departure of the Durrani in December 1762, Sikhs sacked the Afghan principality of Kasur in May 1763, over ran Jalandhar Doab during June, defeated in November near Wazirabad and expeditionary force sent by Ahmad Shah and invested Malerkotla, killing its Afghan chief, Bhikham Khan (December 1763). They followed these successes with the reduction of Morinda and Sarhind in January 1764. Ahmad Shah made yet another (his last) bid to regain Punjab and Delhi during the winter of 1766-67, but failed. He died at Qandahar on 23 October 1772. Ahmad Shah`s son and successor, Taimur Shah (1746-93), attempted five successive incursions, but could not reach Lahore. His successor, Shah Zaman, also made several attempts to regain a foothold in India and did enter Lahore twice (January 1797-December 1798) but was forced to evacuate it within a few weeks on each occasion. Ranjit Singh, the chief of the Sukarchakia Misl of the Dal Khalsa was destined finally to clear Punjab of the Afghans.

Sikh Confederacy (Misl)

Singhpuria Misl

Kapur Singh was the founder of this Misl. He commanded a force of 2500 Horse. "This force" says Latif "though small, was fiercest and most dreaded of all the Sikh soldiers." Kapur Singh attacked and occupied Faizullahpur. He changed the name of Faizullahpur to Singhpur, and the Misl began to be called Singhpuria Misl. On his death in 1755, his nephew Khushal Singh succeeded him. He was a powerful Sardar who further expanded the Misl in power and territories. Khushal Singh died in 1795 and was succeeded by his son Budh Singh.

Ahluwalia Misl

Jassa Singh Ahluwalia was the founder of Ahluwalia Misl. Jassa Singh started seizing villages and towns in the Punjab and established the system of Rakhi or protection. In 1777, he defeated Rai Ibrahim, the Bhatti chief, and took from him the present town of Kapurthala, converting it into the capital of the Ahluwalia Misl. His successor Fateh Singh was the chosen companion of Maharajah Ranjit Singh, with whom he, in 1802, exchanged turbans in a permanent bond of brotherhood. In the majority of Ranjit Singh's campaigns Fateh Singh served him with his contingents. Jassa Singh Ahluwalia died in 1837.

Bhangi Misl

The founder of the Jatha, i.e. band of warriors, that later acquired the dimensions of a Misl was Chajja Singh of Panjvar village, near Amritsar who had converted to Sikhism. He was succeeded by Bhuma Singh, a Dhillon Jatt of the village of Hung, near Badhni in present day Moga district, who won a name for himself in skirmishes with Nadir Shah's troops in 1739. On Bhuma Singh's death in 1746, his nephew and adopted son, Han Singh, assumed the leadership of the Misl. At the formation of the Dal Khalsa in 1748, Hari Singh was acknowledged head of the Bhangi Misl as well as leader of the Taruna Dal. He vastly increased the power and influence of the Bhangi Misl which began to be ranked as the strongest among its peers. He created an army of 20,000 dashing youths, captured Panjvar in the Tarn Taran parganah and established his headquarters first at Sohal and then at Gilvah, both in Amritsar district. Hari Singh kept up guerrilla warfare against the invading hosts of Ahmad Shah Durrani. In 1763, he along with the Kanhaiyas and Ramgarhias sacked the Afghan strong hold of Kasur. In 1764, he ravaged Bahawalpur and Multan.

Sikh Confederacy

Bhangi Misl (Contd)

Crossing the River Indus, he realized tribute from the Baluchi chiefs in the districts of Muzaffargarh, Dera Ghazi Khan and Dera Ismail Khan. On his way back home, he reduced Jhang, Chiniot and Sialkot. Hari Singh died in 1765. Hari Singh was succeeded by Jhanda Singh, his eldest son, under whom the Bhangi Misl reached the zenith of its power. In 1764, Jhanda Singh had invaded Multan and Bahawalpur, but failed to drive out the Durrani satrap Shuja Khan Suddozai. Jhanda Singh marched on Multan again in 1772 forcing the Nawab to flee. Multan was declared Khalsa territory and the city was parcelled out between Jhanda Singh and his commander Lehna Singh. Jhanda Singh subdued Jhang, Kala Bagh, and Mankera. He built a brick fort at Amritsar which he named Qila Bhangian and laid out fine bazaars in the city. He then preceded to Rasulnagar, where he recovered from the Muhammadan Chattha rulers the famous gun Zamzama which came to be known as Bhangian di Top. He was killed in 1774. He was succeeded by his brother Ganda Singh who, dying of illness at the time of a battle with the Kanhaiyas at Dinanagar, was in turn succeeded by his minor son, Desa Singh, under whose weak leadership began the decline of the dynasty. In January 1797 Ahmad Shah's grandson, Shah Zaman, led out an expedition and seized the city. But soon after the departure of the Durrani Shah for Kabul, Lehna Singh and Sobha Singh (Gujjar Singh had died in 1791), returned and re-established their rule. The same year, 1797, Lehna Singh died and was succeeded by his son Chet Singh and about the same time Sobha Singh died and was succeeded by his son Mohar Singh. But the new rulers failed to establish their authority. Reverting to the main branch of the Bhangi Misl Desa Singh, son of Ganda Singh was succeeded by his minor son Gulab Singh, who administered the Misl through his cousin Karam Singh. Gulab Singh enlarged the city of Amritsar where he resided, and, on attaining years of discretion, overran the whole Pathan colony of Kasur, which he subdued, the Pathan chiefs of Kasur, Nizamuddin and Qutb-ud-Din Khan, brothers, entering the service of the conqueror. In 1794, however, the brothers, with the aid of their Afghan countrymen, recovered Kasur. Gulab Singh died in 1800 and was succeeded by his son, Gurdit Singh, a 10-year old boy who conducted the affairs of the Misl through his mother and guardian, Mai Sukkhan. The last Bhangi chief to fall was Sahib Singh of Gujrat who was in possession of a few villages. At its height, the fighting strength of this Misl has been estimated to be nearly ten thousand horsemen.

Sikh Confederacy

Dallewala Misl
At the formation of the Dal Khalsa in 1748, Gulab Singh had a he plundered Panipat, Rohtak, Hansi and Hissar. On his death in 1759, Tara Singh Ghaiba succeeded him as head of the Misl. In 1760, he crossed the Satluj and seized the towns of Dharamkote and Fatehgarh. On his return to the Doab, he took Sarai Dakkani from Afghan chief Saif Ud-din of Jalandhar and marched eastwards seizing the country around Rahon. He made Rahon his headquarters. He next captured Nakodar from Manj Rajputs and several other villages on the right side of the Satluj, including Mahatpur and Kot Badal Khan. He joined other Sikh Sardars in laying siege to Sarhind and razing it to the ground after defeating its Faujdar Zain Khan. Its military strength has been estimated at eight thousand horsemen. Tara Singh died in 1807 at the age of 90.

Kanhaiya Misl
The Kanhaiya Misl was founded by Sardar Jai Singh. He seized part of Riloki comprising the district of Gurdaspur and upper portions of Amritsar. Jai Singh extended his territory to Parol and hill chiefs of Kangra, Nurpur, and Datarpur became his tributaries. In 1781, Jai Singh and his associate Haqiqat Singh led an expedition to Jammu and received a tribute from its new ruler, Brij Raj Dev. On Jai Singh's death in 1793, the control of the Kanhaiya clan passed into the hands of his daughter-in-law Sada Kaur. Sada Kaur whose daughter Mehtab Kaur was married to Ranjit Singh was instrumental in the Sukarchakia chief's rise to political power in the Punjab. The Kanhayas Misl United with The Sukarchakia Misl in 1796. The fighting strength of this Misl was nearly eight thousand horsemen.

Karora Singhia Misl
The founder of this Misl was Karora Singh. His descended, Baghel Singh, in February 1764, captured Saharanpur. In April 1775, Baghel Singh, overran the country ruled by Zabita Khan. In March 1776; he defeated the imperial forces near Muzaffarnagar. On 11TH March 1785, Sikhs entered the Red Fort in Delhi and occupied the Diwan-i-Am. The Mughal emperor, made a settlement with them, agreeing to allow Baghel Singh to raise Gurdwaras on Sikh historical sites. He located seven sites sacred to the Sikhs and had shrines risen thereon. Baghel Singh died in 1806 at Amritsar. The fighting strength of the Misl was estimated to have been twelve thousand horsemen.

Sikh Confederacy

Nakai Misl

Nakai Misl was founded by Hira Singh. He led a band of notoriously brave young men on great plundering raids. He was part of the Khalsa, when the Sikhs sacked Kasur in 1763 and conquered Sarhind in 1764. Hira Singh occupied Bahirval, Chunlan, Dlpalpur, Jambar, Jethupur, Kanganval and Khudian, establishing his headquarters at Chunian. In 1767, he was killed in an expedition to Pakpattan. His successor Ran Singh died in 1781 and was succeeded by his eldest son Bhagvan Singh. Kahn Singh succeeded Bhagvan Singh. The fighting strength of this Misl remained at two thousand only.

Nishananvali Misl

Nishananvali Misl owed its origin to Dasaundha Singh, whose Jatha was the standard-bearers of the Dal Khalsa. The Misl was originally based in Amritsar where it guarded the Holy Harmandir and also served as a reserve force of the Dal Khalsa. In January 1764, Dasaundha Singh took possession of Singhanvala, Sahneval, Sarai Lashkari Khan, Amloh, Doraha, lirfi, and Ambala. On his death, Mohar Singh became the leader of the Misl. Its territories included Ambala, Shahabad, Saunti, Kheri, Morinda, Amloh, Khanna, Doraha, Sahneval, Machhivara and Zira. The fighting force of this Misl consisted of twelve thousand horsemen

Shahid Misl

The Shahid Misl was mostly made up of Nihangs, a class of Warriors who owed their origin to Baba Fateh Singh, son of Guru Gobind Singh. The Shahids under Dip Singh had their headquarters at Talwandi Sabo. They also held control of the Harmandir at Amritsar. After Dip Singh's death, the leadership of the Misl passed on to Karam Singh, a Sandhu Jatt belonging to the village of Marahka in Sheikhupura district, now in Pakistan. In January 1764, at the conquest of the Sarhind province by the Sikhs, he seized a number of villages in the Parganahs of Kesari and Shahzadpur in Ambala district. In 1773, he overran a large tract of land belonging to Zabita Khan Rohilla in the upper Gangetic Doab. He captured a number of villages in Saharanpur district. After Karam Singh's death in 1784, his elder son, Gulab Singh, succeeded to the headship of the Misl. On Gulab Singh's death in 1844, his son Shiv Kirpal Singh succeeded to the family estate. The fighting strength of the Misl was two thousand horsemen.

Sikh Confederacy

Ramgharia Misl

Ramgarhia Misl took its name from Jassa Singh Ramgarhia. He gained reputation as a soldier of daring and skill. He, along with his brothers Jai Singh, Khushal Singh and Mali Singh, took up service under Adina Beg, faujdar of the Jalandhar Doab, which he quit when the Sikhs taunted him with betrayal of the Panth. To begin with, Jassa Singh joined hands with Jai Singh of the Kanhaiya Misl and seized large slices of territory in four out of the five Doabs. Within a decade Jassa Singh became one of the leading figures of the Dal Khalsa. In 1770, he led plundering expeditions into the hills. Jassa Singh Ramgarhia, along with other Sikh Sardars, fought many pitched battles against Ahmad Shah Durrani, the Afghan invader. As the Afghan threat receded, Sikh Sardars began fighting among themselves and Ramgarhia Sardar had to flee the Punjab. Driven out of the Punjab, Jassa Singh became a soldier of fortune. He took possession of Hissar and raised a large body of irregular horse, his depredations extending to the gates of Delhi and its suburbs, and into the Gangetic Doab. Once he penetrated into Delhi itself, and carried off four guns from the Mughal arsenal. The Nawab of Meerut agreed to pay him 10,000 rupees a year on his agreeing to leave his district unmolested. He soon, with a body of 30,000 horse and foot under him, and Karam Singh Shahid, crossed into Saharanpur district, ravaging it at will. On the death of Jassa Singh Ahluwalia in 1783, Jassa Singh Ramgarhia returned to the Punjab and recovered his lost possessions. He allied himself with the Sukarchakias, and their combined forces broke the power of the Kanhaiyas. At the height of its power, Ramgarhia Misl's territories in the Bari Doab included Batala, Kalanaur, Dinanagar, Sri Hargobindpur, Shahpur Kandi, Gurdaspur, Qadian, Ghuman, Matteval, and in the Jalandhar Doab, Urmur Tanda, Sanh, Miani, Garhdivala and Zahura. In the hills Kangra, Nurpur, Manndi and Chamba paid tribute to Jassa Singh.

Jassa Singh died in April 1803 at the ripe age of 80, leaving two sons, Jodh Singh and Vir Singh, the former of whom succeeded him. Jodh Singh was a deeply religious person. He built the Ramgarhia Bunga on the premises of the Harmandir at Amritsar and supplied blocks of perforated marble that served as parapets on both sides of the causeway leading to the sanctuary. On the height of its power there were over one hundred fortresses in the Misl's territories. The fighting strength of the Misl has been estimated at three thousand horsemen.

Sikh Confederacy

Sukarchakia Misl

Buddha Singh laid the foundation of the Sukarchakia fortunes. When Buddha Singh died in 1718, there were scars of forty wounds by spear, sword and matchlock counted upon his body. Buddha Singh's son Naudh Singh was killed in a battle in 1752. Charhat Singh, the eldest son of Naudh Singh, moved his headquarters from Sukarchakia to Gujranwala and erected battlements round the town. The Afghan governor of Lahore came to apprehend Charhat Singh but was repulsed by the Sardar and forced to retreat, leaving behind his guns and stocks of grain. Charhat Singh extended his domains by capturing the towns of Wazirabad, Eminabad and Rohtas. Charhat Singh more than settled his account with the Afghans by chasing them on their return march and plundering their baggage trains. His last foray was into Jammu in 1770, where in one of the skirmishes he fell mortally wounded by the bursting of his own matchlock. Charhat Singh's young son, Mahan Singh, inherited his father's spirit and ambition. He launched upon a career of conquest and expansion of his territory. He captured Rasulnagar from a Muslim tribe, the Chathas, and took Pindi Bhatian, Sahival, 'Isa Khel and Jhang. In 1782, he proceeded to Jammu and with the loot of Jammu; Mahan Singh raised the Sukarchakia from a position of comparative obscurity to that of being one of the leaders of the Sikh Confederacy. At his death, his 10-year-old son, Ranjit Singh, became the head of the Sukarchakia house. Young Ranjit Singh had inherited from his ancestors a sizeable estate in North-western Punjab, a band of intrepid horse and matchlock men, and an ambition that knew no bounds.

Phulkian Misl

Ala Singh laid the foundation of Phulkian fortunes by carving out the principality of Patiala. By 1732, he had conquered a vast territory around Barmala. Ala Singh extended his hold over a number of villages in the Sarkar of Sarhind and occupied important towns such as Sunam, Samansa, Sanaur and Tohana. Phulkian Misls of the Cis-Satluj territories did not serve under the banner of the Dal Khalsa. Baba Ala Singh died in August 1765 and was succeeded by his grandson, Amar Singh. His son Sahib Singh, like other Cis-Satluj Chiefs, accepted the British protection in 1809.

Sikh Confederacy

The Misls

The united strength of the Sikhs was approximately seventy thousand horsemen. It was with this massive force that they began adding to their conquests. As has been stated earlier there was no central authority which could exercise control over these different chiefs and consolidate the Sikh government. Each chief was independent within his own principality, and did as he willed. Of course in the event of foreign invasion all these chiefs united and fought under the flag of the Dal Khalsa for the protection of the Panth. In the absence of common danger they did not hesitate to fight among themselves. The boundaries of the possession of another of Misls were not clearly defined, and usually overlapped with one another's territory, and this situation usually remained a major cause of their wrangling. There was absence of cohesion within the Misls as well the germs of discord remained ever active. Everyone within the Misl nursed an ambition within himself to become a Misldar. Ahmed Shah Abdali's invasions had stopped for ever and their remained no other internal power within the country that could equal the might of the Sikhs. The Sikhs were war-like people and therefore could not remain silent. Their restless nature led to conditions of civil war. On any pretext they would attack their neighbouring chiefs and fight relentlessly. Self-aggrandisement became the reigning principal and 'might is right' the order of the day. Thus history of the Punjab of the last quarter of the eighteenth century is the story of internecine warfare. The chief of one Misl would invade the other. Sometimes united armies of two or three Misls would establish hegemony over the other's possessions. In short Punjab presented a dismal picture bordering anarchy. The traveller George Foster in 1783, shortly after the birth of Ranjit Singh could foreshadow this change:

'Should any future cause call forth the combined efforts of the Sicques to maintain the existence of empire and religion, we may see some ambitious chief led on by his genius and success, and absorbing the power of his associates displays from the ruins of their commonwealth the standard of monarchy. The page of history is filled with the like effects, springing from the like causes. Under such form of government, I have little hesitation to saying that the Sicques would be soon advanced to the first rank among the natives of Hindustan, and should become terror to the surrounding states'.

Maharajah Ranjit was such a man. Let us find out who he was and to which lineage belonged.

Ancestry of Ranjit Singh

Kalu & Bara

Ranjit Singh was descended from Bhatti Rajputs. Bhatti Rajputs trace their history back to Jaisalmir, in the great Thar Desert. Bhatti moved and established themselves across the fertile plains of the Punjab. As time passed most Bhatti married Jat women, simply because there were no Bhatti families around in the region to whom they were not related. As a consequence, Rajputs refused them recognition and all the future generations were known as Jats. The head of this clan which had moved north was known as Kalu the Bhatti. He established his family in 1470 at a village about forty miles south-west of Lahore, which he called Mouza Pind Bhatian. The family lived for three generations, except for Kalu who quarrelled with the rest of the family and moved to a village called Sansi, where he died in 1488. Many generations later, his descendant Bara, at the age of twenty-five, visited Amritsar and entered the Sikh faith. He died in 1679 after spending the rest of his life preaching the faith in the adjoining villages of Kiali and SukarChalk. His nine year son Budha succeeded him.

Sardar Budha Singh

Sardar Budha Singh was an affluent Jat farmer of the village of SukarChalk in the Majha tract of the Punjab. His original name was Desu. He was born in 1670. He possessed 25 acres of land and three ploughs and a well. On this land he had built a couple of houses for his family and cattle. The place was named SukarChalk. SukarChalk was situated near Gujranwala, 70 Kms, and north of Lahore. One of his ancestors was initiated into Sikhism by Guru Gobind Singh in 1692. Budha Singh was a daring adventurer and is said to have taken part in the battles of Guru Gobind Singh and Banda Singh Bahadur. The success, which attended his exploits, won him the reputation of being one of the boldest and the most resolute of the Sikhs of the Punjab He built a fortress-like mansion at his village. He was always held in high esteem by the Sikhs. He used to ride a piebald mare called after him as Desi which had crossed with its rider the rivers of Jhelum, Ravi and Chenab fifty times. The brave and courageous Budha Singh, who was a giant in strength, is said to have received during his life time some forty sword cuts and nine matchlock wounds, without his physical strength failing him. Budha Singh was distinguished for the most intrepid courage; for his sagacity and shrewdness which bore him successfully through all his schemes, and for his ready wit and good humour. He was also famed for his regard to the rights and property of the poor. He died of apoplexy in 1718.

Ancestry of Ranjit Singh

Sardar Naudh Singh
On his death, Budha Singh left behind two sons, named Naudh Singh and Chanda Singh. Naudh Singh grew up into a healthy and beautiful Youngman. During the time of drought he used to bring his cattle to graze to the Majitha village in the present Amritsar district- Gulab Singh, a baptised Sikh of Majitha, married his daughter Lali to Naudh Singh in 1730, on the condition that he should get himself duly baptised. Gulab Singh was a devoted follower of the Khalsa Panth. Under the inspiration of his father-in-law, Naudh Singh joined the Dal Khalsa under the command of Kapur Singh Faizullapuria. He left his home and moved about in the inhospitable jungles along with his companions. He came into prominence when in the accompaniment of Kapur Singh; he relieved Ahmad Shah Durani of his baggage and heavy booty id 1749. Sultan Khan Chattha, Pathan of Rasulnagar, forcibly converted six Sikhs to Islam. Naudh Singh and Chanda Singh attacked Rasulnagar, plundered Sultan Khan's property and brought back the Sikhs and baptised them again. Shahab-ud-Din of Firozwala captured a few Sikhs of village Earyala and removed the hair of their heads and beards. Naudh Singh and Chanda Singh plundered his village and put Shahab-ud-Din to death. In 1749, Naudh Singh was wounded by a gun-shot in the head while fighting against the Afghan invaders. The wound did not prove fatal but he was incapacitated and he lingered on for a few years without participating in the Sikh movement in the Punjab and died.

Sardar Charhat Singh
Sardar Naudh Singh had four sons - Charhat Singh, Dal Singh, Chet Singh and Magahi Singh. The eldest, Charhat Singh was then 20 years old. During the same period, Sardars Jassa Singh Ahluwalia, Hari Singh and Jhanda Singh Bhangis had established their respective Misls and had occupied different territories. Charhat Singh, though young in age, was very intelligent and far sighted. He held consultations with his companions and having collected select brave young men of his area decided to organise a Misl of his own. Charhat Singh was a sagacious and influential young man. Within two years, he succeeded to translate his plans into reality. He raised the flag of his Misl with one hundred horse and foot. His father-in-law Amir Singh and the latter's son Gurbakhsh Singh provided great encouragement and considerable help to him in this matter. Amir Singh at that time was quite old, but had been a great soldier and warrior during his time.

Ancestry of Ranjit Singh

Sardar Charhat Singh (Contd)

The people of Gujranwala trembled at the mention of his name. This facilitated the task for Charhat Singh. Munshi Sohan Lal mentions in his book that Charhat Singh had set the principle that only he who maintained unshorn hair and had taken *Amrit (Khande-di-Pahul)* could be enlisted in his Misl. He himself used to administer *Amrit* to young men before enlisting them. The Muslim governor of Eminabad persecuted his Hindu subjects. Charhat Singh considered it a good opportunity. Soon after the organisation of his Misl, Charhat Singh besieged Eminabad with his young energetic soldiers. The sack of Eminabad brought into the hands of Charhat Singh huge amount of money, valuable goods, many guns and muskets and other munitions from the state magazine and hundreds of horses from the royal stables. Encouraged by this success, Charhat Singh constructed a strong fort at Gujranwala. Gujranwala is situated at a distance of thirty sixty miles (96 Kms) from Lahore. To teach Charhat Singh a lesson for this audacity, Khwaja Obed invaded Gujranwala with a large force. Charhat Singh took refuge in his newly built fort. But during the nights, the Sukarchakia soldiers sallied out of the fort mauled Khwaja's forces and returned safely to the fort. Khawaja Obed was compelled to raise the siege and beat the retreat. Charhat Singh with his young warriors fell upon the enemy's retreating army so as to dispossess them of their provisions and equipment. A large quantity of munitions of war and hundreds of camels and horses fell into his hands. Sardar Charhat Singh further strengthened his position and embarked upon conquest of new territories. He expelled the Muslim *faujdar* of Wazirabad, occupied it and entrusted its *thanedar* (policing) to his brother-in-law Gurbakhsh Singh. He also established his hegemony over Pind Dadan Khan and its surroundings across the river Jehlum and constructed a fort there during the same year. Charhat Singh also occupied the salt mines of Kheora which proved to be a source of income for him. He conquered Dhani and Pothohar regions and subjugated landlords of Chakwal, Jalalpur, etc. Charat Singh was still at Ahmadabad near Jehlum River when he got the news that Ahmad Shah Abdali had reached Attock. He, therefore, attacked the famous fort of Rohtas, expelled Abdali's *Qiladar,* and Nur-ud-Din Khan, occupied the fort and established a *Thana* or post there. In brief, within a short period of fifteen years, Charhat Singh expanded his possessions tremendously.

Ancestry of Ranjit Singh

Sardar Charhat Singh (Contd)

His Misl progressed by leaps and bounds, Gujranwala, Wazirabad, Ramnagar, Sialkot, Rohtas, Pind Dadan Khan, and Dhani territory were included' in the Sukarchakia principality. Its annual income was estimated at three-hundred thousand rupees. Ever since the day Sardar Charhat Singh established his control over Pind Dadan Khan and the salt mines of Kheora, the Bhangi Sardars got envious of him. Hostilities started between the two and skirmishes began to take place quite often. In 1771, the armies arrayed in the battlefield and Sardar Charhat Singh was mortally wounded by the bursting of his own matchlock and died within a few minutes

Sardar Mahan Singh

Sardar Charhat Singh had three children, two sons, Mahan Singh and Sahaj Singh, and one daughter. The elder son Mahan Singh was only ten years old then. Therefore, Charhat Singh's widow, Mai Desan, took the administration of the State in her own hands. In this task, her brothers, Gurbakhsh Singh and Dal Singh greatly helped her. Mai Desan was a worldly-wise, experienced and intelligent lady. To firm up her authority she married her daughter to Sahib Singh, son of the Bhangi Chief of Gujrat. With this, enmity between the two Misls abated for some time. Shortly after this, she married her son, Mahan Singh, to the daughter of Gajpat Singh, Chief of Jind. These matrimonial alliances strengthened the position of Sukarchakia Misl. Besides this, Desan also strengthened the fortifications of Gujranwala.

When Mahan Singh came of age, he took the reins of the Misl in his own hands. He, again wrested Rohtas fort from Nur-ud-Din, and established his hegemony over Kotli Ahangaran near Sialkot. The artisans of this place were skilful manufacturers of shot fire arms. Mahan Singh took full advantage of these craftsmen and armed his men with new versions of muskets. The ruler of Rasulnagar, Pir Mohammad Khan, was from among the notable Pathan chiefs of Chattha clan. He was by nature a bigot and had developed special enmity towards the Sikhs. The youthful Mahan Singh did not tolerate this. He, therefore, attacked Rasulnagar in 1779A.D. Pir Muhammad Khan fought well but was beaten at last. Mahan Singh captured the town and renamed it Ramnagar, the name it bears till today. Although Pir Muhammad Khan had become a tributary of Mahan Singh, the fire of revenge kept smouldering in the heart of the brave Chathas. Therefore they soon rose in rebellion.

Ancestry of Ranjit Singh

Sardar Mahan Singh (Contd)

Sardar Mahan Singh attacked them again after three years. This time he also occupied Alipur, Mancher, etc. He renamed Alipur as Akalgarh. Mahan Singh returned after conquering Rasulnagar. No sooner had he entered the bounds of Gujranwala than he got the happy news of the birth of a son to him. Mahan Singh was overjoyed. Because he had just returned after a victory in the field, he named his son Ranjit Singh during the function held for celebration of the victory. He said that the newborn would always be victorious in field of battle. Later on, it became clear that Mahan Singh's guess proved absolutely correct. Ranjit Singh was born at Gujranwala at midday on Monday, November 13, 1780. Because of his victory over the Chattha tribe, Mahan Singh's fame spread far and near. Among the Khalsa *Jathedars,* his name got included among the front rankers. Therefore, many a notable *Sardar* began joining his Misl. The fighting strength of this Misl increased manifold. Now Sardar Mahan Singh toured the country up to Pindi Bhatian, Sahiwal and Isakhel and collected huge amount of revenue from these territories. Ranjit Deo, Raja of Jammu died in 1782. A dispute for succession arose between his two sons, Brij Raj Deo and Daler Singh. Earlier, the Bhangi Chiefs had tried once or twice to subdue Jammu during a similar situation. Mahan Singh, too, cast covetous eyes on Jammu in midst of this fratricidal feud of the Jammu princes. He invaded Jammu. Brij Raj Deo was overawed and ran away for life taking shelter in the hills of Tarkotah. Mahan Singh's army plundered the wealthy city of Jammu to their heart's content and returned to Gujranwala via Ramnagar with rich booty. During the same year, on the occasion of Diwali, Mahan Singh went to Amritsar for the holy bath. As usual, eminent chiefs including Jai Singh Kanhayas gathered there. Jai Singh was a respectable elderly chief. Mahan Singh went to his residence to pay his respects. There, the mention of the plunder of Jammu by Mahan Singh enraged Jai Singh Kanhayas. In heart of hearts he was jealous of the rising power of Mahan Singh. He used some contemptuous words against Mahan Singh during the conversation. Mahan Singh retorted likewise. The matter got serious and both prepared for war. Mahan Singh thought that it would be difficult for him to humble a veteran like Jai Singh who could elicit support from other *Misldars* as well. Therefore he entered into negotiations with Sardar Jassa Singh of Ramgarhia Misl. Jassa Singh had been ousted from his possessions by Jai Singh and he was loitering in wilderness in the area of Hansi and Hissar across the Sutlej. He was too willing to help Mahan Singh and came back to the Punjab.

Ancestry of Ranjit Singh

Sardar Mahan Singh (Contd)

Therefore Sansar Chand also joined Mahan Singh and Jassa Singh Ramgarhia. The confederacy of the three invaded Jai Singh's territories and occupied Batala. Jai Singh's doughty son Gurbakhsh Singh came forward to face combined forces. A pitched battle ensued in which Gurbakhsh Singh fell fighting and the Kanhayas army lost ground. Jai Singh was left with no other course but to seek peace. Jassa Singh and Sansar Chand got back their possessions. During the combat, Jai Singh was deeply impressed by Mahan Singh's prowess and courage. Moreover, the death of Gurbakhsh Singh left the veteran dismayed. Therefore, he, on the suggestion of his daughter- in-law, Sada Kaur, (the widow of Gurbakhsh Singh), thought it wise to contract relationship with Mahan Singh. Therefore, he engaged the daughter of his late son, Gurbakhsh Singh to Mahan Singh's son Ranjit Singh. Thus a matrimonial alliance came about between the two Misls - which Ranjit Singh fully exploited to his advantage during the time of his early struggle of which mention will be made later on. As has been mentioned earlier, Mahan Sing's sister was married to Sahib Singh Bhangi and both of them vouchsafed for mutual friendship and love. But it is hard to maintain coalescence between authority and personal relationship because authority overcomes relationship. Thus when Sahib Singh's father, Gujjar Singh died and Sahib Singh succeeded to the cheifship of Gujrat, Mahan Singh demanded tribute from him. But Sahib Singh contended that family had always maintained cordial relationship with the Sukarchakias and refused to pay tribute to Mahan Singh. This led to hostilities but Sahib Singh could not give fight. He left Gujrat and shut himself in the fort of Sodharah. Mahan Singh Lald a siege around the fort of Sodharah. During the siege, Mahan Singh fell ill. His health had already deteriorated due to strain of campaigning. With the passage of time, it showed no sign of improvement. At last Mahan Singh entrusted the command of the siege of Sodharah to his son, Ranjit Singh who was only ten years old then. Ranjit Singh continued the siege. Meanwhile, the Bhangi Chiefs dispatched two contingents of troops in aid of Sahib Singh. But Ranjit Singh intercepted them on the way and fell upon them unawares. They were left with no other option but to leave the field. A huge catch of their weapons and several guns fell into Ranjit Singh's hands. The siege had not yet ended when Mahan Singh after a brief illness died at the age of thirty, in the prime of his life.

Sardar Ranjit Singh

Sardar Ranjit Singh

Sardar Ranjit Singh was born in 1780. His birth name was Budh Singh. Sardar Mahan Singh had child's father had his name changed to Ranjit (literally, 'victor in battle' to commemorate his army's victory over the Chatha chieftain, Pir Muhammad. When Sardar Ranjit Singh was with his father in the sack of Jammu he contracted smallpox, which resulted in the loss of sight in his left eye and a pockmarked face. He was short in stature, never schooled, and did not learn to read or write anything beyond the Grumukhi alphabet, however, he was trained at home in horse riding, musketry and other martial arts. At age 15, Sardar Ranjit Singh married his first wife Mehtab Kaur, the only daughter of Sardar Gurbakhsh Singh Kanhaiya and his wife Sardarni Sada Kaur. By virtue of Ranjit Singh's first marriage, an alliance had been forged between Sukarchakia and Kanhaiya Misls. The powerful Sukarchakia and Kanhaiya Misls now became a formidable force. In order to further strengthen his position, Sardar Ranjit Singh, began to make overtures of friendship to the chief of Nakai Misl. As a result, Sardar Ranjit Singh got married to Sardarni Raj Kaur, the daughter of Sardar Ram Singh, chief of the Nakai. Sardar Mahan Singh had performed the rites of dastarbandi (succession) of Sardar Ranjit Singh during his lifetime. After his death Sardar Ranjit Singh inherited Sukarchakia Misl and its estates. Sardar Ranjit Singh was yet a ten years old lad. Although he had seen many a battle along with his father, yet it was difficult for him to carry the burden of leading his confederacy at that young age. He was raised by his mother Sardarni Raj Kaur, (Mai Malawian) who also ruled the Misl in the name of the minor Sardar Ranjit Singh.

Ramnagar

Ramnagar is situated on the left bank of River Chenab, north-west of Gujranwala. Its original name was Rasulnagar and it was the stronghold of Chatha Pathans. It was captured from Pir Mohammed, its Chattha leader by Mahan Singh of Sukarchakia Misl on behalf of Sardar Ranjit Singh in 1795. He granted Sardar Ranjit Singh two villages. He built a fort and a Baradari and laid a fine garden on the banks of the river and used it as a holiday home for himself. Sardar Ranjit Singh was a lover of life, he liked to surround himself with handsome men and women, and he had a passion for hunting, horses, and strong liquor.

Sardar Ranjit Singh

Master of the Misl
When he was seventeen year old, in 1798, he took the reins of Sukarchalk Misl in his own hands. He was in the possession of 18 forts, as regards to the army he had a force of 1,200 horse and 2,000 foot in permanent employment. In case of an emergency he could raise 11,000 horse and 6,000 foot. Sardar Dal Singh was his commander-in-chief, Commander Gulab Khan Afghan commanded the Najib Battalion of 1,000 foot. Mian Ghouse Khan was the Darogha of Topkhana and commanded 1,000 Afghan infantry with six guns. Besides the following feudal chiefs could supply him contingents of varying in strength: Sardar Ahmad Khan Afghan with 1,000 horse, Sardar Fatah Khan Afghan with 100 horse, Sardar Fatah Singh Dhari with 1,000 horse, Sardar Jot Singh with 1,000 horse, and Sardar Liaq Missar with 100 horse.

Shah Zaman's first invasion in 1793
Shah Zaman became the ruler of Afghanistan in May 1793. As soon as Shah Zaman came to the throne, he proclaimed his intention of re-establishing the Afghan sway in India, and founding an Indian Empire. His first attempt brought him to Peshawar. His advance guard of 5,000 crossed the Indus at Attock, and marched upto Hasan Abdal. After a sharp skirmish with Sardar Milkha Singh of Rawalpindi he returned to Afghanistan, to put down a revolt by his brother, Mahmud. Sardar Ranjit Singh did not come into contact with the Shah at this time, though he was present at Pind Dada Khan to watch the Shah's movements.

Shah Zaman's second Invasion in 1795
Shah Zaman's second invasion occurred in November-December, 1795. He advanced and retook Hasan Abdal. His general Ahmed Khan Shahanchibashi marched from Attock and captured Rohtas which belonged to Sardar Ranjit Singh. Sardar Ranjit Singh withdrew his men without any fighting and retired to Pind Dadan Khan along with other Sikh Sardars. A body of Afghans attacked them. Sardar Ranjit Singh and other Sikh Sardars crossed the River Jhelum and gathered on its southern bank. Once again Shah Zaman had to return home, this time to prevent an invasion of his own country from me west. He reached Peshawar on 3RD January 1796 on his way to Afghanistan. By the capture of Rohtak by General Ahmed Khan Shahanchibashi, Sardar Ranjit Singh, the first Sikh chieftain to suffer at the hands of Shah Zaman.

Sardar Ranjit Singh

Shah Zaman's third invasion in 1796

Ranjit Singh did not have much difficulty in recovering Rohtas. In the autumn of 1796 Shah Zaman crossed the Indus for the third time and halted at Peshawar for about a month. He had a well equipped army of over thirty thousand men, and was assured of help from many quarters. Sardar Ranjit Singh lay encamped on the southern bank of the River Jhelum with 10,000 men. He sent womenfolk with cash and jewellery to Patiala. On the advance of the Shah Zaman, Sardar Ranjit Singh's men evacuated Rohtas fort and joined him. He retired to Pind Dadan Khan and then his camp to Miani. Sardar Ranjit Singh at the head of a strong contingent forded the River Jhelum, delivered a surprise attack on the Shah's troops at Pind Dadan Khan and hurriedly crossed the river. On 31st December 1796, Sher Mohammad Khan Wazir at the head of 12,000 troops entered Lahore. Shah Zaman reached Lahore on 1ST January 1797. The Sikhs retired to Amritsar. Sardar Ranjit Singh at the head of 9,000 troops lay encamped to the north of Amritsar. On 11TH June 1797 a detachment of Afghan troops attacked Amritsar. The Sikhs repulsed the attack inflicting heavy loss. The main Afghan army under Shah Zaman arrived at Amritsar on 12TH January. The Shah was defeated and pursued to the very walls of Lahore. In January 1797, Shah Zaman received intelligence that his brother, Mahmud, was again up in arms against him. He left his ablest officer, Ahmad Khan Shahanchibashi, at Rohtas to keep a watch on the Sikhs. He was given thousand Afghan soldiers, 100 pieces of camel artillery, four guns and two lakhs of rupees. Sardar Ranjit Singh and the other Sardars engaged him in a fight and killed him on 29TH April 1797. The Sikhs followed closely at Shah Zaman's heels, as he reached Peshawar on 25TH February 1797, harassing him all the way up to the Jehlum. Sardar Ranjit Singh decimated his columns fleeing towards Gujrat. On 27TH November 1798, Shah Zaman again entered Lahore. An Afghan detachment was sent towards Amritsar. Sardar Ranjit Singh accompanied by other Sikh Sardars met it about 10 km outside the city and, after a fierce three hour encounter compelled the Afghans to retreat. The Afghans were pursued to the walls of Lahore. Shah Zaman was again compelled to return to Afghanistan where his brother, Mahmud, was again stirring up trouble. As soon as the news of Shah Zaman's departure for Afghanistan reached the Sikhs at Amritsar, they broke camp and hurried back to reclaim their estates. Sardar Ranjit Singh quickly went in pursuit of the Afghans. He kept up a running fight with them right up to Attock.

Sardar Ranjit Singh

Shah Zaman fourth invasion in 1798

Shah Zaman led his fourth campaign in the Punjab in September 1798. This time even Muslims were not spared by Shah Zaman's forces and he won Gujarat easily. The Afghans plundered the towns and villages as they had vowed and declared that they would exterminate the Sikhs. However, it was the Muslims who suffered most as the Hindus and Sikhs had already left for the hills. The Muslims had thought that they would not be touched but their hopes were dashed and their provisions forcibly taken from them by the Afghans. Shah Zaman attacked Lahore and the Sikhs, surrounded as they were on all sides, had to fight a grim battle. The Afghans occupied Lahore in November 1798 and planned to attack Amritsar. Sardar Ranjit Singh collected his men and faced Shah's forces about eight kilometres from Amritsar. They were well-matched and the Afghans were, at last, forced to retire. Humiliated, they fled towards Lahore. Sardar Ranjit Singh pursued them and surrounded Lahore. Afghan supply lines were cut, crops were burnt and other provisions plundered so that they did not fall into Afghan's hands. It was a humiliating defeat for the Afghans. Nizamuddin of Kasur attacked the Sikhs near Shahdara, but his forces were no match for the Sikhs. Here too, it was the Muslims who suffered the most. The retreating Afghans and Nizamuddin forces plundered the town, antagonizing the local people. The Sikh cordon was so strong that it was impossible for the Afghans to break it and proceed towards Delhi. Sardar Ranjit Singh terrorized the Afghans. Sardar Ranjit Singh treated the Shah's demands for submission with contempt. The moment Zaman Shah left, Sardar Ranjit Singh pursued his forces and caught them unawares near Gujranwala. They were chased further up to Jhelum. Many Afghans were put to death and their weapons and supplies taken. The rest fled for their lives. Sardar Ranjit Singh combined with Sardar Sahib Singh of Gujrat and Milkha Singh Pindiwala and a large Sikh force. They fell upon the Afghan garrison while Shah Zaman was still in vicinity of Khyber Pass. Ultimately, the shah's withdrawal gave a choice to the Sikhs to obliterate all semblance of Afghan authority between Ravi and Jhelum. The Afghan forces fled towards north after having been routed by the Sikhs. Shah left the Punjab and reached Kabul on 17TH March 1799, leaving his general Ahmad Shah Shahanchibashi, as his deputy, with an army of 12,000. The general attacked the Sikhs, but his force was routed and the general was killed in the battle. Sardar Ranjit Singh then aged 17, distinguished in the battle and began his rise to prominence.

Sardar Ranjit Singh

Jan Muhammad Chattha
Jan Muhammad Chattha fled to Kabul on the eve of the conquest of the fort of Mancher in 1790 by Mahar Singh Sukarchakia. He accompanied Shah Zaman to India in 1797 and recovered his possessions, with the aid of the Afghans, but this was a short lived gain, for Sardar Ranjit Singh attacked his headquarters, Rasulnagar, after the Shah's return to Afghanistan. The besieged Chathas, under Jan Muhammad, made a gallant resistance. Jan Muhammad was killed by a cannon shot and the fort surrendered. Ranjit Singh granted small Jagirs to the sons of Jan Muhammad and employed them in the irregular cavalry.

Sayyid Imamuddin Hussaini
Sayyid Imamuddin Hussaini spy of the British Government, stayed in the Punjab in the last quarter of 1796, and returned to Lucknow by the end of 1798. His account confirms that Sardar Ranjit Singh was the most powerful Sikh in the Punjab territory.

Lahore 1799
The capture of Lahore had been one of Sardar Ranjit Singh's most cherished desires; it was the centre of power in the region. It was at that point in time was ruled by three brothers of the Bhangi Misl, Lehna Singh, Gujar Singh, and Sobha Singh. Muslims joined Hindu and Sikh residents of Lahore in making an appeal to Ranjit Singh to free them from the tyrannical rule. A petition was written by the leading citizens of Lahore to Ranjit Singh, to liberate them. Sardar Ranjit Singh deputed Qazi Abdur Rahman of Ramnagar with the emissary. The adroit Qazi met Mian Muhammad Ashiq, Mehar Mohkamuddin, Mohammad Azim, Hafiz Mohammad, Mehar Shadi Katarband, Ahmed Khan Bhinder, Hakim Rai, and Bhai Gurbakhsh Singh. Muhammad Baqar, Muhammad Tahar, Maulvi Muhammad Salim, Mufti Muhammad Mukarram, Mian Muhammad Jan, the religious guide of Moran Kanjiri and Abid Khan of Atari all of them agreed to accept Ranjit Singh as the chief of Lahore. In order to assure him of their fidelity, they all signed a petition and sent by Hakim Rai who accompanied the Qazi. Sardar Ranjit Sing mobilised an Army of 25,000 and marched towards Lahore on July 6TH, 1799. In the early morning of July 7TH, 1799, Ranjit Singh's men took up their positions. Four Guns, under Mian Ghouse, glistened and bugles were sounded. Sardar Ranjit Singh rode along the walls of the city setting mines. It was July 7TH, 1799 when the victorious Sardar Ranjit Singh entered Lahore.

Sardar Ranjit Singh

Lahore 1799 (Contd)

Ten days later Sardar Ranjit Singh held a great durbar in the Lahore fort which was attendant by principal personalities of the city. He assured them that their persons, honour, property and rights would be quite safe, and no lawlessness would be permitted under any circumstances. A strong contingent roamed inside the city in main bazaars to maintain peace and order. He richly rewarded all those who had helped him in the enterprise. Mehar Mohkam-ud-Din, was honoured with the title of Baba, and was appointed the administrator of the City of Lahore. Other leaders received the titles of Sahib and Mehrban. After three decades of Bhangi misrule the city was desperately in need of peace and stability. Trusted people were appointed to government offices and charities were opened. The city's defences were reinforced by a moat. Ranjit Singh displayed his tolerance to accommodate Lahore's large Muslim community, decreeing protection for their legal system and appointing and Imam Baksh as the chief of police. Muhammad Shahpur and Sadullah Chishti were named as muftis. Panchayats were established in villages to settle disputes and to handle some aspects of local administration. An order was issued for the establishment of a mint at Lahore, and a coin was struck in the name of Sardar Ranjit Singh, Lahore was inundated with people seeking work with the new regime. They included young men from the families of chastened chieftains, scholars, skilled craftsmen and most important the doctors. Ranjit Singh was obsessed with his health and liked to seek remedies for his ailments. A doctor called Ghulam Muhiddin, whose ancestors were from Bokhara and was born at Rahila on river Beas, who treated an eye condition. He brought with him trainee-clinical son, Faqir Azizuddin, whose charm and words mesmerised Sardar Ranjit Singh. Faqir Azizuddin accepted Sardar Ranjit Singh's prompt offer of employment with further flowery language. He became Sardar Ranjit Singh's principal confidant and foreign minister. Sardar Ranjit Singh further favoured the Faqir family by employing Faqir Azizuddin and his two brothers, Faqir Nuruddin and Faqir Imamuddin. Imam Shah was appointed the commander of reserve artillery posted inside the fort of Lahore.

Sarkar-i-Khalsa

Maharajah Ranjit Singh

After prolonged efforts by Sikhs, starting with Guru Gobind Singh, then Banda Bahadur, Nawab Kapur Singh, Jassa Singh Ahluwalia, Jassa Singh Ramgarhia, and other Sikh warriors, finally Sardar Ranjit Singh was able to consolidate the gains made by earlier Sardars. Now it was time for Sardar Ranjit Singh to declare himself the Maharajah of Punjab and treats all his subjects Hindus, Muslims, Sikhs equally. On April 12TH 1801, Ranjit Singh declared himself Maharajah of Punjab on the same auspicious day of Baisakhi when Lahore forces were made by Guru Gobind Singh. The investiture ceremony was performed by Sahib Singh Bedi, who was the direct descendant of Guru Nanak. A commemorative coin was issued, Nanakshahi rupee as it was called. It was a grand gala occasion. Maharajah Ranjit Singh rode on the elephant and passed through the streets of Lahore. He won popular acclaim and earned a lasting place in the hearts of the people. At night the town was illuminated with oil lamps and there was display of fireworks. Many Chiefs and Sardars offered nazarana and in return receive Khilat. The fort was garrisoned. The Maharajah ordered that no interference be made with the personal and public law of Muslims. Cases of Muslim were ordered to be decided according to their religious law, the Sharia. Salaries were fixed under the rules for Qazis, Muftis and Ulema. Nizamuddin was appointed chief Qazi at Lahore. Muhammad Shahpur and Sad Ullah were appointed muftis. Costly robes were bestowed upon them. The city was divided into wards and a Chaudhri was appointed for each ward. A Kotwal was also appointed and police force was posted for the protection of the city under him. Imam Bakhsh Kharswar was named as first Kotwal. A department of health was organised and hospitals were opened where free treatment was given through Unani system of medicine. Faqir Nuruddin, younger brother of Faqir Azizuddin, was appointed director of health services. Faqir Nuruddin also looked after the upkeep of the royal palaces and gardens. The majority of Maharajah Ranjit Singh's subjects were Muslim and had an intense loyalty towards him and his Sikh's. Many decisions were taken by the Maharajah concerning the Muslim populace, which led to the emergence of a partnership between the Muslims and their new rulers. Maharajah Ranjit Singh felt it significant to give positions of importance in his government to the Muslims.

Sarkar-i-Khalsa

Lahore forces in 1799:
The Sikhs prior to 1799, continued with their old desultory methods based on horsemen. Maharajah Ranjit Singh was totally convinced by the European system. His ambition was to form a mighty Sikh Empire not only by annexing other Sikh Confederacies but also by annexing Muslim states patronised by Afghanistan. So he planned to organise his army to meet his ambitions. In trying to reorganise, he decided to go slow, as he wanted the Sikh chieftains to understand and gradually absorb the new system and he also wanted time to examine the European System in much greater detail. During the formative period of expansion of his army, he kept control of the artillery arm directly under him, and did not place it under various chiefs who were allowed to keep cavalry and infantry. Keeping control of the guns was a sound political decision, because during the early stages he was doubtful of his subordinate chiefs. Cavalry lost its primacy, giving way to artillery and infantry, the latter being formed into regular and irregular units while the artillery remained regular under the Maharajah. He had to import officers and men for the artillery from outside. During the initial period his gunners were mostly from Hindustan. They were mostly Muslims and Poorbia Telingas, as Sikhs had no liking for this arm, for that matter they were reluctant to join even the infantry. They had gained their knowledge while serving with the British, French, Marathas and Mughals. By end of this period the total number of guns is estimated to have been between 35 and 40 made of brass as well of iron. These included 5, 6, and 12 pounders and even heavier guns, most being country made. Besides these guns, there were about 100 Swivel guns. Sometime in 1807, factories were established at Lahore, and other places for manufacture and repair of guns. Within a period of less than ten years, Ranjit Singh managed to form the nucleus of regular artillery around 40 guns and 100 camel swivels centrally controlled under his direct supervision.

Yusuf Ali 1799
As well as displaying quick military mind, Maharajah Ranjit Singh showed political mind as well. He appeared to take the Afghan so seriously, that British were compelled the British to send an agent, Yusuf Ali, to try to persuade Maharajah Ranjit Singh to keep his distance from the Afghans. Maharajah Ranjit Singh invited Yusuf Ali to Lahore, Which was assertion of his own importance. Maharajah Ranjit Singh knew as well as Yusuf Ali how untrustworthy the Afghans were, but he did want to be seen doing Britain's bidding.

Sarkar-i-Khalsa

The Punjab in 1800
Casting a close look at the political map of Punjab of the time, it will be found that a major part of the Central Punjab had remained under the Sikh Misls. Kasur was peopled chiefly by Pathan emigrants. Multan was under Nawab Muzaffar Khan Suddozai. Dera Ismail Khan with Abd-us-Samad Khan, Mankera, Hot, Bannu and Kohat remained in possession Muhammad Shah Nawaz Khan and Tonk was under Nawab Sarwar Khan. In the beginning; all these Nawabs used to be governors ruling in the name of the Amir of Kabul. But after the fall of Durrani government, they became independent. Bahawalpur remained with Nawab Bahawal Khan Daudputras and Peshawar and its vicinal areas were with Fateh Khan Barakzai. Afghans of Wazirkhels tribe headed by Jahandad Khan had taken possession of the Attock Fort and its vicinities. Kashmir and Hazara were ruled by Sardar Azim Khan Barakzai, brother of Fateh Khan. The hilly areas of Kangra and Jammu were fragmented into petty Rajput states of Kangra, Kullu, Chamba, Basoli, Mandi, Suket, Jammu, etc. These hill rajas were feudatories of the erstwhile Mughal emperors. Now, they feigned to be independent.

Sikh Misls 1800
The twelve Sikh Misls occupied the plains of Central Punjab and Sarhind and the foothills from Kangra to Jammu. The Misls through the years of intern cite quarrels had reduced each other to political impotence. The Bhangis were the most powerful of the Misl fraternity and held Amritsar, Gujarat, and a large portion of Western Punjab. Maharajah Ranjit Singh decided to break the Bhangis and force other Misldars to accept his suzerainty.

Muslim Nawabs 1800
In the Punjab the Muslim Nawabs ruled their states on behalf of the Kings of Kabul and since the Afghan demise, for all practical purposes were independent. As sovereign of the Punjab, Maharajah Ranjit Singh a legal right to demand that territories which had at any time paid revenue to Lahore, should pay tribute to him and owe allegiance to Lahore Durbar. As regards the petty chiefs, there was no need for the Maharajah to go to war with them. He went often on tour of the country accompanied by a huge army. The small chiefs were overawed by this cavalcade and quietly submitted, offered some gifts and promised recruits for the Lahore forces when required. The others yielded after some resistance.

Sarkar-i-Khalsa

Hill States 1800
The hill states were feudatories of the Mughal Emperors since 1612, until they were wrested from the Mughals by Sikhs in 1783. There was no need for the Maharajah to go to war with them as all the hill states north of the River Satluj accepted his suzerainty, and he appointed Desa Singh Majithia as his nazim or governor of the territory. Jammu was the principal state lying between the Rivers Ravi and Chenab and Maharajah Ranjit Singh conquered Jammu in 1800 and it became part of the Kingdom of Lahore.

Cavalry 1801
While appreciating the flexibility and manoeuvrability of traditional Sikh organization and tactics, the Maharajah had to harness the great fighting skill and fervour of their troops. At the same time he was quick to recognize the advantages enjoyed by armies which had adopted British military systems, and he was determined to organize an army of his own on similar lines. Though still holding the predominant position, cavalry was set on the way to becoming a subordinate arm to Infantry and Artillery.

Jagirdari Cavalry 1801
Apart from inherited the Jagirdari cavalry contingents, as the Maharajah conquered more territory, number of Jagirdars increased. They were required to furnish cavalry and infantry, at their own expense, but no guns were allowed to them. They were allowed guns, after he had established firm control over them, and assured their loyalty.

Infantry 1801
The infantry used to form a negligible portion of the army before 1799. Maharajah Ranjit Singh had inherited an irregular Najib Battalion of infantry under Gulab Khan Afghan. However, in 1803, as the Punjabis were not coming forth, he recruited Najibs for his infantry. He recruited some deserters from the ranks of the English Company, who were tempted with the higher pay and adventure, and raised two battalions of Najibs, under Commandant Raushan Khan and Commandant Shaikh Ibadullah. Gradually these troops were formed into another five Battalions, four of Telingas or Poorbias and one of Hindustanis or Rohillas. The Maharajah began to show special favour to the newly created branch of the army in every possible way. He used to attend its parades in person, and as his marks of pleasure, he would not infrequently distribute gifts of money to the men with his own hands.

Sarkar-i-Khalsa

Artillery 1801

Artillery like infantry received then maximum attention of the Maharajah, who looked upon as an indispensable plank in his scheme of military reforms. The artillery was organised under Ghouse Khan, whose services he had inherited when he took control of Sukarchakia Misl. During the formative period of expansion of his army, he kept control of the artillery arm directly under him. His gunners were mostly Hindustani Muslims. They had gained their knowledge while serving with the British, French, Marathas and Mughals, as Sikhs had no liking for this arm, for that matter they were reluctant to join even the infantry. Muslims loved their guns and were excellent gunners.

Maharajah Ranjit Singh's conquests upto 1808:-

Jammu 1800

Formerly Jammu was tributary to the Sukarchakia Misl, but the tribute had not been paid for many years. In 1800, on his way to Jammu, Maharajah Ranjit Singh conquered Mirowal and realized tribute from Narowal. He then laid siege to Chaprar. The Maharajah called upon the garrison to surrender. On their refusal he stormed the fort and captured it. Because of the stiff resistance he met, he massacred all the inhabitants. In consequences the Raja of Jammu submitted without any opposition and offered tribute and together with elephants and Jewellery.

Kasur 1801

Kasur, situated south of Lahore, was a Pathan colony. During the Afghan invasion, and the upheaval it caused, Nizam-ud-din had and occupied Kankipura, Haveli, Atari, Nadian, Mahmonki, Khem Karan, Rukhanwala, and Chunian belonging to Tara Singh Churiarivala and the Nakai. Maharajah Ranjit Singh sent Fateh Singh Kalianwala against him. The Afghan force opposed the Sikhs a few kilometres from Kasur. On being defeated, they took shelter in a fort inside the town. As Fateh Singh Kalianwala besieged the town, Nizam-ud-din sued for peace. He paid a large indemnity, accepted Maharajah Ranjit Singh as his overlord and agreed to pay tribute and furnish troops whenever required. In 1802 when Ranjit Singh was busy reducing Chiniot, Nizam-ud-din carried his depredations up to the gates of Lahore and planned to seize the capital. Maharajah Ranjit Singh sent Fateh Singh Ahluwalia to punish him for his treachery. In a pitched battle the Pathans were defeated and the town plundered. Nizam-ud-din submitted again on payment of a heavy fine and became tributary to Maharajah Ranjit Singh.

Sarkar-i-Khalsa

Moran Sarkar 1802
She was a Muslin nautch girl, and used to dance for Maharajah Ranjit Singh, he fell madly love with her. Through his marriage to Moran, the Maharajah also wanted to uplift the community of Tawaifs who were social outcasts. He married Moran against the wishes of the entire community and despite the conditions that were laid down by Moran's father and the head of her community Mian Samdu. The community was rehabilitated in Sharifpura, near Amritsar. Moran and the Maharajah went to Hardwar for a dip in the Ganga after their marriage in 1802. The marriage incurred the wrath of the entire Khalsa Panth and Ranjit Singh was called to the Akal Takht for retribution. He was proclaimed guilty and condemned to public flogging. He bowed before the Akal Takht and accepted the punishment. He was exempted with one kora and a fine. He never minted a coin in his own name but he struck one in Moran's name. She became known as Moran Sarkar and became a window to the common people who often brought their problems to her. There is also a Masjid in Moran's name in Lahore that was renamed from Masjid-e-Tawaif to Masjid Moran (built it in 1809). Deeply spiritual, Moran had a spiritual guide called Mian Jaan Mohammad of Laverian, who told her that a madrasa would benefit more people than a Masjid. Moran was instrumental in setting up a school for Persian and Arabic studies for students who would be spared the trouble of travelling all the way to Persia. Post the death of Maharajah she spent most of her time and money trying to set up Persian and Punjabi language schools. Historic accounts state that she passed away somewhere in 1862 and was buried in the Miani Sahib Graveyard. Her grave location has been a mystery whereas many people claim that they found her grave. An out of the ordinary looking mosque is located in the Walled City of Lahore, inside the Shah Almi Gate near Pappar Mandi, which is called the Moran Tawaif Masjid. Historic references say that the mosque was built by Moran and her mother, and Tehqeeqat-e-Chishti. Whereas some references say that Maharajah Ranjit Singh at Moran's request, built a mosque called as Masjid-e-Tawaifan in 1824, which was renamed in 1998 as Mai Moran Masjid in Lahore. Tawaif in local language of Urdu means a 'dancing girl'. And this Moran (dancing girl) was Maharajah Ranjit Singh's favourite. Till date, the mosque is red in colour, which was once the symbol of passion and love of Moran Tawaif for the religion of Islam and it showed the standards of religious harmony prevalent back then. If we talk about the structure of the mosque it is built on a raised platform and one has to climb a few steps to enter inside it.

Sarkar-i-Khalsa

Moran Tawaif Masjid

Though the mosque was built in a simple structure but you will not see the original fabric today as it has been completely changed over the passage of time but the name and historic value remains there. Like many other mosques inside the walled city of Lahore, this one too is not open for the general public and is only limited to the entry for those who go there for the five prayers, as it is a functional mosque. Also, let me tell you here that this mosque is one of the known ones inside Lohari and Shah Almi area and you will always see hustle and bustle there during the prayer hours. If by any chance you manage your way inside the mosque you will see that there are rooms inside the Mosque for the residences of the Imam and Moazzen of the Mosque. On one side there is an area for the ablution and people say that the placement of this ablution area is the same which Moran constructed. The mosque has three domes and Maulana Ghulam Rasool was deputed as the first Moazzen of the mosque by Maharajah Ranjit Singh. This mosque and the religious school (madrasa) associated with it gained popularity in those times and people from far flung areas would come there to attend classes and for research on religion. The mosque was known for the Islamic education, calligraphy and diversified religious studies. No doubt, that it attracted foreigners and locals of the sub continent in those times. Unfortunately the school was closed down during the British era but the Mosque is still intact. At present the mosque is hidden behind many encroachments and perfume shops and one has to look for it amidst them, as it is comparatively a smaller structure and cannot be compared with Wazir Khan Masjid or Begum Shahi Masjid in its grandeur and space covered. You must be thinking about the name of the mosque and history associated with it, so let me tell you a little about that too as you might not find much information regarding this mosque on internet as not much has been written on it because it remained a hidden piece and so it is till now. Firstly we need to know about the character of Moran and observe her role in the Sikh History and Lahore. She was known to be the beloved of Sher-e-Punjab, Maharajah Ranjit Singh and later he married her out of love and respect. Now here is something interesting for my readers that Maharajah Ranjit Singh in his entire regime here at Punjab did not mention his name on a coin but yes, the coin of Moran Tawaif was issued as a currency of that time. The coins were the origin of the term Moran Sarkar, and were called Moran Shahi currency. The court decisions were not made in the chamber or court of Maharajah Ranjit Singh, but in the drawing room of Moran Tawaif.

Sarkar-i-Khalsa

Moran Tawaif Masjid (Contd)
Soon she got popular as Moran Sarkar and became a window to the common people who often brought their problems to her and she was the one who ordered the courtiers and other officials to resolve those issues. According to references, she was also considered to be very cultured in arts. She was known for her philanthropic acts and in bringing Maharajah's attention to many problems which he and his ministers would overlook otherwise. This is the importance of the Moran in the Sikh history and Lahore.

Raja Sansar Chand 1802
In 1802, Raja Sansar Chand of Kangra, tried to extend his authority into the plains of Hoshiarpur and had seized some villages in the estates of Sardarni Sada Kaur. She appealed to Maharajah Ranjit Singh for help. Sansar Chand's Kardar on hearing of the Maharajahs approach fled, and the Rani obtained the possession of the territory that had wrested from her. Maharajah Ranjit Singh proceeded and captured a portion of Kangra territory, which he gave back to Sardarni Sada Kaur. He then marched to Nurpur, which he subdued.

Khewra 1802
Khewra was a small village near Pind Dadan Khan, famous for its salt mines. During the Mughal era the salt was traded in various markets, as far away as Central Asia. On the downfall of the Mughal Empire, the mine was taken over by Sikhs. The salt mines were seized by Maharajah Ranjit Singh in about 1802. The salt quarried during Maharajah Ranjit Singh's time was both eaten and used as a source of revenue.

The Kharals 1802
The Kharals had their chief settlements in the swampy jungles of the Montgomery district. There were many of them in Jhang, and they held some forty villages in Lahore, chiefly about Sheikhupura. Through all historic times the Kharals have been a turbulent, savage and thievish tribe, ever impatient of control, and delighting in strife and plunder. More fanatic than other Muhammadan tribes they submitted with greatest reluctance to Maharajah Ranjit Singh's rule. For whenever an organized force was sent against them they retired into the marshes and thick jungle, where it was impossible to follow them. There are many of them in Jhang, and they hold some forty villages in Lahore, chiefly about Sheikhupura. Kamal Khan founded Kot Kamalia, in the sixteenth century, forty miles into south Jhang, where lived the Sials, whom Karallas claimed as kinsmen, but with whom they were always fighting.

Sarkar-i-Khalsa

Saadat Khan 1803

In 1803 Saadat Khan was compelled after a fruitless struggle to submit to Maharajah Ranjit Singh who annexed Kamalia to the Lahore Kingdom. Saadat Yar khan fled to the protection of Nawab Muzaffar Khan of Multan. Maharajah Ranjit Singh recalled him and gave him proprietary rights over forty villages, in which he succeeded by his son Muzaffar Khan. In 1810 the Maharajah gave him the village of Muhammad Shah. Muzaffar Khan was succeeded by his brother Muhammad Sarfaraz Khan, who was able man and a brave soldier. He held the family Jagir throughout the reign of Maharajah Ranjit Singh.

Jhang 1803

Mai Khan had obtained the territory of Jhang as hereditary possession, from the Imperial rulers the Lodis. His family continued to rule Jhang until the beginning of the 18TH century until the Sikhs had begun to show muscle and immediately set out to conquer Jhang. Karam Singh Dulu, a chief of the Bhang! Confederacy had conquered Chiniot. In 1803 Maharajah Ranjit Singh took the fort there and marched on Jhang, but was bought off by Ahmad Khan, the last of the Sial chieftains, on promise of a yearly tribute, amounting to Rs. 70,000 and a mare. Three years later, however, the Maharajah again invaded Jhang with a large army, and took the fort, after a desperate resistance. Ahmed Khan had collected around him a large number the Mohammand tribes, and had also with him two pieces of artillery. The battle lasted from noon till evening, when Ahmed Shah retired to the city with his two guns. Ranjit Singh besieged the city by night. The fighting lasted for three days. The Nawab seeing his cause hopeless, fled with his family to Multan. The Maharajah took possession of the immense wealth which the Sial chief had been accumulating for many years. The Maharajah farmed the territories of Jhang to Sardar Fateh Singh Kalianwala. Shortly afterwards, Ahmad Khan returned with a force given him by Muzaffar Khan, Nawab of Multan, and recovered a large part of his previous dominions, which Ranjit Singh suffered him to retain on payment of the former tribute, as he found himself too busy elsewhere to attack Jhang. After his unsuccessful attempt on Multan in 1810, the Maharajah took Ahmad Khan a prisoner to Lahore, as he suspected him of favouring his enemy, Muzaffar Khan. He afterwards bestowed on him a Jagir, which descended to his son, Inayat Khan. On the death of the latter, his brother, Ismail Khan, endeavoured to obtain succession to the Jagir, but failed through the opposition of Gulab Singh.

Sarkar-i-Khalsa

Bhera 1803

Bhera was the most notable town in the west Punjab. After the final success of the Sikhs against Ahmad Shah in 1763, Sikhs of Bhangi Misl took control of this region, after their final success against Ahmad Shah Abdali in 1767. In 1783 Maha Singh Sardar of Sukharchakia Misl took control of the town, from Tara Singh of Bhangi Misl. Later on his son, Maharajah Ranjit Singh continued his march to expand his state and took possession of Bhera and Jhawrian in 1803, then in control of Sardar Jodh Singh Bhangi, and annexed to the Lahore Kingdom.

Amritsar 1803

Maharajah Ranjit Singh was keen to unite the political capital Lahore with Amritsar, the religious capital of the Sikhs. The only formidable family was that of a Bhangi chief. The last notable Bhangi chief of Amritsar was Gulab Singh Bhangi who died in 1800, leaving behind his widow, Mai Sukkhan. She was in possession of the Lohgarh fort, on whose ramparts was the Bhangi Gun. Maharajah Ranjit Singh demanded from Mai Sukkhan the famous Bhangi Gun, Zamzama. It was captured from the Durranis in 1764 by the Bhangis and it came to be known as Bhangian Di Tope. In 1802, Maharajah Ranjit Singh marched towards Amritsar at the head of the troops. A fierce fighting took place but in the end the gates could not stand the heavy cannonade of Lahore guns, and the marching army entered city in triumph, with the Maharajah at the head. He captured considerable war material, including the Zamzama and the area which yielded handsome revenue. More important than the capture of the fort was the acquisition of the services of the gallant warrior, Akali Phula Singh. He belongs to the militant order of the Nihangs and had devoted his life to the protection of the Sikh shrines. He rendered necessary help to the Maharajah in capturing the city. With him were about three thousand Nihangs who joined the army of the Maharajah. The fanatical Akalis fought in the fore-front of the military campaigns. The Zamzama gun is perhaps the largest specimen of Indian cannon casting, and is celebrated in Sikh historical annals more as a marvel of ordnance than for its efficiency in the battlefield. Yet for its effectiveness it has been called "a fire raining dragon" and "a gun terrible as a dragon and huge as a mountain." It was employed by the Lahore army in the campaigns of Daska, Kasur, Sujanpur, Wazirabad and Multan. In these operations, the cannon were severely damaged and it had to be brought back to Lahore, unfit for any further use. (It was placed outside Delhi Gate, Lahore, where it remained until 1860.

Sarkar-i-Khalsa

Attar Khan 1803

Maharajah Ranjit Singh also encouraged other arts, reflecting his secularism. A Muslim craftsman was chosen to fulfil the Durbar's decision to build an impregnable wall around Amritsar. He liked to have the Satirist Attar Khan play for him during the rainy season, and would suspend court proceedings to go with his advisors to admire the beauty of gathering monsoon clouds.

Multan 1803

At the time of Maharajah Ranjit Singh's accession to power, Multan was held by Muzzafar Khan who was a tributary of the ruler of Kabul, but independent of every external control. Maharajah Ranjit Singh led his first expedition against Multan in 1802, and exacted a large tribute from its ruler and returned to Lahore. He sent other expeditions to Multan in 1803, and again exacted a large tribute from Muzzafar Khan. Multan, however, retained its independence.

Khattars 1803

Little can be said the history of the Khattars. Like their neighbours the Ghebas and Awans, they resisted Maharajah Ranjit Singh, as long as they could, like them they resisted in vain. Maharajah Ranjit Singh subdued them in 1803. Maharajah Ranjit Singh allowed them the fourth of the revenue as lords of the soil.

Khan Muhammad Khan 1803

Khan Muhammad Khan of Nurpur Tiwana was engaged in constant hostilities with his neighbours. For some time Khan Muhammad Khan defended himself; but his enemies were too powerful and in 1803 he applied to Maharajah Ranjit Singh for succour. Maharajah Ranjit Singh was no means secure; but on the promise of subsidy, he consented to tackle Khan Beg Khan. When Maharajah Ranjit Singh's troops caught Khan Beg Khan, he was made over to his brother, who put him to death. Now Khan Muhammad Khan's second son Ahmad Yar Khan, rebelled against him, having won over most of the tribe to his side, induced his father to make a virtue of necessity and yield the cheifship to him.

Chaudhry Qadar Buksh 1803

Chaudhry Qadar Buksh was a member of Maharajah Ranjit Singh's court. Maharajah Ranjit Singh couturiers came from the whole spectrum of races and religions. Two other Muslim brothers, Sarfaraz Khan and Zulfikar Khan, were prominent at court.

Sarkar-i-Khalsa

Sansar Chand 1804
Sansar Chand Katoch Rajput Raja of Kangra who ascended the throne in 1775. He was an ambitious ruler and began extending his influence over the neighbouring hill states as well as over the plains lying at the foot of the Sivalik ranges Sansar Chand left his hill possessions in 1804, and renewed his ravages on Hoshiarpur and Bajwara. He found himself unable, however, to cope with the Sikhs, and two descents upon the Sikh possessions in the plains, in 1803 and 1804, were repelled by Maharajah Ranjit Singh.

Gobindgarh fort 1805
Gobindgarh fort, raised in the time of Maharajah Ranjit Singh on the ruins of an old fortress built at Amritsar by Gujar Singh was named in honour of Guru Gobind Singh. Shamir Singh Thethar, was also appointed its first qiladar (commandant). The Fort, an imposing structure with a gilded dome, was surrounded by a high wall. It had eight towers. The moat around it was lined with bricks. The huge wooden door on the eastern side marked the main entrance. The Fort contained magazines, arsenals and royal stables, besides a mint. The Fort also served as the State treasury. Here were kept the crown jewels as well as the Maharajah's gold and silver. Political prisoners were sent here for detention. Imamuddin, one of the renowned three Faqir brothers, remained in charge of the Fort for many years.

Anglo-Sikh relations 1805
Anglo- Sikh relations need to be traced to the transformation of the British East India Company, a commercial organization, into a political power in India. Robert Clive the victor of Plassey and governor of Bengal during 1765-67, watched with interest the repeated invasions of India by Ahmad Shah Durrani and rejoiced at his final repulse at the hands of the Sikhs. Since the fall of Sarhind to them in January 1764, the Sikhs had extended their area of operations to Ganga Yamuna Doab and Ruhilkhand bordering on the territories of the Nawab of Oudh. Jhanda Singh Bhangi a powerful Sikh Sardar, in a letter dated 19TH August 1771 addressed to General Robert Barker sought friendly relations with the British. Warren Hastings governor of Bengal since 1772 and made governor general in 1773, was however deeply perturbed at the increasing power of the Sikhs. The Sikhs audaciously continued their raids into the Doab and Ruhilkhand. The latter territory had been conquered by the Nawab of Oudh with British help in 1774, and thus formed part of the British protectorate.

Sarkar -i- Khalsa`

Anglo-Sikh relations 1805 (Contd)

In December 1778, the entry of the Sikhs into Ruhilkhand was resisted by British troops who were able to force the Sikhs to retire. In January 1783, Sardar Beghel Singh, at the head of a large force, approached Anupshahr; some British battalions also arrived on the scene. The Sikhs retreated, changed direction and plundered, during February 1783, the southern districts of the Doab up to Shikohabad and Farrukhabad, pillaging Agra on their way back. In the following month they raided the northern parts of Delhi itself. Major James Browne, the British Agent at the Mughal court, got in touch with several Sikh Sardars including Baghel Singhs. In response to Browne's overtures leading Sikh Sardars expressed their willingness to form a friendly alliance with the British, but the latter were too apprehensive of their power. In January 1784, a body of 30.000 Sikh horse and foot crossed the Yamuna. The British government was alarmed and strengthened their garrisons at Bareilly and Fatehgarh. James Browne informed Warren Hastings about the threatening attitude of the Sikhs, but said that Karam Singh, the leader of the expedition, had regard for British friendship. Karam Singh persuaded the other Sikh Sardars not to cross the Ganga into the territories of the Nawab of Oudh, an ally of the English. Warren Hastings prepared, in December 1784, his own plan to checkmate the Sikh influence at Delhi. Emperor Shah Alam was to be instigated to organize opposition to the Sikhs at the imperial court while the Emperor was to receive military help from the British and the Nawab of Oudh. This plan, however, also failed partly because Mahadji Scindia, the Maratha chief, would not allow a passage to British troops to reach Delhi through his Trans Yamuna territory. On 30TH March 1785, Ambaji Ingle, one of Scindia's generals, made a provisional treaty of peace and friendship with the Sikhs. Warren Hastings left India on 1ST February 1785. George Forster, who had already travelled through the Sikh territories, to establish contacts with the Sikhs and collect intelligence about their future designs. The new governor general, Lord Cornwallis favoured a policy of caution and persuasion in dealing with the Sikhs and instructed the British Resident at Lucknow to please the Sikh vakil or agent posted there. At the same time he cautioned the Nawab of Oudh to ensure stricter vigilance at Anupshahr and Daranagar ferries and assured him of British reinforcements as and when needed. In December 1790, a Sikh band of 300 men attacked Longcroft, an Englishman in indigo business, at village Jalauli in `Aligarh district, but retired as their leader was killed by the villagers.

Sarkar -i- Khalsa'

Anglo- Sikh relations 1805 (Contd)

Soon after, Bhanga Singh of Thanesar assuming the leadership advanced on Anupshahr where he captured, on 3RD January 1791. The local British commander, Lieutenant Colonel Robert Stuart, whom he brought to Thanesar and demanded 2, 00,000 rupees as ransom for his release. Many Englishmen offered to collect this amount but Lord Cornwallis did not agree. Ultimately a sum of Rs 60,000 was paid through Begam Samru and the Colonel was set free on 24TH October 1791. With their conquest of Delhi on 11TH September 1803, the British had established their supremacy in the region. Meanwhile, Maharajah Ranjit Singh had emerged as the ruler of the Sikhs, overpowering the Misl chiefs. The Sikh raids into the Doab and the region north of Delhi came to an end. The Cis Sutlej Sikh chiefs accepted the suzerainty of the British who now entered into direct relationship with the Sikh monarch, Maharajah Ranjit Singh.

Rao Holkar 1805

Jaswant Rao Holkar, Maratha chief of Indore, crossed into to the Punjab in 1805, after he was defeated at Fatehgarh and Dig in December 1804 by the British. Accompanied by Rohilla ally, Amir Khan and a Maratha force estimated 15,000, Holkar arrived at Patiala, but on hearing the news that the British general Lake, was in hot pursuit, both the refugees fled northwards, entered Jullundur Doab and ultimately reached Amritsar. Maharajah Ranjit Singh hastily came to meet Holkar. The Maharajah was hospitable and sympatric towards the Maratha chief and kept him in royal style. He was shrewd enough not expouse a forlorn cause, and come to conflict with the British, especially when he was far from securely established on the throne. Through diplomatic negations, he brought about the reconciliation between Holkar and the British Commander-in-Chief, as a result of which the Maratha ruler secured the greater part of the territory which had been seized by the British.

Anglo-Sikh Treaty of 1806

Maharajah Ranjit Singh had kept the Punjab for becoming a theatre of war between two foreign armies, and led to the Anglo-Sikh Treaty of 1806. The treaty brought the Sikh chief into direct contact with the British government. This treaty of friendship and amity between East India Company and Maharajah Ranjit Singh was signed by both the parties on January 1ST, 1806. Jaswant Rao Holkar was to be removed from Amritsar and, in return, the English were not to enter the Punjab and seize any possession of the Sikh Kingdom of Lahore.

Sarkar-i-Khalsa

The Ghebas 1806

Ghebas came to the Punjab same time after both Sials and Tiwanas, and settled in the wild hilly country between the Indus and Sohan rivers, now known as the Paragons of Fatehjang and Pindi Gheb. Here they held their own against the neighbouring tribes of Awans, Gakhars, and Jodhras, till the days of Sardar Charat Singh Sukarchakia, grandfather of Maharajah Ranjit Singh. They had subdued by the Afghan invaders of India, for they were just off the highway, and their country was difficult to access; nor did they ever invite attack by their demeanour, but presented a small tribute such as a horse or a few head of cattle as the invader passed, and thus secured his goodwill. Sardar Gujar Singh Bhangi of Gujrat, who for a time held the country as far north as Rawalpindi, made but a little impression on the Gheba country. Charat Singh Sukarchakia, after he had seized Pind Dadan Khan, overran the southern part of Rawalpindi and made Rai Jalal tributary, leaving him one fourth of the revenue. But neither Sardars Charat Singh nor his son Mahan Singh was able to get much out of the Ghebas, and their supremacy was little more than nominal. Rai Jalal managed his old territory and gave up a certain proportion to the Sikh chiefs. In 1806 Maharajah Ranjit Singh sent Sardar Fateh Singh Kalianwala as the governor of Rawalpindi District, and he continued the farm of Kot and Khunda itakas to Rai Muhammad Khan, the nephew of Rai Jalal. The village of Sardar Rai Bahadur was conferred on Rai Muhammad with a revenue free grant. The great rivals of the Rais of Kot were the Maliks of Pindi Gheb, who farmed the Sil itakas from the Sikhs. Their jealousy at length ended in bloodshed, for during a year of scarcity, when both had failed to pay the revenue, they were summoned to the Durbar at Lahore. There they quarrelled, and Rai Muhammad cut down Malik Ghulam Muhammad almost in the presence of the Maharajah himself and fled to his home. It was not thought politic to punish him at that time, as his services were urgently needed on the side of government in a wild country where the Sikh Kardars never gained full power. In 1830 Rai Muhammad served against Sayad Ahmad, the fanatic leader who having been compelled to retire from Peshawar, which he had for some time absolutely ruled, had made Balakot in Hazara his headquarters. Here he was attacked by the Sikh army, commanded by Prince Sher Singh and utterly defeated. Rai Muhammad much distinguished himself in thus battle, and for his services received the village of Garn. Jodh Singh, Dhana Singh Malwai, Attar Singh Kalianwala and Prince Nau Nihal Singh successfully governed the Gheba country, and all found Rai Muhammad difficult to control.

Sarkar-i-Khalsa

The Ghebas 1806 (Contd)
Sardar Attar Singh during his tenure of office determined for the sake of peace to get rid of him. He invited Rai to his fort of Pagh. Muhammad Khan did not suspect treachery and went to Pagh, attended Ghulam Muhammad Khan and two followers. No sooner he had entered the fort than the little party was attacked by Budha Khan Malal an old enemy of his family and the retainers of Attar Singh and were killed. Fateh Khan succeeded his father, and avenged the death upon Budha Khan whose family he almost extirpated.

Multan 1807
The Nawab of Multan was known to have extended help and support to the Nawab of Kasur. Nearing Multan, Maharajah Ranjit Singh's forces destroyed all the buildings that lie outside the walled city and ready to assault the citadel. Nawab Muzzafar Khan found himself incapable of facing the assault, when he made terms with the Maharajah by paying him an expensive tribute.

Kasur 1807
Nawab Nizamuddin of Kasur had died and his brother Qutabuddin was not prepared to accept allegiance to Ranjit Singh and declared his independence. The territory was invaded in February 1807. It contained many small forts, all of which were well stored with munitions and provisions. The Maharajah sent Faqir Azizuddin to bring Qutabuddin to obedience, to no avail. The Maharajah invested the town and the invading troops, and their artillery levelled to the ground a great portion of the city walls. Qutabuddin was compelled to surrender and retire to his territory of Mamdot, holding a Jagir subject to supplying the Maharahaja.100 horsemen for services when required. To Fateh Din Khan, nephew of the chief, Maharajah Ranjit Singh gave a Jagir at Marup, subject to the same military conditions were imposed on his uncle. Kasur was taken away from the ruling family and given over to Sardar Nihal Singh Attariwala.

Mian Ghouse Khan 1807
In January 1807, 4,000 troops were sent under Mian Ghouse Khan, commandant of the Maharajah's artillery to reduce Haran Minar, chiefs of which place, had greatly disturbed the public peace, by their depredations throughout the country. After fierce fighting the chiefs were put in irons and taken to Lahore, and their fighting men were transferred to Maharajah Ranjit Singh' service, and the country was bestowed upon Prince Kharak Singh as Jagir.

Sarkar-i-Khalsa

Jasrota 1808

Jasrota was a small state situated in the outer ranges of the Shivalik hills. It occupied a fertile tract of land. Its rulers were powerful and often came into conflict with the Rajas of Jammu.

The first written record of Jasrota is probably that found in the *Ma'asir-ul-Umara*. The state was bifurcated following a dispute between the twin sons of Kailesh Dev, who had been ruling in 1320. Pratap Dev and Sangram Dev both sought to succeed their father but it was impossible to prove which brother was the older. Eventually, the rulers of neighbouring hill states negotiated a settlement, leading the lands being divided and Sangram becoming the first ruler of the new state of Lakhnaur in 1350. In 1594-94, the ruler of Jasrota, Bhivu Dev, used his army comprising over 100,000 men and 10,000 horses to ally in a rebellion involving some other hill states against the Mughal emperor Akbar. The revolt is referred to in the *Ma'asir-ul-Umara* and *Akbarnama* but the history of Jasrota in the following years, up until the arrival of Sikh forces in the region, is obscure. It appears to have taken little part in the various regional upheavals of the 17TH and 18TH centuries and the recorded genealogy of the ruling family is incomplete. Ajab Dev was ruler of Jasrota between 1790-1800. He arranged the construction of Jasmergarh Fort, in order better to protect Jasrota from Sikh incursions. The last member of the Dev dynasty to rule Jasrota independently was Randhir Singh, who reigned from 1805 to 1820 and had to acknowledge Ranjit Singh, the founder of the Sikh Empire, as his superior. Although Randhir Singh's brother, Bhuri Singh, was nominally recognised as his successor, Ranjit Singh annexed the territory in 1834 and converted it into a jagir that was gifted to Hira Singh, a son of Dhian Singh, the Dogra Prime Minister of Lahore, who was also a nephew of Gulab Singh. It was Hira Singh who built the present fort at Jasrota, although its foundations date from around the 12th or 13th century and had been developed as a fortified town by Dev rulers thereafter with "palatial buildings, Baradaris, shrines, water tanks etc". Hira Singh was mostly an absent ruler but he aspired to develop Jasrota in the image of Jammu, with which it shared a similar topography. He went some way towards achieving this, and named many of its places and structures after those of Jammu, but the fort was razed by the Sikh Khalsa Army in 1845 and abandoned thereafter. The descendants of the Jasrota family migrated to Khanpur, near to Nagrota

Sarkar-i-Khalsa

The Lahore forces in 1808:-

Commander-in-Chief
Maharajah Ranjit Singh

Regular Cavalry (6,000)
Original Dehras (2,500)
New Dehras (3,500)
Derah Chaudhari Quda Bakhsh
Derah Amir Shah
Derah Abdul Rehman Khan
Derah Sujan Ali

Irregular Cavalry
Derah Mir Abdul Rehman Khan
Derah Nasiruddin Khan
Derah Chaudhari Quda Bakhsh
Derah Qadirabad
Derah Muriwala

Artillery
Forty cannons
Derah Ghouse Khan
40 guns various calibres
One hundred Zambooks
Derah Ibadullah Khan
Derah Ghulam Mohd Khan
Derah Abdul Rahim Khan
Derah Khair Ali Khan
Derah Muhammad Shah

Guards and constabulary of
Irregular Cavalry
Derah Sayyad Ahmad Shah
Derah Shadi Khan
Derah Shah Baksh
Derah Shahbaz
Derah Shaikh Haidar
Derah Wazir Kundan
Derah Yusuf Ali Khan
Derah Raushan Shah,
Derah Sardar Khan

Jagirdari forces (1,500)

Regular Infantry (1,500)
Paltan Aziz Khan
Paltan Khair Ullah
Paltan Misri Khan Rohilla
Paltan Pir Bakhsh;
Paltan Qadir Baksh
Paltan Raushan Khan;
Paltan Shadi Khan ;
Paltan Shaikh Basawan;
Paltan Sher Ali
Paltan, Shaikh 'Ibadullah;
Paltan. Shamshir Ali
Derah Ahmad Ali Khan

Guards and constabulary of
Irregular Cavalry
Derah Ahmad Khan Afghan
Derah Almat Khan
Derah Bakhtawar Khan
Derah Didar Baksh
Derah Dhuman Khan
Derah Fateh Khan
Derah Ghani Sham
Derah Gul Khan
Derah Hidayat Khan
Derah Himmat Khan
Derah Hussain Khan
Derah Imam Baksh
Derah Imami
Derah Khairullah Shaikh
Derah Malu Khan
Derah Mian Mauju
Derah Misri Khan Rohilla
Derah Mohammad Khan Rohilla
Derah Muhammad Yar Khan,
Derah Pir Shah

Sarkar-i-Khalsa

The Janjua Tribe 1809

Raja Shabbat Khan, the great-grandson of Malik Khan Janjua, allied with Maha Singh in many campaigns of the late 18TH century. Upon his death, the Sikh chief Attar Singh Dhari assassinated Khan's heir, Raja Ghulam Muhiddin Khan. The Janjua then rebelled, having realised that the intent was to replace the old aristocracies. The lucrative salt mines in possession of the Janjua Sultans of Makrach and Khewra made the territory too important for the Sikh Maharajah to ignore. The expansion of the Sikh empire, spearheaded by Maharajah Ranjit Singh, was met with a rebellion by the Janjua Sultan of Wali, Sultan Fateh Muhammad Khan. A six month siege of Kusuk Fort in Wali followed and this was ended when the inhabitants ran short of water. The Kala Khan branch of Rawalpindi Janjuas fortunes were also eclipsed by the rise of the Sikh Empire. The fiercely independent Khakhas branch of the Janjua Rajput fought against the Sikh expansion into their Kingdom in Kashmir. The bold and warlike tribes of Bombas and Khakhas, who now and then carried out looting incursions into the Valley, were a constant source of anxiety and danger to the Sikhs. In fact many times during their rule Bombas and Khakhas looted the valley as far up as Pattan When the Sikh Empire's attention turned towards Kashmir, they encountered the other formidable Janjua branch of the Khakhas Janjua warlords, renowned as the most troublesome tribe of Kashmir. Sardar Raja Ghulam Ali Khan and his brother Raja Sarfaraz Khan openly revolted against the Sikh Governor of Kashmir Dewan Moti Ram resulting in attracting the attention of Hari Singh Nalwa the Sikh General who was deputised to subdue the rebels. Raja Ghulam Ali Khan openly defied the repeated orders to pay revenues, leading to a fierce battle with Hari Singh Nalwa known as the Battle of Khakhas at Uri. Both brothers were captured and taken prisoner by the Sikh general Hari Singh Nalwa who viewed the united Khakhas Bombas uprising as detrimental to their peace and stability in Kashmir. On 1ST February 1821, information was received at the (Sikh royal) court that Hari Singh Nalwa had suppressed the uprising of Khakhas and captured their chief, Ghulam Ali. The Maharajah wrote to Hari Singh to lose no time in sending the captive with appropriate security to Lahore. There was great rejoicing in Lahore for this was a troublesome man. A celebratory firing of cannons was ordered. Both Khakhas Rajput chiefs were taken to Lahore under heavy escort, where they were later butchered alive by Nalwa in prison captivity for refusing to instruct their tribe to give up the rebellion. The Khakhas Rajas now intensified their raids in consequence to the weakening Sikh power after Maharajah Ranjit Singh's death.

Sarkar-i-Khalsa

Cis-Satluj States 1809
It would be proper to mention here that some of the Cis-Satluj chiefs had maintained relations with the British for several years. When the British occupied Delhi in 1803, Raja Bhag Singh of Jind, Bhai Lal Singh of Kaithal and Sardar Bhanga Singh of Thanesar had helped them. Their relations with the British had become more firm. The British did not think it proper to meddle in the mutual relations of these states. That is why during the Maharajah's visitations of these states, the British had given no help to these chiefs. But they themselves had strengthened their only fort at Karnal as a precautionary measure. Right at the time and ambassador of the Cis-Satluj Sikh chiefs called upon the British Residence and requested him that their states be granted British protection against Maharajah Ranjit Singh.

Anglo-Sikh Treaty 1809
The British decided to win the Sikhs over to their side and sent a young officer, Charles Metcalfe, to Maharajah Ranjit Singh's court with an offer of friendship. Metcalfe met the Maharajah in his camp on 12TH September 1808, and presented to him the draft of a treaty. Maharajah Ranjit Singh rejected Metcalfe's terms and made his own, seeking the British to recognize his authority over the Sikh country to the south of the Satluj. As the danger of Napoleon's attack lessened, the British became arrogant in their attitude. On his return to Lahore, Ranjit Singh received a message from the Governor-General that the British had taken the Sikh chiefs south of the Satluj under their protection. The British sent a force under the command of Colonel David Ochterlony who, passing through Buria and Patiala, came very close to the Satluj and stationed himself at Ludhiana. Ranjit Singh also started making warlike preparations. Metcalfe, who had followed Ranjit Singh to Lahore, presented a new treaty which was based on terms first offered by the British and the proposal made by Ranjit Singh. The treaty in this form was acceptable to the Sikh ruler. Although it stopped him from extending his influence beyond the Satluj, he was left master of the territories, south of the river, which was in his possession before Metcalfe's visit. The treaty was signed at Amritsar on 25TH April 1809. Although the treaty of 1809 halted Ranjit Singh's ambitions at the Satluj and prevented the unification of the Majha and Malwa Sikhs into a new commonwealth, it gave the Sikh sovereign one clear advantage. Security on the southern frontier allowed him freely to consolidate his power in the Punjab, build up a powerful army, and pursue unhampered his conquests in the north, northwest and southwest.

Sarkar-i-Khalsa

Hakim Mohammad Ali Khan 1809
It is of interest that Maharajah Ranjit Singh with an iron constitution was nonetheless preoccupied with his body. Mohammad Ali Khan was a personal physician to Maharajah Ranjit Singh. On Wednesday 9TH January 1809, he showed his pulse to Hakim Mohammad Ali Khan who administered aperients to him.

Lahore army 1809
The pace of development was greatly accelerated after 1809. The constant Afghan challenge kept Maharajah Ranjit Singh on the alert and made him increase both the strength and efficiency of his army. The period 1809-1821 is noted for considerable changes in almost every aspect of the military organization, particularly in the strength, constitution and composition of the army.

Maharajah's conquests from 1809 to 1821:-

Kangra 1809
The Kumaon Kingdom having been incorporated into Nepal in 1791, he endeavoured to add the hill country to its west as far as the river Sutlej. This expedition was entrusted to the Amar Singh Thapa, who was later reinforced by the Nain Singh Thapa. In 1807, Kangra Fort, on the west bank of the Sutlej, was put under siege. By early 1809, most of the land of Kangra *jagir* had been incorporated into Nepal, although the fort still held out in dire straits. Raja Sansar Chand of Kangra deputed his younger brother, Fatteh Chand, as an envoy to Lahore, to ask the Maharajah Ranjit Singh's aid in expelling the Gurkhas from his territory. On 28TH May, he marched to the relief of the citadel of Kangra. The duplicity of Sansar Chand at this juncture, in entering into negotiations with the Gurkhas, and promising them the surrender of the fort in the event of himself and his family being permitted to withdraw unmolested, excited the anger of the Maharajah Ranjit Singh. He suddenly made his appearance at the head of a chosen body of his troops and demanded admission to the fort and his demand being rejected, he attacked the fort and the troops. Maharajah Ranjit Singh made his triumphant entry into it on 24TH August 1809. Amar Singh after the defeat retired to Malakra, the fort of which he besieged but was compelled by the Lahore troops to raise the siege and driven to Char Bagh, and forced the Gurkhas across the Satluj. Ultimately the Nepalese General was forced to retire back to Nepal.

Sarkar-i-Khalsa

Kulu 1809
Sansar Chand was the overlord of Kulu, and when in 1809 he invited Maharajah Ranjit Singh to expel the invading Gurkhas from Kangra. At this time the Raja of Kulu became feudatory of Maharajah Ranjit Singh. Three years later, the Sikhs demanded an annual payment, on the Raja Ajit Singh's refusal, marched upon his capital of Sultanpur and sacked his palace. Raja Ajit Singh at length bribed the Sikhs to withdraw, by paying them all the money he could collect. Eventually Raja Ajit Singh retired across the Sutlej to his fief of Shangri, which he had held from the British Government, and so placed him beyond reach of vengeance from Lahore. A Sikh army soon after marched into Saraj, but found it completely deserted, the inhabitants having fled into the inaccessible forests on the mountain-sides. Accordingly the Sikhs handed over the country in farm to the Raja of Mandi, leaving a garrison in Kulu to enforce their supremacy.

Datarpur 1809
Datarpur was a small state situated in a tract in the of Hoshiarpur district.
In 1786, it came under the control of Sansar Chand from whom it passed to Maharajah Ranjit Singh by conquest in 1809. When the Raja of Datarpur died, his territory was annexed to the Lahore Kingdom's territory and his son was granted a Jagir.

Gujrat 1809
Faqir Azizuddin occupied the town of Gujrat without encouraging any resistance. The Faqir prohibited the soldiers, who were greedy of plunder. Faqir Azizuddin thereupon levied a moderate contribution from the town's people, and gave the money to the soldiers, who were thus pacified. The Maharajah was greatly pleased, and showed his appreciation of the excellent rendered by his secretary, by conferring on him a valuable Khilat. Faqir Nuruddin, Azizuddin's younger brother was appointed governor of Gujrat.

Fazaldad Khan Chib 1810
Maharajah Ranjit Singh, after seizing Gujrat in 1810, attacked Raja Umar Khan Chib, chief of Mangla, and annexed his territory. Fazaldad Khan Chib son of Raja Umar Khan Chib was recipient of a pension from Maharajah Ranjit Singh which was originally granted to his elder brother Amir Khan as compensation for the confiscated territory of his father. Fazaldad Khan was taken into service by Prince Kharak Singh to whom the area of Khari Kariali, the territory which had belonged to Fazaldad Khan`s ancestors, was given in jagir.

Sarkar-i-Khalsa

Raja Muhammad Akbar Khan Chib 1810

Raja Muhammad Akbar Khan was the great-great grandson of Raja Sultan Khan the second last ruler of Bhimber. In 1810 the first attempt by Maharajah Ranjit Singh was made to subdue the States of the Chiban, as a necessary preliminary, and a force was sent against Bhimber. At that time the ruler was Raja Sultan Khan a brave and resolute man, who made a determined resistance, but had finally to submit and pay Bs. 40,000 in tribute. A large portion of the territory was at the same time made over to a relative, named Ismail Khan, probably with the idea of weakening the State. For two years Sultan Khan was left in peace, but in 1812 a conflict took place between him and Ismail Khan, in which the latter was killed. On hearing of this Ranjit-Singh at once dispatched a force from Lahore, under the nominal command of Prince Kharak Singh. Sultan Khan took up a strong position on a height above the town of Bhimber, which was practically unassailable, and the Sikhs were defeated and had to retreat. Another force was dispatched in support, but meanwhile negotiations had been opened with Sultan Khan by the Sikh Commander. The terms offered were that the territory should be restored and that the Raja should be treated with honour. On these terms he was persuaded to accompany the Sikhs to Lahore and on his arrival Ranjit-Singh refused to be bound by the conditions entered into, and committed Sultan Khan to prison in the Lahore Fort, putting him in irons. There he remained for six years. The State was annexed and conferred in jagir on Prince Kharak Singh! In 1819 Ranjit-Singh made his final and successful advance on Kashmir, Ranjit Singh liberated Raja Sultan Khan and furnished him with a large contingent of Dogras for the conquest of Kashmir. The brothers Dian Singh and Gulab Singh were alarmed at the prospect of an extension of Sultan Khan's territories, and determined to be rid of him. He was invited to visit Jammu, and was there assassinated by Gulab Singh's servants while engaged in prayer on the walls of the newly-built Mandi Palace. The Maharajah- professed great anger at the news of this treacherous murder, and permitted Sultan Khan's son Faiz Talib Khan to succeed to the chief ship, then worth nearly nine lakhs of rupees per annum. But he was dispossessed by Raja Gulab Singh on the death of Ranjit Singh, though subsequently reinstated in a portion at the instance of Maharajah Sher Singh. At the conclusion of Anglo-Sikh wars, he took up his abode at Shahdara near Lahore; and be it recorded to his credit that he and his relatives have ever since proved themselves thoroughly loyal to the new Power

Sarkar-i-Khalsa

Multan 1810
After his unsuccessful attempt on Multan in 1810, the Maharajah took Ahmad Khan of Jhang prisoner to Lahore, as he suspected him of favouring his enemy, Muzaffar Khan. Ahmad Khan's son Inyat Khan fled to Hyderabad in Sind. Maharajah Ranjit Singh feared that Inyat Khan would excite the Sind Amirs against him, and promised Ahamad Khan his release from prison if he would recall his son and leave him at Lahore as security for his good behaviour. This was done, and Ahmad Khan received a Jagir at Mirowal in the Amritsar district.

The Gakhars 1810
The Gakhars territories were taken over by Maharajah Ranjit Singh in 1810. The Gakhars were allowed to manage their territories right upto the annexation of the Punjab, when they were able to claim their homelands bordering Jammu and Kashmir.

Chib chiefs 1810
The Chib chiefs held the district of Khari Kariali, stretching along the Jhelum, below the fort of Mangla and Nowsher. In 1810 after Maharajah Ranjit Singh had seized Gujrat, and marched northwards and reduced the fort of Chunian, held by Raja Umar Khan, who retired to his strongest fort of Mangla. The Lahore army marched against Mangla, when Umar Khan, thinking resistance useless, sent his son Akbar Ali Khan to sue for peace. Before the answer could be received the chief died, and the Maharajah Ranjit Singh, not wishing to drive Akbar Khan to extremities, left him half of his father's possessions, which he had only six months to enjoy. All was then confiscated; but to Amir Khan, the second son, a pension was assigned and his cousin Sher Jang Khan was also awarded a pension. Some years later Amir Khan died, and the pension was continued to his younger brother Fazaldad Khan.

Shah Shuja 1810
Shah Shuja was the youngest son of Taimur Shah and grandson of Ahmad Shah Durrani. Shah Zaman, his elder brother, appointed him governor of Peshawar. In 1800, Shah Zaman was defeated and dethroned by his half brother, Shah Mahmud, but Shah Shuja defeated Shah Mahmud in 1803 and occupied the throne of Kabul. In 1809, Shah Mahmud again rose to power and defeated Shah Shuja. In February 1810, Shah Shuja escaped towards the Punjab. Maharajah Ranjit Singh received him with honour at Sahiwal and provided .him with a residence at Rawalpindi.

Sarkar-i-Khalsa

Shah Zaman 1810

Shah Zaman was captured by his brother Mahmud, blinded and imprisoned in Kabul, in the Bala Hissar. He managed to escape to Lahore and sought asylum from Maharajah Ranjit Singh in 1810. This was the same Sikh Emperor, whose lands he had invaded only a decade earlier. Ranjit Singh was magnanimous, and received him with full state honours at Lahore. After sometime, Zaman Shah moved to Ludhiana where he lived with a pension of Rs 24,000 from the British.

Sahiwal 1810

Fateh Khan the chief of Sahiwal, had in 1809, agreed to give Maharajah Ranjit Singh, 25 horses and 25 camels annually as a tribute. He had in January 1809, his tribute been commuted for an annual payment of the sum of Rs.12, 000 which having recently failed to remit the tribute punctually. Accordingly Maharajah Ranjit Singh invested Sahiwal in 1810, and summoned the chief to his presence. The Baluch chief suspecting treachery sent his minor son, Lal Khan, with rich presents to the Maharajah who received the boy with great cordiality and withdrew, apparently satisfied. The Maharajah preceded to Khushab, which place was finally reduced, after a siege of several days, the chief Zafar Khan being expelled. Having thus lulled the suspicions of Fatteh Khan, who thought himself secure, Maharajah Ranjit Singh at once returned to Sahiwal by night, when he immediately assaulted and captured the fort, having succeeded in completely taking the defenders by surprise. Fatteh Khan was put in chains and sent to Lahore, his castle at Kachi, and all his estates being confiscated to the Lahore state. After a year Fatteh Khan was released and given a Jagir in Jhang, with which he was to furnish fifty horsemen.

Bhimber 1810

Maharajah Ranjit Singh had seized Gujrat in December 1810. Raja Sultan Khan of Bhimber was a tributary of Gujrat. Maharajah Ranjit Singh invited Sultan Khan to attend court at Lahore. The Raja feared imprisonment and evaded compliance. The Maharajah despatched battalions of Najibs under Faqir Azizuddin to Bhimber to deal with Sultan Khan. Sultan Khan after an engagement with the Lahore army suddenly fled away into the higher mountains. Faqir Azizuddin occupied Bhimber and appointed Ismail Khan, as the head of the government, and returned to Lahore.

Sarkar-i-Khalsa

Multan 1810
Muzaffar Khan ruled the Durrani province of Multan independently. With the relatives of the deceased Fateh Khan engulfed in a power struggle with Mahm Shah, no Durrani force would be able to relieve him. During 1810, Maharajah Ranjit Singh called upon Muzaffar Khan to surrender Multan to him. In short time, the whole Lahore army was encamped before Multan and took possession of the city on the following day. The fort of Multan was now closely besieged, but the Pathans offered a stout resistance, and the most strenuous attempts of the Lahore soldiers to carry out the fort by assault signally failed. The Maharajah seeing his case hopeless, retired on the 19TH of April, and was to accept now the very terms which he had on many previous occasions rejected with scorn.

Ahmed Khan 1810
Ahmed Khan was the last of the Sial chiefs. After Maharajah Ranjit Singh had unsuccessfully attacked Multan in 1810, he visited his chagrin on Ahmed Khan, whom he suspected of favouring Muzaffar Khan, chief of Multan. Having captured Ahmed Khan at Sarai Siddhu took him to Lahore, while his son Inayat Khan fled to Hyderabad in Sindh. The Maharajah feared that Inyat Khan would excite the Sindh Amirs against him, and promised Ahmed Khan his release from prison if he would recall his son and leave him at Lahore as security for his good behaviour. This was done, and Ahmed Khan received a Jagir at Marwal in Amritsar district.

Inyat Khan 1818
After Maharajah had taken Multan in 1818, he granted Ahmed Khan a Jagir. On the death of Ahmed Khan his son Inyat Khan, succeeded to the Jagir. He exchanged for one of the same value at Sarai Siddhu in the Multan district and was again exchanged for a Jagir at Mustanwali in Leiah. Inyat was killed near Risalpur, fighting on the side of Diwan Sawan Mal against Raja Gulab Singh. His brother Muhammad Ismail Khan went to Lahore to endeavour to obtain the confirmation of the Jagir in his favour, but the Maharajah was paralytic and Gulab Singh his enemy, in the ascendant, but he only obtained a pension. He remained at Lahore four years till his pension was discontinued, and returned to Jhang, where he lived upon a monthly allowance granted to the family by Sawan Mal.

Sarkar-i-Khalsa

Suket State 1810
Mandi and Suket were originally held by a common progenitor of the present chiefs. Suket is the senior branch of the family; the ancestor of the Mandi Raja having separated early in the thirteenth centaury. The two States have been on friendly terms.

Mandi State 1810
Mandi is a leading Hill State of the Kangra Range, ` It is bounded on the on the north and east by Kangra and Kulu, and on the south by Suket and Bilaspur. During the rule of Raja Sheo Man Sen, of forty seven years, Mandi became successive prey of the Katochs, the Gurkhas, and the Sikhs and lost her independence for ever. Finally Maharajah Ranjit Singh appeared on the scene, and Mandi was made to pay a tribute to Maharajah Ranjit Singh.

Bambas 1811
Bamaba tribe were the descendants of Alexander's Greek soldiers who had deserted him and had settled in the lower Kashmir hills. In medieval times most of them had embraced Islam. They lived on the right bank of the River Jhelum, in the hills with headquarters at Muzaffabad. Maharajah Ranjit Singh conquered them in 1811, and annexed their territory to the Lahore Kingdom.

Kakas 1811
The Kakas were a branch of the greater tribe of the Chibhalis. They inhabited the left bank of River Jhelum opposite Bambas between Gingal and Muzaffabad, and up the lower part of the Kishan Ganga Valley. The Kakas were a strong and bold people, but somewhat surly of temper. Maharajah Ranjit Singh conquered them and annexed their territory to his kingdom. The country was farmed out to Sahib Singh Bedi. In order to make these people peaceful inhabitants, Bedi hanged their holy man, a Faqir, who was held in high esteem by the tribe.

Shah Mahmud 1811
The Maharajah Ranjit Singh was told of the advance of Shah Mahmud of Kabul at the head of 12,000 Afghans in the direction of the Indus, which he had crossed. The Maharajah moved in force to Rawalpindi, and sent to ascertain his intentions. He deputed his Foreign Secretary Faqir Azizuddin to the Shah's camp to make enquiries as to the object of his majesty's expedition. The Shah stated that his only object in visiting the country was to punish or overawe Ata Muhammad Khan, the governor of Kashmir, for aiding Shah Shuja-ul-Mulk, on his late attack on Peshawar.

Sarkar-i-Khalsa

Sultan Khan 1812
Sultan Khan came back to Bhimber, slew Ismail Khan and resumed his authority. In March 1812, Maharajah Ranjit Singh sent a larger force under Prince Kharak Singh to punish Sultan Khan. On reaching the vicinity of Bhimber, the Prince opened negotians for his peaceful surrender. The Raja quietly submitted, and accompanied the Prince to Lahore at the head of a small force of his own in 1812. Maharajah Ranjit Singh received Sultan Khan with great distinction. He was given a mansion to live in with a handsome allowance and made a regular durbari (courtier). After sometime Sultan Khan sent back his escort to Bhimber and he was at once imprisoned, his territory annexed. He was eventually set free.

Mitha Tiwana 1812
Tiwanas of Shahpur used to commit decoities in Lahore terror. Maharajah Ranjit Singh sent a force against them under Dal Singh and General Hari Singh Nalwa in 1812. The Tiwanas fought bravely under their leaders Ahmad Yar Khan, but was compelled to submit to the Lahore forces. General Hari Singh Nalwa was granted the Jagir of Mitha Tiwana

Kashmir 1812
In late 1812, Fateh Khan, the Vizier of Kabul, crossed the Indus River under orders from Mahmud Shah Durrani to raid Kashmir and to free Shuja Shah Durrani from its renegade vizier, Atta Muhammad Khan. In an 1812 interview with Maharajah Ranjit Singh, Fateh Khan agreed to a joint invasion of Kashmir. He could not invade Kashmir if he was opposed by the Sikh Empire. He agreed that a small Sikh force, which would receive one third of the plunder. Both invasions began at Jhelum, but once the armies reached the Pir Panjal Range, Fateh Khan used a heavy snowfall to double march his veteran mountain troops through the range. However, the Sikh commander was able to have a small body of troops present at the captures of Hari Parbat and Shergarh. The vizier of Kashmir, Atta Muhammad Khan, had offered no resistance to either army. While the Afghan were busy looting, the Lahore troops stole Shah Shuja away to their camp. When Wazir Khan discovered what had happened, he demanded the custody of the Shah and on the refusal to deliver the royal hostage, attempted to take him by force. The attempt was frustrated; but it gave Fateh Khan an excuse and refused to share the spoils and occupied rest of Kashmir. Shuja Shah Durrani chose to be escorted to Lahore, out of fear of becoming a prisoner at Kabul.

Sarkar-i-Khalsa

Raja Raheem Ullah Khan 1812

Rajouri town was built on the right bank of River Tawi. The Lahore troops captured the fort of Rajouri in 1812, and confirmed Aghar Khan as the ruler. In the Kashmir expedition Aghar Khan had misled Maharajah Ranjit Singh. Bhayya Ram Singh, a deserter from the British army, was in the service of the Lahore Durbar. Through the treachery of Aghar Khan and cowardice of Ram Singh the expedition had failed. Ram Singh was sent to subdue Rajouri. In the battle Ruhullah Khan's son was killed and victory remained undecided. Aghar Khan sought for peace. Maharajah Ranjit Singh rejected the peace proposal, plundered the town and razed the fort to the ground. Aghar Khan paid some tribute and agreed by treaty to help the next expedition to conquer Kashmir. He was raised in his position and during the last Kashmir expedition Aghar Khan took to flight. His younger brother Rahimullah was installed as Raja of Rajouri, by Maharajah Ranjit Singh in 1803, and he was allowed a Jagir of Rs. 12,000. He made friends with the Maharajah and was employed in many military expeditions, including one against Kashmir which proved successful, for which he received a Jagir of 50,000.

Attock 1812

When the joint expedition to Kashmir of Sikh and Afghan was planned in December 1812, Jahandad Khan, governor of Attock, felt sure that after the defeat of his brother in Kashmir, he would be the next target of Barakzai Wazir Fatah Khan. Ata Muhammad Khan from Kashmir advised his brother to negotiate a deal with Maharajah Ranjit Singh for the surrender of Attock to him. When Ranjit Singh was still at Rohtas, negotiating with Wazir Fatah Khan, about the joint expedition to Kashmir, Jahandad Khan sent his confidential messengers to the Maharajah. He demanded security against Kabul, a Jagir in Punjab and a handsome allowance. The Maharajah warmly received the agents, approved of the proposal, and asked to meet him at Wazirabad. The terms were amicably settled and the bargain was confirmed. Both parties appointed their spies to report the result of Wazir's Kashmir campaign at the earliest. When the fort of Attock passed into possession of Ranjit Singh, Qazi Muhammad Khan, who was at Attock to decide religious cases, crossed the Indus and took refuge in Khattak country. Amir Singh Sandhawalia called him back and restored a portion of his old Jagir and granted him a Jagir in the Khattak country.

Sarkar-i-Khalsa

Firozuddin Khan 1813
The head of the family claims to have descended from Shamir Khan, who founded the village of Shamsabad. The residents of Shamsabad to have thought themselves too open to attack, to meddle much in district or imperial politics, and lived quietly at their village, while the army marched past without molesting them. At last in 1813, the Kabul army, part of which was investing Attock, chose Shamsabad for their camp, and after the Lahore army of Maharajah Ranjit Singh, had defeated the Afghans and destroyed the village, which the Maharajah considered had favoured and assisted the Afghans. The Maharajah, however, restored the estate to the family, and the village was rebuilt at considerable expense. Up to 1844, the affairs of the family were managed by the eldest brother Ghulam Ahmad; but about the time he retired in favour of the youngest brother, Firozuddin Khan and devoted himself to the study of the Koran. Firozuddin Khan had been in the Lahore service and owing to his superior intelligence and education, he soon took the lead in private and public affairs; and it was chiefly owing to the his exertions that the family property was much increased and improved.

Allahyar Khan 1813
With the collapse of Mughal authority after the death of Aurangzeb, the Pindigheb Maliks under Aulia Khan's son Malik Amanat Khan reached their zenith. It during his rule Attock became focus of Sikhs raids. After brief attempt by Ahmed Shah Abdali, the Afghan rule to establish his authority, Attock slipped back into the control of local tribes. By the end of the 18TH Century, Sikh superiority was established. The arrival of the Sikh also saw the decline of the Malik of Pindigheb. The Malik of Pindigheb became nominally subject to the Sukarchakia chiefs and paid but a small tribute. Consequently the Nawab held the farm from Maharajah Ranjit Singh the itakas of Sil and Bala Ghebb. In 1813 he rebelled, but was not able to hold his own against the Lahore troops, and fled to Kohat, where he died in exile. His brother Ghulam Muhammad Khan succeeded him, being allowed one-fourth of the revenue of Sil. In the battle of Akora, Ghulam Muhammad Khan fought under Attar Singh and Budh Singh Sandhawalia against Sayad Ahmad, and no long time afterwards he was assassinated by his rival and enemy Rai Muhammad Khan Gheba at Amritsar., wither both had been summoned by the Maharajah Ranjit Singh. Allahyar Khan succeeded to the estate; but of this chief there is little to record.

Sarkar-i-Khalsa

Battle of Hasan Abad 1813
Wazir Fatah Khan, was deeply perturbed the loss of Attock. The rulers of Kabul attached the greatest importance to the possession of to Attock which dominated the passage across the Indus to Kashmir. He arrived at Muzaffabad towards the close of May 1813. The advance party under Dost Muhammad Khan arrived in Hazara not far from Hasan Abad. He gathered information about the position of the Lahore troops and stopped supplies sent from Lahore from reaching the fort. The Wazir joined him there. Daya Singh was in the fort of Attock, while Bhayya Ram Singh Purbia, and was at Hasan Abad. Wazir Fatah Khan attacked Hasan Abad on 7TH June 1813 with 2,000 Afghans. Bhayya Ram Singh had only 500 horse and foot. About 50 men were killed on both sides. Bhayya Ram Singh Purbia and his Najibs took to flight. His entire baggage, horses and camels fell to Wazir's hand. The Wazir and Dost Muhammad Khan closely besieged the fort of Attock, and cut off all supplies to it.

The Battle of Attock 1813
(Also known as the Battle of Chuch or the Battle of Haidru)
Wazir Fatah Khan and Dost Muhammad invested Attock fort with 15,000 cavalry. The vanguard under Dost Muhammad Khan consisted of fanatic frontier tribes supported by Afghan cavalry. At the same time Ranjit Singh rushed Ram Singh with a force of cavalry, artillery, and a battalion of Najib infantry to meet the Afghans. The Sikhs encamped 8 miles from the Afghan camp, unwilling to risk a decisive engagement, although both sides engaged in numerous skirmishes and took losses. On 12TH July 1813, the Afghans' supplies were exhausted and Diwan Mokham Chand marched 8 kilometres from Attock to Haidaru, on the banks of the Indus River, to offer battle. On 13TH July 1813, he split the cavalry into two divisions, giving command of one division to General Hari Singh Nalwa and taking command of one division himself. The lone battalion of infantry formed an infantry square protecting the artillery, with Gouse Khan commanding the artillery. The Afghans took up positions opposite the Sikhs, with a portion of their cavalry under the command of Dost Muhammad Khan. Fateh Khan opened the battle by sending his Pathans on a cavalry charge which was repulsed by heavy fire from the Sikh artillery. The Afghans rallied under Dost Muhammad Khan, who led the Ghazis on another cavalry charge which threw one wing of the Lahore army into disarray and captured some artillery. When Mokham Chand detected Afghan pressure weakening, he ordered his cavalry to charge.

Sarkar-i-Khalsa

The Battle of Attock 1813 (Contd)
The Afghans broke ranks and fled, leaving over two thousand of their comrades dead on the field and all their heavy guns and equipment to The victors. Fateh Khan, fearing his brother, Dost Muhammad Khan, had died, fled the field and halted only at Peshawar. Nihal Singh Attariwala had exhibited great valour in the battle. He was awarded a cash award and two villages in Jagir on the banks of River Jhelum on August 1813. It was the first victory the Lahore forces had won over the Afghans and Pathans in a pitch battle. That it should have been on the field of Attock was even greater significance. Attock had been wrested from Raja Jaipal in 1002 by Muhammad Ghazni and since then had remained in foreign hands. Its capture meant the liberation of northern India from Pathan and Afghan menace.

Kazi Ghulam Muhammad 1813
When Maharajah Ranjit Singh took the Attock fort in 1813, Kazi Ghulam Muhammad fearing for his safety, fled across the Indus to Khattak, where he took refuge with Firoz Khan, while his house was burnt and his property plundered by the Sikhs. Sardar Amir Singh Sandhawalia recalled him, and restored a portion of his old Jagirs and giving him a new one in Khattak. Soon after this Maharajah Ranjit Singh made him an agent on the part of the Government in the Yusafzai and Khattak territories, and this office he held till 1824, when he was assassinated by a Nihang whom he had offended. His eldest son Fazl Ahmed succeeded him in Wakilship which he held, enjoying considerable authority and influence among the Pathans of the district.

Kashmir 1812
A month after the victory at Attock, the Maharajah Ranjit Singh resolved to wrest Kashmir from the Afghans. In October 1813, he invaded Kashmir. Local Kashmiri Rajas, under the leadership of Raja Agar Khan, joined him. He met his first resistance at Bahram Galla Pass by Wazir Ruhullah Khan. The Maharajah bypassed him. Raja Agar Khan led the Lahore forces to the rear of Ruhullah Khan through a different route. Because of the heavy snow and rain the Maharajah could not cross Pir Panjal Pass. Further operations were suspended. The Maharajah, having made arrangements for strengthening the newly captured passes returned to Lahore.

Sarkar-i-Khalsa

Firozuddin 1813

Shamsabad lies just off the high road, and the residents seem to have thought they too open to attack to meddle much in district or imperial politics, and lived quietly at their village while the army after army marched past, Delhi wards, without molesting them. At last in 1813, the Kabul army, part of which was investing Attock, chose Shamsabad for their camp, and after the Lahore army had defeated the Afghans, it destroyed the village, which it considered had favoured and assisted the Afghans. Maharajah Ranjit Singh restored the estate to the family, and the village was rebuilt at considerable expense. Upto 1844, the affairs of the family were managed by the eldest brother, Ghulam Ahmad; but about that time he retired in favour of the youngest brother, Firozuddin, and devoted himself to the study of the Koran, whence he obtained the designation of Hafiz. Firozuddin had been in the service of Maharajah Ranjit Singh and owing to his superior intelligence he soon took the lead in private and public affairs; and it was chiefly to his exertions that the family property was much increased and improved.

Nawab Khan 1813

The ancestor of Nawab Khan, the chief of Sil, was nominally the subject to the Sukarchakia chiefs, paid but a small tribute, and with his troops held the country his father had ruled. In 1813 he rebelled, was not able to hold his own against the Lahore troops and fled to Kohat, where he died in exile. His brother Ghulam Muhammad Khan succeeded him.

Kashmir 1814

On June 6TH, 1814, the Lahore forces army marched towards Kashmir; the main body advanced through the Poonch route, towards the Toshu Maidan Pass, while another force passed through Baramulla towards Supin in the heart of the valley. However, the expedition could not succeed as the rains had set in. Maharajah's division reached Poonch, the supplies were replenished and the force marched towards Mandi. On July 18TH, they reached Toshu Maidan. Here, Ata Muhammad Khan, the Governor of Kashmir, was ready to face the Lahore army. The Lahore forces attacked the well-defended town but did not succeed in breaching its defences. Meanwhile, Azim Khan's cavalry reached there. A fierce battle was fought and Lahore forces suffered heavy losses. The worsted army returned to Pir Panjal. Azim Khan attacked the Lahore force at Toshu Maidan. No defence could be offered and the Sikh soldiers retreated to Mandi. The Afghans pursued the Lahore forces. Many Lahore soldiers were slain. Much of the war material was lost.

Sarkar-i-Khalsa

General Mian Ghaus Khan 1814

Ghaus Khan was an artillery officer under Mahari Singh Sukarchakia, and after his death, under his son, Maharajah Ranjit Singh. He knew something about casting guns, was skilful in his profession, and was rewarded with jagirs at Van and Bharoval in Amritsar district, with a large house in Lahore. When, in 1812, the Maharajah reorganized the artillery wing of his army into Topkhanai Khas and Topkhanai Mubarak, General Ghaus Khan was put in charge of both, with the designation of Daroghai Topkhana. General Ghaus Khan distinguished himself in several of the Maharajah's early campaigns. In 1807, he reduced the fortress of Sheikhupura and secured the surrender of its defiant chiefs. In 1810, he captured Patti and the villages in the vicinity of Tarn Taran. In 1813, he was put in charge of operations against Attock whose Afghan governor, Jahari Dad Khan, eventually surrendered. General Ghaus Khan commanded the artillery in the severely contested battle of Haidru, in which the Lahore forces routed the Afghan forces of the Kabul Wazir, Fateh Khan. In 1814, General Ghaus Khan took part in Maharajah Ranjit Singh's expedition against Kashmir. The Lahore army under the Maharajah reached Purichh but rain and sickness caused havoc. Cholera broke out and General Ghaus Khan fell a prey to the epidemic and died on his way to Lahore. Sardar Sultan Mahmud, son of General Mian Ghaus Khan, succeeded his father as Commander of artillery.

Commander Sultan Mahmud Khan 1814

Sultan Mahmud Khan, son of General Ghaus Khan, was a commander of a section of heavy artillery during the regime of Maharajah Ranjit Singh. After the death of General Ghaus Khan in 1814, although the chief command of the artillery was entrusted to Misr Divan Chand, the battery under the former's command was placed in the charge of Sultan Mahmud. Sultan Mahmud accompanied Maharajah Ranjit Singh on his expeditions against Multan and Kashmir. After the reorganization of the Sikh army into Brigades, when a horse battery was attached to each brigade, the heavy siege train continued to be commanded by General Sultan Mahmud as a separate corps. Sultan Mahmud was of exceedingly intemperate habits, and his drunkenness brought him more than once into trouble with his master, but he was a useful officer and was generally treated with favour. At the death of Maharajah Ranjit Singh and Maharajah Kharak Singh, when Nau Nihal Singh secured power, Sultan Mahmud lost his command and was sent in charge of a troop of artillery, to Mandi in the hills.

Sarkar-i-Khalsa

Mazhar Ali 1814
Mazhar Ali, an artillery officer in Sikh times who commanded the horse battery of Maharajah Ranjit Singh's Topkhanai Khas. For a time, he served under General Ghaus Khan with command of a battery of 10 light guns. He took part in the Attock operations in 1813. The Maharajah often called upon him to display on ceremonial occasions the skill and effectiveness of his artillery. He is described in contemporary chronicles as a skilful gunner who served his royal master with devotion and loyalty

Shamir Khan 1814
The head of the family claims to have descended from Shamir Khan, who founded the village of Shamsabad. The residents of Shamsabad to have thought themselves too open to attack, to meddle much in district or imperial politics, and lived quietly at their village, while the army marched past without molesting them. At last in 1813, the Kabul army, part of which was investing Attock, chose Shamsabad for their camp, and after the Lahore army of Maharajah Ranjit Singh, had defeated the Afghans and destroyed the village, which the Maharajah considered had favoured and assisted the Afghans. The Maharajah, however, restored the estate to the family, and the village was rebuilt at considerable expense.

Raja Ali Khan 1816
In preparation of the conquest of the strongly fortified Mankera, Ranjit Singh decided to approach it from its southern extremity. After the Baisakhi of 1816, Illahi Bakhsh, Fateh Singh Ahluwalia, Nihal Singh Attariwala and General Hari Singh Nalwa accompanied by seven paltans and the Topkhana went towards Kot Maharajah to capture it. When news of its conquest arrived, it left the Maharajah so elated at the success of Lahore arms that he celebrated this victory with the firing of cannons. Its chief Raja Ali Khan was sent to Lahore as a prisoner, and his estates were annexed to the Lahore Kingdom.

Jaswan 1816
Jaswan is a valley in Una district, intervening between the Shivalik hills and outer Himalayan range. The valley was the seat of an ancient Rajput family, Jaswal, closely allied to the royal Katoch house of Kangra. In 1815, the Sikh Maharajah Ranjit Singh ordered all his available forces to assemble at Sialkot. The raja of Jaswan, Umed Singh failed to obey the summons and was fined a sum beyond his means. The raja was forced to relinquish his state to the Sikh emperor, and accepted a jagir of 21 villages and 12,000 Rs per annum.

Sarkar-i-Khalsa

Uch 1816
Uch is situated at the confluence of five rives of the Punjab. It was the seat of the holy Sayyid Pirs, held for sanctity by both Hindus and Muslims. Maharajah Ranjit Singh reached Uch on 15TH February 1810. The holy men waited on the Maharajah with horses, and offered their blessings. They were left in possession of their estates on the promise of paying an annual tribute. In April 1816, Uch was annexed by Maharajah Ranjit Singh, and the Sayyids were given a Jagir for maintenance.

Ahmad Yar Khan 1817
In 1817, the Maharajah dispatched troops against the Tiwana chief at Nurpur. After a short resistance the fort was conquered, and Ahmad Yar Khan fled to Jhandavala in the Mankera territory. On the withdrawal of the Lahore army, some troops were left behind in Nurpur for guarding the fort under Jaswant Singh Mokal. Ahmad Yar Khan came back and recovered control of the country; but he was a second time compelled to fly to Jhandavala, from which he was driven by the Mankera Nawab, who threw his sons into prison. He now yielded to the authority of the Maharajah, who granted him a jagir worth Rs 10,000, subject to the service of sixty horsemen.

Assad Khan 1818
When the farm of the district was taken away from the Nawab of Bahawalpur, and general Ventura put in charge by Maharajah Ranjit Singh, Assad Khan refused to come in, or as the Nutkanis say, delayed in paying the Nazarana due by him. In any case, the Sikh army under Prince Kharak Singh marched against them, and Haji Muhammad Khan was encouraged to claim the Tummandarship of the tribe. Assad Khan fled to Bozdars hills, and remained there for some time, while Haji Muhammad Khan joined Prince Kharak Singh's army, but the arrangement broke down, for the Haji would not undertake to pay the heavy annual Nazarana demanded. Assad Khan was afraid to venture into the plains, but he deputed his son Zulfikar Khan after some time to sue for terms. He was sent as a prisoner to Lahore, and ultimately released by the Maharajah. Assad Khan shortly afterwards

Hafiz Sarbuland Khan 1818
Hafiz Sarbuland Khan had always stood high in the favour of Multan Nawabs. Hafiz Sarbuland Khan had fought bravely against the Lahore forces. Notwithstanding his brave conduct against the Lahore forces, Maharajah Ranjit Singh gave him the command of two hundred horses, and was sent to watch the frontiers of Bahawalpur.

Sarkar-i-Khalsa

Saifullah Khan 1818

Saifullah Khan is of the Babar branch of Multani Pathans who settled in Muzaffargarh towards the end of the 18TH Century. They were established in this country by their relative Muzaffar Khan, Suddozi Afghan, who held the Multan Nawabship, until coming of Maharajah Ranjit Singh in 1818, when they became his tributary, and were farmed out to the Kangra Rajas.
Paid a visit to the Suddozai Nawab Sher Muhammad Khan at Dera Ismail Khan, and while there arrested and sent to Lahore. The Sikh governor, called him to Multan, and granted him an annual allowance.

Mirza Ghulam Murtaza 1818

In 1530, last year of the Emperor Babar's reign, Hadi Beg, a Mughal of Samarkand, had immigrated to the Punjab and settled in the Gurdaspur district. For several generations the family held offices of respectability under the imperial government, and it was only when the Sikhs became powerful that if fell into poverty. Gul Muhammad and his son Ata Muhammad were engaged in perpetual quarrel with the Ramgharia and Kanhaiya Misls, who held the country in the neighbourhood of Kadian; and at last, having lost all the estates, Ata Muhammad retired to Begowal where, under the protection of Sardar Fateh Singh Ahluwalia, he lived quietly for twelve years. On the death of Ramgharia Sardar, Maharajah Ranjit Singh, who had taken possession of all the lands of Ramgharia Misl, invited Ghulam Murtaza to return to Kadian, and restored to him a large portion of his ancestral estates. He with his brothers entered the army of the Maharajah and performed efficient service on the Kashmir frontier and other places.

Multan 1818

The Maharajah had made four attempts to take Multan, but had so far only succeeded in capturing the outlying bazaars. The capture of the fort had defeated them every time. The Lahore forces had already severed the chain of small states around Multan. All remained was Multan itself. A force of twenty thousand men immediately set out for Multan. Artillery, which had to play a major role in reducing the fort, was under the command of General Elahi Baksh. On their way to Multan the Lahore forces took the forts of Khangarh and Muzaffargarh. Nawab Muzaffar Khan planned to defend the city in three stages; the countryside, the city and the fort. The first engagement was in the open, where he let his Ghazis, armed only with swords and spears, gain the martyrdom they sought at the hands of well-disciplined troops equipped with cannon and musket.

Sarkar-i-Khalsa

Multan 1818 (Contd)
This battle only lasted one day, and Muzaffar Khan withdrew the remnant of his forces behind the city walls. The second round began with the Lahore troops surrounding the city and bombarding the walls. The defenders held them at bay for a few weeks, when the city walls crumbled; the defenders retreated into the fort to fight the third and last rung. The fort was surrounded by a large deep moat. It was broad enough to keep cannon at a safe distance from the battlements; it was also deep enough to make the task of miners very hazardous. For a whole month Elahi Baksh's batteries pounded the massive walls without making any impression. The Zam Zama arrived in April, and it proved more effective. With each shot it sent eighty pounds of solid metal hurtling into the wall and tore huge holes in it. When the defenders energies were concentrated in blocking the damage, a party of Nihangs stole down the moat under cover of darkness and laid a mine under another portion of the wall. The next morning a huge segment of the battlement was blown sky high. The battle recommenced. The Nihang leader, Sadhu Singh, led his band in a desperate charge through one of the breaches and closed in on the defenders. Muzaffar Khan, his two sons, and a nephew were killed fighting; two younger sons were taken prisoner by the Lahore forces. The fort capitulated on June 2ND, 1818. The conquest of Multan was the most remarkable achievements of Maharajah Ranjit Singh and had far reaching results. He has now hailed as a conqueror and a general. Maharajah Ranjit Singh's occupation of Multan gave a death-blow to the Afghan influence in the Punjab. Henceforth the Afghans did not remain a power to be reckoned with in the politics of Punjab. It increased the revenues resources of Maharajah Ranjit Singh. It has been calculated that Multan alone yielded an annual income of nearly seven Lakh rupees. This increase in the income of the Maharajah further facilitated his conquests of North-Western territories and provided him with resources for other expeditions. The occupation of Multan by Maharajah Ranjit Singh opened the road to Sindh. It quickly sharpened his appetite for Sindh and he now began to toy with the idea of expanding his kingdom in the direction of sea. Lastly, the possession of Multan also proved to be useful to Maharajah Ranjit Singh from commercial and strategic importance as it lay on the direct route from Delhi to Khandhar. It had a commercial importance as it was through Multan that the trade with Sindh and Khandhar territories was carried on.

Sarkar-i-Khalsa

Makkhum Shah Mahmud 1818

After Maharajah Ranjit Singh had conquered Multan in 1818 he assigned cash allowances to the Shrines of Bahauddin and Rukn-i-Alam. After the death of Maharajah Ranjit Singh and the ensuing Anglo-Sikh war of 1848, Makkhum Shah Mahmud remained faithful to the government of Lahore. His influence and information he furnished were very valuable to the Lahore forces. And after the Anglo-Sikh wars, and annexation of the Punjab by the British, the allowances of the Shrines of Bahauddin and Rukn-i-Alam were conferred. Makkhum Shah Mahmud was an energetic man, and with the help and money of his disciples, he restored the shrines to their former glory.

Peshawar 1818

Maharajah Ranjit Singh was aware that as long as Peshawar remained outside his domain, the Afghan would not reconcile to the Lahore conquest of these territories. The Maharajah set out for Attock with powerful army in October 1818. When the Afghan Khattak tribe learnt about these movements, they at once mobilised a mob of seven thousand. They laid an ambush in the hills of Khairabad, and elimated almost the entire detachment. The news of this incident he drew his sword and hurled a trayful of gold coins into the Attock as an offering and rode his elephant into the swirling waters, and a fierce battle ensued. The tribesmen could not withstand the wrath of the Lahore troops. Tribal strongholds at Khairabad and Jehangiria were occupied. The news of their success against the Khattaks disheartened Yar Muhammad Khan the Afghan governor of Peshawar, who fled the city, leaving behind fourteen guns and other equipment. In November 1819 the Lahore troops entered the famous citadel of the Afghans. Contrary to the practice of most Afghans and Pathans who had usually plundered the towns and cities of Northern India, the Maharajah forbade his soldiers to lay their hands on any person or property. For the first in eight hundred years the city saw and Indian conqueror ride through the streets. Jahan Dad Khan was appointed the governor of Peshawar. But no sooner the Lahore troops withdrawn, when Dost Muhammad expelled Jahan Dad Khan from Peshawar. Dost Muhammad offered to pay tribute every year and accept Maharajahs sovereignty over Peshawar. `The Maharajah agreed to accept the offer and spare his troops and another troublesome campaign.

Sarkar-i-Khalsa

Aliani Laghari 1818
The Tumadars of the Laghari tribe belong to the Aliani section; and the chieftainship has been held in an unbroken line for fifteen or sixteen generations. When the Sikhs took possession of the Dera Ghazi Khan, the Lagharis became allies of the Sikhs, and reaped the reward in obtaining the assistance of Diwan Sawan Mal against their old enemies, the Gurchanis and Khosas. Chata Khan Gurchani had usurped the Tummandarship from Bijar Khan his nephew; but the later surprised and killed him, and recovered his rights. The Lagharis, who supported Chata Khan, took up the quarrel and obtained the assistance of Diwan Sawan Mal, who had an old grudge against Bijar Khan. He was seized and sent to Multan, and there made over to the Lagharis by whom he was slain. The enmity that arose out of these events after slumbering for some time again became active and the murder of Allahdad Khan, son of Rahim Khan Laghari, in Bahawalpur territory, is said to have been instigated by the Gurchanis in revival of the old feud. Rahim Khan, cousin of the late chief, usurped the Tummandarship after the death of Muhammad Khan, and finally driven out with the assistance of Mazaris, and went to Bahawalpur, obtaining a Jagir from the Nawab of Rahimabad in the Sadikabad Tahsil. His sons, Ghulam Haidar Khan and Mir Alam Khan, lived there and retained the grant.

Fateh Khan Tiwana 1819
Fateh Khan Tiwana served General Hari Singh Nalwa and held the Tiwana jagir of Mitha Tiwana since 1819. He held a command under the General's authority until his death in 1837. The following year Prime Minister, Raja Dhian Singh rewarded him control of Mitha Tiwana and the salt mines to the south of the country. His administration was unsuccessful and he was placed under house arrest by Nau Nihal Singh until arrears were paid. On the death of Nau Nihal Singh, his fortunes rose once again, and he was made Manager of the Kachhi country. In 1843 his patron Raja Dhian Singh was assassinated, and Fateh was accused of conspiracy to the murder. The murdered minister's son, Hira Singh, himself now Prime Minister, placed a bounty on Fatah's head. Fateh escaped to Bannu where he sought refuge and thereafter returned to rally fellow Muslims to take up arms against the government. In 1844, on the fall of Hira Singh from power, Fateh went to Lahore to seek the assistance of Jawahir Singh, the new Prime Minister. Jawahir Singh made him governor of Mitha Tiwana, of portions of Jhelum and Rawalpindi, and of the whole province of Dera Ismail Khan and Bannu.

Sarkar-i-Khalsa

Fateh Khan Tiwana 1819 (Contd)

In return, Fateh was requested to assist Jawahir Singh in defeating Peshaura Singh, a reputed son of Maharajah Ranjit Singh and popular choice to succeed as Maharajah of the Punjab. Peshaura had, with the help of local Muslim tribes, secured the fort of Attock. Together with Chattar Singh Attariwala, and some 8,000 men, Fateh was ordered to the fort. Unable to seize Peshaura by force, they promised him safe passage if he surrendered the fort and Peshaura obliged. That same night they placed him in chains and marched him back to Attock. Here he was placed in the lower chamber of a tower, and strangled to death the following night. His body was thrown into the Indus River. After the murder of Peshaura, Fateh took possession of Dera Ismail Khan and sought to secure his position. He had the two of the chief Jagirdars of Tank killed, namely Painda Khan and Ashiq Muhammad Khan, whilst a third Hayat Ullah Khan narrowly escaped. The killings caused uproar across the province and Fateh had to pay a high price for immunity. He was however replaced as governor of Dera Ismail Khan by Daulat Rai.

Mazari Tribe 1819

The Mazari tribe is one of the oldest tribes of the Baloch. The Mazaris continuously defeated, overwhelmed and annihilated the Nahars, Machis, Bugtis and Chandios and fought many battles against the Sikhs In 1836, Mitthankot, by then a strong Sikh garrison fortress, was attacked by the Mazari Baloch tribal forces under the command of Sardar Karam Khan, the younger brother of the Mazari Chief, Sardar Mir Bahram Khan. The attack came as result of the constant threats of Maharajah Kharak Singh to Rojhan Mazari. The garrison was burnt to the ground. Any prisoners captured were skinned alive. Maharajah Ranjit Singh retaliated attacking Rojhan. Rojhan was burnt. Despite this, casualties on the Mazari side were minimal as the Sikh army lost the element of surprise and the Mazaris were able to evacuate their city in time. They then took refuge in the Suleiman Mountains and continued to harass the Sikhs from there. This Eventually Karam Khan was invited to Multan where he entered to a mutual agreement which was to be ratified at Lahore. Finally, in 1838 Mir Bahram Khan visited Lahore on the invitation of the Maharajah Ranjit Singh. This meeting between the two leaders officially brought an end to the long war between the Mazari Baloch and the Sikh Empire that started with the attack on Mitthankot.

Sarkar-i-Khalsa

Kashmir 1819

The Mughal Emperor Akbar conquered Kashmir from 1585-86, taking advantage of Kashmir's internal Sunni-Shia divisions, and thus ended indigenous Kashmiri Muslim rule. Kashmir became the northern-most region of Mughal India. The Afghan Durrani dynasty's Durrani Empire controlled Kashmir from 1751, when weakling 15TH Mughal emperor Ahmad Shah Bahadur's viceroy Muin-ul-Mulk was defeated by the Durrani founder Ahmad Shah Durrani. The Afghan rulers brutally repressed Kashmiris of all faiths. In 1819, the Kashmir Valley passed from the control of the Durrani Empire of Afghanistan to the conquering armies of the Sikhs under Ranjit Singh of the Punjab, thus ending four centuries of Muslim rule under the Mughals and the Afghan regime. When the Lahore army entered the city of Srinagar after the battle, Prince Kharak Singh guaranteed the personal safety of every citizen and ensured the city was not plundered. The peaceful capture of Srinagar was important as Srinagar, besides having a large Shawl-making industry, was also the centre of trade between Punjab, Tibet, Iskardo, and Ladakh. After taking Srinagar, the Lahore army faced no major opposition in conquering Kashmir. Kashmir was an important acquisition for the Punjab. It extended the frontiers of the state to the borders of China and Tibet.

Sardar Kaura Khan 1819

Dera Ghazi Khan was conquered by Maharajah Ranjit Singh in 1819, and was farmed out the Nawab of Bahawalpur, Sadik Muhammad Khan. Lal Khan the expelled chief of the Nutkanis, now sought his patron's aid in attacking his old enemy the Khosas. The Nawab gave him an army of two thousand men. But the Khosas were victorious, and Lal Khan was killed. The defeat let the Bahawalpur Nawab to resolve on the humiliation of the Khosas, and he accordingly demanded that Ghulam Haidar Khan should give him his daughter in marriage, which the Laghari, Gurchani, and Nutkan chiefs, refused with scorn. The Nawab was determined to enforce submission and laid a siege to the fort of Gujri. After two year Ghulam Haidar Khan and a few followers were surprised on the open plain and killed by the Nawab's troops. He was succeeded by his brother Kaura Khan, who found it necessary to submit. In 1830, Maharajah Ranjit Singh took over the direct administration of Dera Ghazi Khan. Kaura Khan then went to Lahore to make his submission and was awarded a pension. In 1832 Sawan Mal became a governor. Kaura Khan gave him active support against the Bozdars and Khetrans.

Sarkar-i-Khalsa

Punch 1819

Ruhullah Khan was the Raja of Punch. In 1814 during Maharajah Ranjit Singh's Kashmir expedition he had played a treacherous part in thwarting the attempt of the Maharajah to conquer Kashmir. In 1819 Lahore forces occupied Punch, and Ruhullah Khan was granted an annual Jagir.

Dera Ghazi Khan 1819

The Sikhs first made them felt in Dera Ghazi Khan in 1819. Between that year and 1830, Nawab Sadiq Muhammad of Bahawalpur farmed the revenue from Maharajah Ranjit Singh. General Ventura was the first Sikh governor after 1830, and was followed in 1832 by Diwan Sawan Mal who held the charge for twelve years. The wild independence which had reined among the Baluch tribes was not put down without difficulty. Nawab Sadiq Muhammad had a long struggle with the Khosas, and they were on good terms with the Sikhs. The Gurchanis were at perpetual war with the Lahore government and Diwan Sawan Mal had himself to march against the Mazaris. The Lagharis and Nutkanis is found their proud profession by loyalty to the Sikhs, although chiefs of the latter tribe fell into arrears with their nazarana payments, and got into much trouble as if they had been all the while in active opposition. When Mul Raj rebelled the tribes which had been most opposed to Sikhs naturally took the lead in joining Edwards and of those the Khosas were most forward. The Lagharis and Nutkanis, as might had been expected, held back and waited for the result; but all submitted cheerfully in the end, and welcomed the establishment of a government which proclaimed peace and order.

Lund Tribe 1819

The Lund tribe of Baluchis under their chief Sori are stated to have settled in the plains at the end of the fifteenth century. They occupy the tract of country known as Sori; for which they had taken the name Sori Lunds. When Maharajah Ranjit Singh conquered Dera Ghazi Khan, the Lundi Chief made his submission and was taken into favour. He assisted the Sikh governor, Diwan Sawan Mal an expedition against the Bozdars, who were forced to submit. In reward for his services to the Diwan, freed the Lundis from the payment of grazing dues, and restored the arrangements made in the time of the Durranis. On the eve of the Second Anglo-Sikh war, Fazl Ali Khan joined Lieutenant Edwards with two hundred sowars, and was with him through the siege of Multan. He was rewarded with a valuable Khilat and rent free grant of twenty wells in Jiwani and Paki.

Sarkar-i-Khalsa

Sardar Mitha Khan 1819
Under the administration of the Sikh governor, Sardar Mitha Khan received half the produce of the Kasrani villages, the whole Nazarana, six wells in Bet Ladha and the right of levying a duty on every camel and donkey using the Pehar and Kawan passes. When Lieutenant Edwards marched down the frontier in May 1848, on the outbreak of Second Anglo-Sikh war, the fort at Mangrotha, dominating the whole Kasrani country, was held for Mul Raj by Chatan Mal the governor of Sangarh.

Hazara 1820
Hazara lies at the foot of the Himalayas in the north-west corner of the Punjab. Ranjit Singh turned his attention to Hazara after his aquision of Attock. It was a difficult in fact to retain possession of Attock without the occupation of Hazara. The tract could not be left unconquered on account of its strategic value. It was situated on the highroad leading from Afghanistan to Kashmir which could be conquered by securing this road. Further Maharajah Ranjit Singh's main aim was to close the Khaibar Pass which had served as the gateway to India during the past two thousand years. Hence the subjugation of Hazara was imperative for Maharajah Ranjit Singh. The Pathans are the dominant people throughout the whole of Hazara. The whole tribe was armed to the hilt. They were armed with heavy matchlocks and long spears. Both were used with singular dexterity. The success of the Lahore troops against the Pathans was due to their superior military organisations, solidarity among their ranks, and the erection by them of a number of forts at strategic points. Galaxy of Sikh generals were appointed by the Lahore government to govern Hazara.
When the Lahore Kardar was besieged in Hazara by the insurgents, Malik Ghulam Khan and Fateh Khan came to his aid and rescued him. Fateh Khan was granted by Maharajah Ranjit Singh Jagir the villages of Bahtar, Bhagwi, Kot Sadullah and Landi.

Faiz Ali Khan 1820
When Maharajah Ranjit Singh conquered Dera Ghazi Khan in 1820, he gave the district to Faiz Ali Khan, the Nawab of Bahawalpur to farm. The Lund chief made his submission and was taken into favour by the Maharajah. He assisted the Lahore governor in an expedition against Bozdars, who were soon made to submit. In reward for this service the Lahore government freed the Lunds from the payment of grazing dues, and restored the arrangements made in the time of the Durranis, by which they paid only half of the revenue due on their villages.

Sarkar-i-Khalsa

Shaikh Ghulam Muhiyddin 1820

Shaikh Ghulam Muhiyddin was the son of Shaikh Ujala, a Munshi or accountant in the service of Sardar Bhup Singh of Hoshiarpur. At a young age, Ghulam Muhiyddin took up service under Diwan Moti Ram, the governor of Kashmir, later shifting to Lahore. He exhibited great diplomatic skill when in 1823, under Maharajah Ranjit Singh's instructions, he persuaded Sardar Muhammad Azim Khan of Kabul, who had marched upon Peshawar, to retire without firing a shot. In 1827, he was appointed a governor of Kashmir.

Mian Qadir Bakhsh 1820
Makhe Khan

The ancestors of Mian Qadir Bakhsh and his cousin Makhe Khan were among Bhatti Rajputs who migrated from Bikaner and Jaisalmir to the Punjab, about the year 1500. They settled at Batala in Gurdaspur district of the Punjab. They received Jagirs from the Mughal Emperor Babur, which they retained under Emperors Sher Shah Suri and Shah Jahan. The close of the eighteenth century saw the decline of Mughal power m the Punjab, and the rise of the Sikhs. The Diminution of Mughal authority in the Punjab injured the Mughal satraps most, and their assistant administrators soon found themselves dispossessed of their valued position. In this upheaval Mian Qadir Bakhsh, the successor of Mian Muhammad Ashraf, lost his hereditary office and his Jagir, and nothing beyond a small holding and a redential house was left of the large ancestral estate. His younger brother, Mian Imam Bakhsh, and his cousin Makhe Khan, both of whom were tried military officers and offered their services to Maharajah Ranjit Singh.

Allahdad Khan 1821

Allahdad Khan was the last ruler of Khattak family of Tonk, situated in Bannu district, on the northwest frontier. When Maharajah Ranjit Singh conquered this region in 1821, Allahdad Khan became a tributary of the Lahore government. As the tribute had fallen in arrears, an expedition was sent against Tonk in 1836. Allahdad Khan fled, but continued his intrigues against Maharajah Ranjit Singh. In 1843, Fateh Khan Tiwana was sent to curb his revolt, proposed that Allahdad Khan be appointed governor of Tonk to secure peace in the territory. The proposal was still under consideration of the Lahore Durbar when Allahdad Khan died 1843.

Sarkar-i-Khalsa

Langar Khan 1821

The Baluch family of Sahiwal came to India in 1527. Malik Beg Khan was a petty chief of Kach Makran, the most westerly province of Baluchistan. The descendent of Malik Beg Khan, Muhammad Khan found it difficult to make head against the Sikhs, who were at this time overrunning the country. Sardar Jhanda Singh Bhangi attacked Sahiwal, but was repulsed, though he took possession of a portion of the territory. Muhammad Khan at length succeeded in recovering this with some loss, but was assassinated soon afterwards by some Sikhs and Baluchis who had come to Sahiwal on pretence of paying him a complimentary visit. Allayar Khan having punished his father's murderess turned his attention to the improvement of the country, and was engaged in cutting a canal from the Jhelum, when he was killed by a fall from his horse. Fateh Khan the fourteenth chief was a minor at the time of his brother's death. When the boy grew up he was determined to seize power, and his bold policy was completely successful. He then turned his arms against the Sikhs and recovered from them the forts of Nahang and Shaikh Jalal. From Sardar Mit Singh Bhangi he took Dera Jara, and soon became dreaded for his energy and courage. On all sides he recovered ancestral possessions and acquired new ones, till he at length ruled over a larger tract of country than any of his predecessors. When Sardar Mahan Singh rose to power Fateh Khan thought it politic to pay him a small tribute; and in 1804 he agreed to give Maharajah Ranjit Singh yearly twenty–five horses and twenty –five camels. In the spring of 1810, having collected his forces, Maharajah Ranjit Singh marched to Sahiwal, and summoned Fateh Khan to his presence. The Baluch fox had noticed many footprints going to the den of the lion, but no sign of returning step, and hesitated to comply; but Maharajah Ranjit Singh expressed such devoted friendship for him, that at length that he sent his son Langar Khan, a child of four years of age with rich presents. The Maharajah received the boy the great cordiality, and having again expressed his friendship for Fateh Khan. The Maharajah then marched against Zafar Khan, chief of Khushab, which place he reduced after days siege. Fateh Khan thought himself secure; but Maharajah Ranjit Singh returned at night to Sahiwal, and took the fort by surprise and carried the chief prisoner to Lahore. After a year he was released, and Jagir was given to him at Jhang, with which he was to furnish fifty horsemen. In 1812 he returned to Lahore, and for three years remained at Court; but this life was not to his taste. He fled to Mankera to the protection of Muhammad Khan, the great and wise Baluch governor.

Sarkar-i-Khalsa

Langar Khan 1821 (Contd)

He remained here for nine months, but Muhammad Khan could do much to assist him, and then he left for Multan, where he lived for two years supported by Muzzafar Khan. But when his old enemy marched on Multan in 1818, he retired to Bahawalpur where in the town of Ahmadpur he died in 1820. Langar Khan his eldest son was fourteen years old at his father's death, and Sadik Khan the chief of Bahawalpur, took him and his horsemen into his own service. After three years Maharajah Ranjit Singh, who had heard of Fateh Khan's death, invited Langar Khan to Lahore gave him a Jagir in Jhang and Sahiwal, with allowances for fifty horsemen into in his own service, and stationed him at Multan where he remained for ten years. Shortly before the Maharajah's death he granted a new Jagir to Langar Khan at Munglanwala, Nun, Jhok and Manjur with the old Sahiwal Jagir. Besides this, Langar Khan was allowed cash, for services of himself, his two sons, and forty-two troopers. Maharajah Sher Singh ordered him two hundred horsemen to accompany the camp of General McCaskil through the Punjab during the Afghan War, and in July 1841, commanding the same force; he went with Major Lawrence as far as Charbagh in Laghman. After the assassination of Sher Singh, Langar Khan was sent by Hira Singh against Fateh Khan Tiwana, who was the country between the Chenab and the Indus; but the expedition had not much success and it was not until the death of Hira Singh that Fateh Khan submitted and came to Lahore, where he offered his services to Sardar Jawahir Singh the new Wazir. Under this minister Langar Khan was stationed at Pind Dada Khan, and at the close of 1847 he was sent under Lieutenant Edwards to Bannu. In June 1848, during the first Anglo-Sikh war, he did good service against the insurgent Bhai Maharaj Singh. For three days and nights from Jandiala to Jhang, did Langar Khan, with other Muhammadan chiefs, hang on his tracks till being joined by the fresh troops of Misri Sahib Dayal; they drove the rebel force into the swollen Chenab. Two months afterwards Langar Khan joined General Whish's camp at Sardarpur and served the whole siege of Multan with great credit.

Malik Baksh Khan

Malik Baksh Khan and his son Malik Jahan Khan served in the army of Maharajah Ranjit Singh. He held some villages in Jagir from Maharajah Ranjit Singh.

Sarkar-i-Khalsa

Mankera 1821

In October 1821, the Maharajah personally led the troops that besieged Mankera. The siege lasted for twenty-two days and at a great cost to the invaders. Mankera, fortified by the brick wall had a distinct advantage of its position being in the middle of a desert. The besieging army had not only to deal with the gallant musketry of the Mankera troops but had to find out ways to deal with the natural difficulties as well. Water had to be carried for the troops from considerable distances. Maharajah Ranjit Singh's ingenuity saved the day, as he ordered his army to dig several wells. Twelve such wells were dug. The siege dragged on for twenty-two days during which time the Nawab held his own; however the desertions of his Sardars and the demolition of one of the minarets of Jamia Masjid—taken as a bad omen—forced the Nawab to surrender the fort to the Sikhs. The fort of Bhakkar capitulated without firing a shot, as the commander of the fort could not face the attack of Lahore troops. The Maharajah, treated the Nawab with respect, and sent across the River Indus and annexed his territory and established a permanent military post in the territories. The iron ball shot from the big guns, including the Zam Zama employed by Ranjit Singh during the Mankera expedition is still preserved in the mosque's compound.

Hafiz Sarbuland Khan 1821

After the capture of Mankera in 1821, by Maharajah Ranjit Singh, Hafiz Sarbuland Khan received a Jagir in Leiah Tehsil, which he retained till 1829, when it was exchanged for one of the same value in Multan.

Commandant Ibadullah 1821

The Commandant Ibadullah was killed in action at the battle of Mankera. He had led the Najib Battalion with great distinction in all the battles of Lahore forces since its inception in 1810. The adjutant Imam Shah was promoted to succeed him in the command of the Najib battalion in 1821.

Derah Ismail Khan 1821

This district is situated on the western bank of River Indus. It was annexed by Maharajah Ranjit Singh on 9TH November 1821. In January 1822, Maharajah Ranjit Singh made it over to Nawab Hafiz Ahmad Khan. The Nawab died in 1825, and was succeeded by his 32 year old son Sher Muhammad Khan. He took little interest in administration and voluntarily retired into private life on receiving a handsome Jagir from Maharajah Ranjit Singh. A Kardar was appointed to administer the state.

Sarkar-i-Khalsa

The Lahore forces in 1821:

Commander-in-Chief
Maharajah Ranjit Singh

Ghorchurras (11,000)
Original Dehras (2,500)
2ND Generation Dehras (3,500)
6 New Dehras (3,500)
Regular Cavalry
Derah Amir Shah
Derah Abdul Rahman Khan
Derah Sujan Ali
Derah Nasiruddin Khan
Irregular Cavalry
Derah Abdul Rehman Khan
Derah Nasiruddin Khan
Dehra Pir Daulat Khan
Dehra Sarbuland Khan
Dehra Qamaruddin
Dehra Ahmed Khan Yar Tiwana
Dehra Bakhurdar Khan
Dehra Jalal Khan
Dehra Qamar Uddin
Dehra Karam Illahi
Dehra Nasiruddin Khan
Dehra Jalal Khan
Dehra Hakim Shah
Dehra Qamar Uddin
Dehra Karam Illahi
Dehra Game Khan
Dehra Illahi Baksh
Dehra Imam Shah Sayyad
Dehra Mohammad Haji
Dehra Hussain Ali Khan
Dehra Ali Khan
Dehra Nawab Qadir Dad Khan
Dehra Karam Illahi
Dehra Game Khan
Dehra Nasiruddin Khan

Regular Infantry (10,000)
16 Regular Infantry Battalions
Paltan Shaikh Basawan
Paltan Shaikh Ibadullah
Paltan Aziz Khan
Paltan Bakhtawar Khan
Paltan Ghulam Hussain
Paltan Najaf Khan
Guards and constabulary of
Irregular Cavalry
Paltan Allah Yar Khan
Paltan Imami Baksh
Paltan Bakhtawar Khan
Paltan Babat Khan
Paltan Khazana Shaikh
Paltan Shahbaz
Paltan Shadi Khan
Paltan Qadir Baksh
Paltan Yusuf Ali Khan
Paltan Misri Khan Rohilla
Paltan Mir Khan
Paltan Khair Ullah Shaikh
Paltan Dhuman Khan
Paltan Mohammad Khan Rohilla
Paltan Faqir Mohammad
Paltan Mian Mauju
Paltan Mawajib Shahzada
Paltan Imam Baksh
Paltan Sultan Mahmud
Paltan Imdad Ali
Paltan Shaikh Haidar
Paltan Ahmad Khan
Paltan Ahmad Ali Khan
Paltan Himmat Khan
Paltan Shaik Haidar
Paltan Waris Khan

Sarkar-i-Khalsa
The Lahore forces in 1821(Contd):-

Commander-in-Chief
Maharajah Ranjit Singh

Artillery Dehras (554)
Dehra Illahi Baksh
Dehra Mazhar Ali Beg
Derah Fattu Khan

Zamburkhana (100 Zambruks)
Derah Ibadullah Khan
Derah Ghulam Mohammad
Derah Abdul Rahim Khan
Derah Khair Ali Khan

Jagirdari ` (20,000)
Feudal Horse
Feudal Infantry

Artillery 1821
It may be seen that even end of this period, the artillery branch was headed by only by Muslims. It seems that Sikhs were still not fully integrated with this arm.

Maliks of Kala Bagh 1822
Kala Bagh the home for generations of the local Awan Maliks is one of the most ancient towns in this part of the Punjab. Malik Yar Khan was the chief when the Sikhs annexed the district in 1822. He was made responsible for the revenue, and had to give an annual tribute the Maharajah Ranjit Singh of two horses, eleven camels, five dogs, two third of the salt tax and two fifths of the revenue of the Masan lands held by him. The countenance of the Sikhs enabled Ali Yar Khan to strengthen and extend the hold he had lately acquired on certain Cis-Indus villages, and his family generally benefited largely under the comparative secure rule of Lahore Durbar.

Malik Ali Ya r Khan Tiwana1822
When Maharajah Ranjit Singh annexed the district in 1822, Malik Ali Yar Khan Tiwana was made responsible for the revenue, and had given an annual tribute to the Maharajah of two horses, eleven camels, five dogs, two-thirds of the Salt tax and two-fifths of the revenues of the Masan lands held by him. The countenance of the Maharajah Ranjit Singh enabled Malik Ali Yar Khan Tiwana to strengthen and the hold he had lately acquired on certain Cis-Indus villages, and his family generally benefitted largely under the secure rule of Lahore Durbar.

Sarkar-i-Khalsa

Nowshera 1823

In the autumn 1822, Faqir Azizuddin, was sent to Peshawar to collect the tribute for Lahore Durbar. He was well received by Yar Mohammed, who ordered the city to be illuminated in the Fakir's honour. Yar Mohammed paid the tribute in cash and horses. Faqir Azizuddin returned to Lahore well satisfied with his mission. Mohammed Azim who was ruling Kabul taunted Yar Mohammed for paying tribute to infidels. Azim Khan marched out of Kabul and the cry of jihad echoed at Khyber. Over Forty-five thousand Khattaks and Yusafzai tribesmen under the leadership of Sayyid Akbar Shah of Balmer volunteered to fight. Yar Mohammed abandoned Peshawar and went into hiding. Maharajah Ranjit Singh ordered his army to move towards Peshawar. Prince Sher Singh was leading their battalions of infantry. General Hari Singh Nalwa, Phula Singh, Fateh Singh Ahluwalia, Desa Singh Majithia and Attar Singh Sandhawalia were leading the cavalry while artillery was in charge of General Illahi Baksh. Recently trained and incorporated battalion of Purbia and Gurkha Soldiers were also sent. Total number forces were about 25,000 men. In December 1822 orders were given to Prince Sher Singh, to lead the march with his battalions of Cavalry and Infantry. General Hari Singh Nalwa whose Sher-e-Dil Rajaman battalion was replenished by additional soldiers making it the largest Cavalry regiment of about 5000 men and horses in the Lahore army was closely following Prince Sher Singh. These advance columns of Lahore army reached Attock River a month ahead of other forces. They crossed the Attock River using a pontoon bridge and occupied the fort of Jehangiria. Mohammed Azim and his Afghan Jihadis soon surrounded the fort of Jehangiria. Other men helping Mohammed Azim to lead their 45,000 forces of Mujahedeen were his brothers, Dost Mohammed, Sayyid Akbar Shah and Jabbar Khan, the ex-governor of Kashmir. They destroyed the pontoon bridge over River Attock so that Lahore's forces could not cross and started pounding the fort with their guns. General Hari Singh Nalwa and Prince Sher Singh with much grit and determination held the fort with their total of less than 10,000 men. Since this fort was right on the banks of a river, there was no shortage of water or other supplies. General Hari Singh Nalwa led his cavalry in numerous sorties outside fort destroying two of the invaluable guns of Afghanis. Meanwhile, Maharajah Ranjit Singh and rest of the Lahore forces force which was following his advance columns arrived in January to found that only pontoon bridge across the river was destroyed.

Sarkar-i-Khalsa

Nowshera 1823 (Contd)

The Maharajah decided to wait for his heavy guns to arrive which were due by mid-day (March 14, 1823) but, at the morning Sikh service, which was always held at times of war or peace, a Gurmata (Resolution) had already been passed that the Ghazis shall be attacked the same morning, before they could gather more force. The Akalis, therefore, refused to wait in view of the Holy Resolve (Gurmata), and wanted the attack launched without delay. The Maharajah had also to yield and ordered prince. Fortunately, the artillery also arrived before time under Illahi Baksh. General Hari Singh Nalwa and Prince Sher Singh had already taken on the enemy earlier crossing the river before the bridge was destroyed and capturing the fort of Jehangiria. They were exerting powerful pressure on the enemy but badly needed reinforcements which had arrived on the other side of that river, but could not wait for the bridge to be constructed under the threat of enemy fire. Maharajah Ranjit Singh one early morning leading himself riding on his white horse he dipped in the freezing water to cross the river. Whole force followed but in this exercise much of the equipment was lost, that included much needed guns. Akali Phoola Singh's suicide squad who was following Ranjit Singh, now took the lead, and, without a moment's thought, plunged their horses in the swollen and turbulent river. Every one followed suit, but before they crossed over, the enemy had taken flight from Jehangiria leaving even their dead or dying in the battle-field and saying in despair: - Toba, Toba, Khuda Khud Lahore forces shud." (God forbid, but it appears, God himself has turned a Lahore forces!). It was believed that no one could cross the river at its full fury. Thus catching the enemy by surprise that were sleeping soundly, Ranjit Singh and his forces broke open the cordon massacring more than 1,000 Afghanis. Afghanis who were mostly belonged to Khattak and Yusafzai tribes, fled and entrenched themselves nearby a city then called Pir Sabak. Main Afghan force under Azim Khan's brothers was separated from the other column of tribal Jihadis by a small swift running stream called Landai. Whatever was left of Lahore's artillery, it by passed these Jihadis and reached the bank of the Landai training its heavy guns on the opposite bank. When Azim Khan knew about this situation he made a dash from Peshawar and joined his brothers on the bank of the Landai River. They could not cross the stream because of constant firing by Lahore guns. Azim Khan and his brothers decided to launch an attack early morning when Punjabi guns were being rested. Lahore forces who were on constant vigil counter attacked on Pir Sabak Hill, where tribal Mujahid were resting.

Sarkar-i-Khalsa

Nowshera 1823 (Contd)

Tribal army fought desperately but was overwhelmed by the Lahore's newly trained battalions of Poorbias. A furious battle raged. The Lahore's guns rained death on the enemy lines and soon the warriors took to hand-to-hand fighting. Meanwhile, seeing their comrades getting killed all Afghanis came together in a desperate effort to hold the attack by Lahore army. The Lahore forces surrounded them from all sides. General Hari Singh Nalwa pressed on his cavalry deploying Guerrilla tactics of attack and retreat of one wave while other attacked and retreated. Raising war cries of Bole So Nihal Sat Sri Akal from time to time, General Hari Singh Nalwa and his disciplined soldiers emptied their muskets on Jihadis. A wave of about 50 soldiers on their horses would charge at Jihadis, firing their muskets and then sending more to meet their creator through their bayonets as they gallop across the battlefield. General Hari Singh Nalwa and Akali Phula Singh with their cavalry regiment of Sher-Dil-Rajman and Nihangs gave them coup de grace. They drove the Khattaks and Yusafzais from Pir Sabak Hill. Heavy artillery on the land surrounded the Jihadis and opened up a barrage to complete the slaughter. While Hari Singh was leading his Sher-Dil-Rajman attacking Jihadis from one end, from other side Akali Phula Singh and his Cavalry of Nihangs, were performing similar feat. Jihadis changed their tactics and decided to go for the leaders in order to demoralize the Lahore forces. Akali Phula Singh's horse was shot. This angered Akali Phula Singh and he made a grave mistake by getting on an elephant. Now Akali Phula Singh's towering torso was seen from all over the battlefield. Ghazi Jihadis saw the General on top of an elephant and immediately trained their muskets on him. Akali Phula Singh's body was riddled with bullets, he collapsed in his howdah exhorting the Nihangs to not to give way. Akali Phula Singh through his dashing feats had inspired other commanders his martyrdom renewed the vigour to fight. Mohammed Azim Khan watched the massacre from the other side of the stream without being able to help his tribesmen brother. He did not have the will to fight till death. By the day's end, four thousand tribesmen were left dead on the field. Probably two times that number were injured and left dying at the battlefield. It was a crushing defeat for Afghanis, General Hari Singh Nalwa whose ideal was Akali Phula Singh, chased the remaining Afghans deep into their territory killing hundreds more. Mohammed Azim was too ashamed to face the people of Peshawar and he returned to Afghanistan, where he died in couple of months. This battle proved the effectiveness of organized military.

Sarkar-i-Khalsa

Nowshera 1823 (Contd)

Death of a great General Akali Phula Singh at this battle was the biggest cost of this battle for Maharajah Ranjit Singh. Azim Khan's Jihadis had lost heart and abandoned their zeal for Jihad in complete disorder. 14 large and 18 small guns were captured by the Sikhs. It showed them the effectiveness of organized artillery and cavalry regiments as well as old tactics of Guerrilla warfare. In this battle not all of Ranjit Singh's forces took part, some regiments just waited for their turn which never came. Afghans after a great massacre submitted and Naushera was captured. Hari Singh Nalwa played a conspicuous role first by inflicting a crushing defeat upon the enemy and secondly by pursuing the enemy after the defeat in order to be sure about the victory of the Lahore troops. The battle made it evident to the frontier tribesmen that the Afghan militia was weaker than those of Lahore troops. This battle sealed the further prospects of Muhammad Azim of Kabul and established the Sikh supremacy over Peshawar. Three days later the Maharajah entered Peshawar the head of his victorious troops. The citizens welcomed him and paid him homage with nazarana (gifts). The Maharajah's sojourn was, however, not a peaceful one. What the tribesmen could not achieve in open combat, they tried to gain by the cold-blooded murder of Punjabi soldiers under cover of darkness. Maharajah Ranjit Singh knew about the tactics of these tribesmen. A few days later both Yar Mohammed and Dost Mohammed presented themselves at court and craved the Maharajah's pardon, he forgave them readily and accepted their tribute of presents and horses. Yar Mohammed was reinvested governor of Peshawar on promising increased annual revenue of Rs. 1,000,000 to the Lahore Durbar. This was first time that Afghanis were totally beaten and humiliated in their own country by the people on whom they had earlier ruled. Ranjit Singh made this possible through his able generals and brilliant military tactics. Ranjit Singh in order to further subdue the Afghanis ordered General Hari Singh Nalwa and Prince Sher Singh to remain in North West Frontier province. He also ordered them to construct series of small forts all along the highway leading to Khyber Pass. He correctly had assessed the importance of Khyber pass., and thus organized the defences of his frontier with Kabul. General Hari Singh Nalwa was given governorship of North West Frontier province which he ruled with firm hand.

Sarkar-i-Khalsa

Ayub Shah 1823
None of his successors of Ahmad Shah inherited his capacity for ruling, and the Suddozi dynasty, was finally over-thrown by Dost Muhammadan 1823. Ayub Shah, the last of the Durrani Kings, together with many of his relatives, sought refuge at the Court of Maharajah Ranjit Singh, who received them kindly and gave many of them liberal allowances. Among others pensioned was Shahzada Faruk Siyar, grandfather of Shahzada Sultan Ibrahim, to whom the Maharajah allowed a pension. After Faruk Siyar's death part of his allowance was continued to his sons by the Lahore Durbar.

Shaikh Ghulam Muhiyddin 1824
After four years, Shaikh Ghulam Muhiyddin returned with him to Lahore where, he was subjected to punishment for his cruel treatment of the people of Kashmir. But within a year he returned to Kashmir as a deputy to Prince Sher Singh. The Shaikh was reported to have followed a repressive policy which, coupled with the outbreak of famine, made the lot of the people extremely miserable. The Maharajah recalled Shaikh Ghulam Muhiyddin, and inflicted a heavy fine upon him besides confiscating all of his property and the hidden wealth which he had amassed at Hoshiarpur. The Shaikh remained out of favour with the Durbar for some time but eventually found a patron in Bhai Ram Singh who helped him to secure service with Prince Nau Nihal Singh.

Painda Khan 1824
Painda Khan, chief of Darband, remained in rebellion against the Sikh government from the time Ranjit Singh had occupied Attock in 1813. Unable to expel the Sikh garrisons established at various strategic places, he set himself up on the western bank of the Indus at Amb, and continued making sporadic raids and plundering the people, especially in the areas of Chach, Hazara, Muzzafarabad and Naushera. A force was sent against him from Peshawar, and he fled away into the hills. Yet he continued to disturb the peace in the region. In December 1824, Hari Singh Nalwa suppressed the revolt of Painda Khan of Darband. In 1825, the Yusafzais gathered in huge body to expel the Lahore troops from their country. The number of rebels was five times greater than that of the Lahore force. General Hari Singh Nalwa rushed upon them and scattered them into the hills from where they had come. General Dhaurikal Singh, commanding officer of the Sikh troops in Hazara, had Painda Khan poisoned to death.

Sarkar-i-Khalsa

Kazi Fazl Ahmad 1824

When Maharajah Ranjit Singh took the Attock in 1813, Kazi Ghulam Muhammad fearing for his safety, fled across the Indus to Khattak, where he took refuge Firoz Khan, while his home was burnt and his property plundered by the Lahore forces. Sardar Amir Singh Sandhawalia recalled him, and restored a portion of his old Jagirs, and giving him a new one in Khattak. Soon after this Maharajah Ranjit Singh made him a Wakil or agent on the part of the Government in the Yusafzais and Khattak territories, and this office he held till 1824, when he was assassinated by a Nihang whom he had offended. His eldest son, Kazi Fazl Ahmad, succeeded to the Wakilship, which he held, enjoying considerable authority and influence among the Pathans of the district.

Bannu 1825

The Maharajah Ranjit Singh conquered Bannu in 1825, and assigned it to the Nawab of Derah Ismail Khan on the payment of an annual tribute. However, it could only be collected with the help of the troops. Tara Singh was sent to restore peace and order there. He was surrounded by a large number of Bannuchis assisted by 4 to 5 thousand Waziris. The Maharajah sent a fresh force to help Tara Singh. Fighting lasted for about two months. All the forts and villages were destroyed, and the rebels driven away.

The Battle of Darband 1825

Darband was both the district and the town. The forts of Shergarh, Darband, Tarbela and Phulra were built to guard the district. In 1825, General Hari Singh Nalwa was stationed at Darband, was so hard-pressed that he could hold his ground with the utmost difficulty against the tribesmen. After sometime a much larger force attacked him. General Hari Singh Nalwa displayed exemplary valour and dispersed the attackers to their hilly hideouts.

John Brown 1826

John Brown, an Englishman, who, deserting the East Indian Company's service in the Bengal artillery, came to Lahore and joined the Sikh artillery in 1826. He was later promoted colonel and placed in charge of the artillery depot at Lahore. During the first Anglo-Sikh war, he acted as a British spy. He continued to serve with the Sikhs and be a secret agent of the British. Later he was taken prisoner by the British. After the annexation of the Punjab, the British rewarded him by giving him a high ranking job in the police department. In 1856, he became blind and was retired from service on pension.

Sarkar-i-Khalsa

Ghulam Muhammad Khan 1827
Ghulam Muhammad succeeded Nawab Khan to the cheifship of Sil in 1813. In the battle of Akora, near Attock in 1827, Ghulam Muhammad Khan fought under Attar Singh and Budh Singh Sandhawalia against Sayad Ahmad, and no long time afterwards he was assassinated by his rival and enemy Rai Muhammad Khan Gheba at Amritsar., wither both had been summoned by the Maharajah Ranjit Singh. Allahyar Khan succeeded to the estate; but of this chief there is little to record

Yar Muhammad Khan 1829
Maharajah Ranjit Singh defeated the Kabul Wazir in the battle of Naushehra on 14TH March 1823, and installed Yar Muhammad Khan, governor of Peshawar. Shortly afterwards, Sayyid Ahmad Barelavi proclaimed a holy war against the Sikhs, Yar Muhammad Khan joining hands with him. A battle was fought between the Ghazis and the Lahore troops on 21ST December 1826, at Akora, 18 km from Attock, across the River Indus. Ghulam Muhammad Khan had fought under Attar Singh and Budh Singh Sandhawalia heroically. The Ghazis were repulsed and Peshawar was reoccupied. Yar Muhammad was pardoned and restored to his old position. Sayyid Ahmad again attacked Peshawar in 1829 and Yar Muhammad was killed in action.

Ahmad Yar Khan Tiwana 1829
In 1817, Maharajah Ranjit Singh dispatched troops under the command of Misr Divan Chand against the Tiwana chief at Nurpur Tiwana. The fort was conquered and Ahmad Yar Khan ran to Mankera territory. On the withdrawal of the Sikh army, with some troops having been left behind under Jaswant Singh Mokal in Nurpur for guarding the fort, Ahmad Yar Khan came back and recovered control of the country, but he had to withdraw for the second time and again run back to Jandiala. The Nawab of Mankera gave him no quarter, turned him out from there and imprisoned his sons. He then yielded to the authority of the Maharajah who granted him a jagir worth Rs 10,000, subject to the service of sixty horses. In 1821, Maharajah Ranjit Singh left on a campaign against Hafiz Ahmad Khan, the Nawab of Mankera, when Ahmad Yar Khan readily took the opportunity to join him in the enterprise just to settle some old scores with the Nawab. The assistance rendered by Ahmad Yar Khan and his tribe, the Tiwanas, during this campaign was of crucial importance. The Maharajah insisted upon a troop of Tiwana horse returning with him to Lahore. Ahmad Yar Khan died in 1829.

Sarkar-i-Khalsa

Sultan Muhammad Khan 1830
In 1830 Sultan Muhammad Khan became governor of Peshawar and a tributary of the Sikhs. In May 1834, he was replaced in by General Hari Singh Nalwa, and granted a handsome Jagir. When in 1835, Dost Muhammad Khan declared war on the Sikhs to recover Peshawar; Sultan Muhammad Khan placed no faith in Dost Muhammad Khan and defected to Ranjit Singh`s camp. When the British government decided to bring Afghanistan under their influence and planned with the help of Ranjit Singh to replace Dost Muhammad Khan by Shah Shuja, Sultan Muhammad Khan supported the Sikhs.

Sadik Muhammad Khan 1830
Sadik Muhammad Khan was placed in command of ten sowars, when sixteen years of age, by the Lahore governor of Multan. He accompanied the governor on his expeditions in 1833 against the Gurchani, Lishari, Laghari and Khosa tribes when they made their incursions into Daji and Khanpur, fought in the skirmish at Kala Pahar. After this he was thought worthy of an independent command, and was sent with forty horsemen to Harappa, and later received the itakas of Kamala and Sayadwala. In 1838 he again had to march against his first enemies, the Gurchani and Lishari, who had descended upon the plains and were ravaging the country, and drove them back to the hills with considerable Loss.

Rai Muhammad Khan 1830
In 1830, Rai Muhammad Khan served against Sayad Ahmad, the fanatic leader, who having been compelled to retire from Peshawar, which he had for sometime absolutely ruled, had made Balakot in Hazara his headquarters. Here he was attacked by the Lahore army, commanded by Prince Sher Singh and utterly defeated. Rai Muhammad much distinguished himself in the battle, and for his services received the village of Guru. Sardar Attar Singh determined, for the sake of peace, to get rid of him. He invited Rai to his fort of Pagh; Muhammad Khan did not suspect treachery and went to Pagh, attended by his son Ghulam Muhammad Khan and two followers. No sooner he entered the fort than the little party was attacked by Budha Khan Malal, an old enemy of his family, and the retainers of Attar Singh were all killed. Fateh Khan succeeded his father, and avenged his death upon Budha Khan whose family he almost exterminated. Fateh Khan taking advantage of the weakness of the Lahore Government rose in revolt, but in August of the latter year he surrendered to Sardar Chatar Singh Attariwala, who thought of employing him to suppress the future disturbances in the district.

Sarkar-i-Khalsa

The Lahore Forces in 1831:

Commander in Chief
Maharajah Ranjit Singh

Ghorchurras (10,000)
Original Dehras
2ND Generation Dehras
3RD Generation Dehras
New Dehras

Regular Cavalry
Rajman Abdul Rehman Khan
Rajman Sujan Ali
Rajman- Nasiruddin Khan

Irregular Cavalry
Rajman Fateh Khan Bloch
Rajman Karam Illahi
Rajman Sarbuland Khan
Rajman Ahmad Yar Khan Tiwana
Rajman Ali Khan
Rajman Ashaq Khan
Rajman Ata Hussain Khan
Rajman Bakhurdar Khan
Rajman Bute Khan
Rajman Fateh Khan
Rajman Fateh Shah
Rajman Fateh Shah Mianwali
Rajman Game Khan Watalia
Rajman Ghulam Shah
Rajman Haidar Shah Mianiwala
Rajman Haji Hussain Ali Khan
Rajman Hakim Shah
Rajman Illahi Baksh
Rajman Imam Shah Sayyad
Rajman Jalal Khan Bhatti
Rajman Karam Illahi
Rajman Khudayar Khan,
Rajman Maqsud Ali Khan ;
Rajman Mohammad Ali Khan

Regular Infantry
Paltan Hussain Khan
Paltan Ibadullah
Paltan Bakhtawar Khan
Paltan Najaf Khan
Paltan Mirza Raushan Beg
Paltan Raushan Khan
Paltan Shaikh Basawan
Paltan Mir Khan

Guards and Constabulary of Irregular Infantry :
Paltan Ahmad Khan
Paltan Amir Khan
Paltan Dhuman Khan
Paltan Haidar Shah
Paltan Himmat Khan Rohilla
Paltan Jan Mohammad Khan
Paltan Karam Khan
Paltan Mahtab Khan
Paltan Mian Bor Naurang
Paltan Mian Mauji
Paltan Mian Naurang
Paltan Misri Khan Rohilla
Paltan Mohammad Khan
Paltan Nawab Ahmad Ali Khan
Paltan Phagu Khan
Paltan Saidi Shah
Paltan Shadi Khan
Paltan Shahbaz Khan
Paltan Shaikh Khazana Khan
Paltan Sher Shah
Paltan Sher Ali
Paltan Sher Dad Khan Rohilla
Paltan Sher Shah
Paltan Sital Shah
Paltan Taj Mohammad Khan

Sarkar-i-Khalsa
The Lahore Forces in 1831 (Contd)

Commander in Chief
Maharajah Ranjit Singh

Irregular Cavalry
Rajman Mohammad Haji
Rajman Mohammad Khan
Rajman Mubarik Khan
Rajman Muhammad Khan :
Rajman Nasiruddin Khan
Rajman Nawab Ata Hussain Khan
Rajman Nawab Qadir Dad Khan
Rajman Paz Khan
Rajman Pir Bakhsh
Rajman Pir Daulat khan
Rajman Qadir Dad Khan
Rajman Qamaruddin
Rajman Shamsuddin Khan
Raman Nasiruddin Khan

Jagirdari : (27,000)
Feudal Infantry
Feudal Horse
Some feudal artillery

Artillery
Topkhana Jinsi
Derah Ilahi Bakhsh.
Derah Sultan Mahmud Khan
Derah Sayyid Imam Shah

Topkhana Jinsi
Derah Ilahi Bakhsh
Derah Mazhar Ali Beg

Zamburkhana
Derah Ibadullah
Derah Khair Ali Khan
Derah Abdul Rahim Khan
Derah Mohammad Shah

The guns earlier allotted to Infantry battalions were withdrawn, and organised under separate artillery park, and placed under Sayyed Imam Shah. The other changes were to standardise the size of Dehras, particularly in Horse Artillery.

Maharajah Ranjit Singh's Army
This period is particularly memorable for a large scale expanding of the Army and introduction of the French mode of training. So many advances had been made that end of the period, that British officers expressed favourably their views, when they reviewed the army on the occasion Ropar meeting in 1831. But inspite of all this progress a number of serious short coming still remained, to name but one, the slow evaluations of the Sikh battalions to supplement the Najib battalions.

Sarkar-i-Khalsa

Jamaluddin Khan 1831

The ancient city of Kasur situated some twenty miles to the south of Lahore, was in 1570 by permission of Emperor Akbar, settled by a colony of Pathans, numbering about 3,500 souls. Among those came from Kandahar the ancestors of Mamdot Chiefs of the Hassanzai tribe, and till the fall of Mughal Empire they lived at Kasur, sometimes as traders, sometime as soldiers, as suited their inclination or their means. When the Sikhs rose to power, they experienced great opposition from the Pathan colony; but in the end the Bhangi confederacy overran and subdued the whole Kasur territory, under Sardar Gulab Singh; and two brothers Nizamuddin Khan and Kutabuddin Khan entered the services of the conqueror. Those young men, however, were energetic and brave, and in 1794, with the aid of their Afghan countrymen, expelled the Sikhs entirely from Kasur and established chieftainship of their own. They were not left unmolested. Sardar Gulab Singh made frequent attempts to recover his lost territory, and later young Sardar Ranjit Singh attacked the brothers several times without success. Nizamuddin Khan joined vigorously in the cabal against Sardar Ranjit Singh in 1800, when that chief obtained possession of Lahore, and the next year Kasur was more vigorously attacked, but Nizamuddin held out, though agreed to pay tribute to Maharajah Ranjit Singh. In 1802 Nizamuddin Khan was assassinated by his three brothers-in-law Wasil Khan, Haji Khan, and Najib Khan, whom he had ousted from their Jagirs. Kutabuddin has generally been accused of having been privy to the murder; but he appears to have been absent from Kasur at that time, and on his return he stormed and took the fort of Azam Khan, whither the murderers had retired, and put Wasim Khan and Najib Khan to death, Haji Khan escaping to the Deccan. Maharajah Ranjit Singh at the close of the year again invaded Kasur, but was not able to make much impression, and Kutabuddin held his own till 1807, when the Maharajah again appeared with a strong army, and after a month's fighting Kutabuddin gave in, and agreed to retire to his territory of Mamdot, on the other side of Satluj, holding in Jagir, subject to the service of one hundred horsemen. Kutabuddin and his brother had conquered Mamdot from Rai of Raikot in the year 1800, with the assistance of Dogars, a turbulent Muhammadan tribe inhabiting the district. Maharajah Ranjit Singh gave to Fateh Din Khan a Jagir at Marup, in the Gugera district, subject to the supply of the same of horsemen as Mamdot. But Fateh Din Khan was not satisfied, and was always appealing to the Maharajah for the grant of Mamdot, which he considered his right.

Sarkar-i-Khalsa

Jamaluddin Khan 1831 (Contd)

At last with the connivance of the Maharajah, he crossed the river in 1831, when his uncle's contingent was absent on service, and attacked him. Dogars ready for any change, joined him, and Kutabuddin Khan was defeated, severely wounded and driven out of the country, and died soon after at Amritsar. Maharajah Ranjit Singh now thought it fit to interfere on the other side. He recalled Fateh Din Khan and confirmed Jamaluddin Khan in his father's position. Once again Fateh Din Khan tried his fortune, but the British agent interfered, and the Maharajah ordered him back to Lahore. The Mamdot chiefs were at no time invested with sovereign power but were merely Jagirdars, feudatory of the Lahore government. Lahore was the high court of appeal; and there are many instances on record of fines imposed on these chiefs. In 1824, Kutabuddin Khan was fined for conniving at, and sharing in the plunder of cattle from the Lahore territories.

Sayyid Ahmad Khan 1831

Sayyid Ahmad Khan aim was to restore Muslim rule in India. He turned against the Sikhs. After his conquest of Multan, and Kashmir, Ranjit Singh was planning to conquer Sind. The British had their eyes on Sind also. They were happy at Maharajah Ranjit Singh's involment on the North-West Frontier. In consequence, the British government did not check the Sayyid from raising funds, recruiting men, and collecting war material in the British territory to fight the Sikhs. Sayyid was joined by all the tribes and their chiefs including Maharajah Ranjit Singh's Barakzai governors of Peshawar. The Sayyids religious reforms, his demand for money from Pathans and Maharajah Ranjit Singh's determination to hold on brought about the Sayyids fall. Within one year of their defeat at Naushera, the tribes of the north-west frontier again challenged the sovereignty of Maharajah Ranjit Singh. The centre of the insurrection was at Sitana, near which General Hari Singh Nalwa had raised a fort named after him as Haripur. Nalwa was reduced to dire straits by the tribesmen until the Maharajah came to his rescue. Yar Muhammad again protested his loyalty and was re-instated at Peshawar. But early in 1827 the whole of the north-west frontier was in ferment. This time they were roused by one Sayyid Ahmed who had come all the way India through Sindh to lead a Jihad against the Sikhs. Before coming to the Pathan country Sayyid Ahmed and his two lieutenants, Shah Ismail and Maulvi Abdul Haye, had gone to an extensive tour of Hindustan and addressed mammoth gatherings of Indian Muslims. They raised corps of volunteers and large sum of money.

Sarkar-i-Khalsa

Sayyid Ahmad Khan 1831 (Contd)
Among the patrons was the Mughal Emperor armed many Muslims rulers of Indian states, notably the Nawab of Tonk. The British government made no attempt to check this crusade against a state which had signed a treaty of friendship. Thousands of volunteers were trained and armed in India and then permitted to cross over to Sindh on their way to the north-west frontier of the Punjab. Organisations collected money for the crusaders were allowed to function without let or hindrance in many cities of India. The Indian crusaders were joined by Pathan tribesmen, mainly Yusafzais. Sayyid Akbar Shah of Bruner gave his blessings to the venture. Yar Muhammad true his fickle nature, decided to throw in his lot with what he believed would be the winning side, and evacuated Peshawar. Maharajah sent Budh Singh Sandhawalia to retake Peshawar. Sayyid Ahmed met Sandhanwalia's forces at Shaidu near Attock. Religious fervour proved poorly match for discipline; crusaders were pushed aside and Peshawar re-occupied. Yar Muhammad was on his knees again, craving pardon. He sent his brother as hostage to the Maharajah and promised to be faithful. Once again he was pardoned by the Maharajah. The crusaders explained away the defeat as a reverse for Yar Mohammad, whom they branded as a collaborator. Sayyid Ahmed started harassing stray columns of Lahore troops. These skirmishes were magnified into victories and the whole Muslim India was kept in a state of Jubilation. Sayyid Ahmed's tactics soon put the Lahore troops on the defensive. The crusaders swarmed all over the country around Peshawar. In the summer of 1829, Prince Sher Singh took the initiative and inflicted a severe defeat on them. But even this reverse did not hold them back. A few months later they killed Yar Muhammadan a skirmish and would have slain his brother Sultan Mohammad, if he had not been saved by the Lahore troops. Sayyid Ahmed got bolder and attacked a force under General Hari Singh Nalwa in the Hazara hills and kept the Lahore troops on the defensive while he went forward and recaptured Peshawar. He was proclaimed caliph and coins were struck in his name with inscription 'Ahmed the Just: the glitter of whose scimitar scatters destruction among the infidels.' Success went to Sayyids head. As Muslims from all over India, Sindh, and Kashmir flocked to his banner, he began to assume the airs of monarch. Pathan tribesmen became restive at the influx of foreigners on their soil and the demands they made for food and women, particularly women. Maharajah's agents exploited the growing feeling of resentment. They bribed some tribal leaders to turn against Sayyid Ahmed and murder the Hindustanis. Sayyid Ahmed was compelled to retire from Peshawar.

Sarkar-i-Khalsa

Sayyid Ahmad Khan 1831 (Contd)
The city was re-occupied by Prince Sher Singh and given to Sultan Muhammad Khan. Sayyid Ahmed found himself sandwiched between the Lahore troops and hostile tribesmen. He was at Balakot at the bottom of the Kaghan Valley when Prince Sher Singh caught up with him. In a short sharp engagement, he completely decimated the small band of Ghazis, including the Sayyid. Sayyid Ahmed died at Balakot in 1831.

Begum Gul Bahar 1832
Begum Gul Bahar, a dancing girl from Amritsar, was married to Maharajah Ranjit Singh in 1832. Ranjit Singh grew very fond other, and eventually admitted her into his harem as a wedded wife. Sohan Lal Sun, the court diarist, recording on 27 September 1832 the marriage in his chronicle, writes: "The Maharajah put on saffron garments, decorated himself with ornaments and jewellery... Gul Begum was dressed in yellow garments, with her hands and feet decorated with henna and bedecked with bejewelled gold ornaments from hand to mouth... the Maharajah took his seat in a chair and made Gul Begum sit in another. Garlands of roses interwoven with pearls were tied around the forehead of the Maharajah and a gold nose ring with a pearl was fixed in the nose of Gul Begum and lovely words of congratulations filled the heart of the audience with pleasure." Renamed Gul Bahar Begum, she rode with the Maharajah on the same elephant, sat in the Durbar without veil and dwarfed the influence of other wives on the Maharajah. Gul Bahar Begum is stated to have the finest figure, the fairest hair and the darkest eyes. Having no issue of her own she adopted a Muslim boy, whose progeny still lives in Lahore. She also built a mosque, which is still extant. Gul Bahar Begum survived the Maharajah and was awarded an annual pension of Rs 12,380 by the British. Gul Bahar Begum died at Lahore in 1863.

Anglo-Sikh Treaty 1832
Maharajah Ranjit Singh had an obsessive appetite for horses and was overwhelmed to receive the prestigious dray horses sent by King of England which Captain Burnes ferried upto Lahore. His meeting with the Sikh emperor paved the way for undertaking treaty of friendship between the British and Sikh Empire and finalised the modalities of navigation in Punjab rivers right upto Ropar in the river Satluj. Lord William Bentinck and Sir Charles Metcalfe were to sign a treaty of friendship with Ranjit Singh at a meeting at Ropar on October 31ST, 1831. It was succeeded by a treaty signed on December 26TH, in Lahore in 1832 which spelt out the details of trade and commerce.

Sarkar-i-Khalsa

Bahalpur State 1833
The Bahalpur State lies to the south-west of the Punjab. The power of the State gradually declined before the rising influence of Maharajah Ranjit Singh, and its territory was considerably diminished. Bahawal Khan, succeeded to the cheifship in 1825, took the only course possible to secure his dominions from the Sikhs, and obtained recognition of his independence in a treaty made with the British Government in 1833, and thus saving his country from the fate of Multan and other Muhammadan States in the Western Punjab. In 1838 this Bahawal Khan loyally repaid the protection by services rendered to the army of occupation in Afghanistan; and he was rewarded with the grant of the district of Sabzalkot and Bhang Bara. A fresh treaty was made with him in this year, when he again came under the protection of the British Government, which recognised his position as an absolute ruler.

Budha Khan 1836
The Malal Malik's were reduced to obedience by the Lahore government of Maharajah Ranjit Singh. They were allowed, like the Rais of Kot and the Malik's of Pindigheb, a fourth share of revenue of their villages. When Prince Nau Nihal Singh held the itakas in 1836, Budha Khan received in Jagir the village of Khadwal. This Malik was one of the men who assassinated Rai Muhammad Khan of Kot in the fort of Pagh by order of Sardar Attar Singh Kalianwala. The son of the murdered man well avenged his father, and killed all Budha Khan's family, with the exception of one or two who contrived to escape. There had always been feud between the families, and these murders did not tend to end it.

Malik Fateh Khan 1836
As with most of Muhammadan or Rawalpindi district, it was flourishing under the Empire, and after fighting for some time with more or less success against the Sikhs, was at last reduce to obedience. The Malal Maliks were allowed like the Rais of Kot and the Maliks of Pindigarh, a fourth share of the revenue of their villages, and when Prince Nau Nihal Singh held the itakas in 1836, Budha Khan received a Jagir in the village of Khadwal. This Malik was one of the men who assassinated Rai Muhammad Khan of Kot in the fort of Pagh by the order of Sardar Attar Singh Kalianwala. The son of the murdered man well avenged his father, and all killed Budha Khan's family, with the exception of one or two contrived to escape. There had been always a feud between the families, and these murders did not tend to end it.

Sarkar-i-Khalsa

Malik Fateh Khan Tiwana 1836
At the time of Sikhs conquest, Ahmed Khan was the chief of Isa Khel. Sanad (deed granted to people confirming them in their states, in return for their allegiance) was given to him in 1836, confirming his possessions but requiring payment of seven-eighth of the collections, thus leaving little for the maintainace of the chief and his family. Ahmed Khan demurred in subscribing to the terms; and he was reported to the Lahore government as a dangerous rebel by Diwan Lakhi Mal, who then had the charge sent to the Derajat Province. A force was sent to eject him under the command of Sardar Fateh Singh Ran and Raja Suchet Singh. Resistance would have been fruitless. He fled to Kot Chanda in the Khattak hills, and thence to Bannu, where he was hospitably received by Sher Mast Khan, chief of the Jhandu Khel. He died shortly afterwards in exile. Fortunate for the family, Prince Nau Nihal Singh had received kindness at the hands of Ahmed Khan and refused to support Lakhi Mal's policy of crushing the clan completely out. He insisted in appointing Muhammad Khan, brother of the deceased Ahmed Khan, to the full rights and privileges of the Chieftainship. But the Diwan had his revenge later on. He persuaded Shaikh Imamuddin who was marching through Bannu and Marwat at the head of a strong Sikh force, to make a descent upon Isa Khel and carry Muhammad Khan away. The measure was not a complete success. Some Muhammad Khan's children were taken prisoners; but fled to the hills, His son Shah Nawaz rode off to Peshawar, and throwing himself at Prince Nau Nihal's feet , secured the kindly intervention of the Prince second time in his father's behalf. The Khan was duly reinstated and his family were allowed to return to Isa Khel. It appears strange that the Diwan, who was subordinate to Prince Nau Nihal Singh, should have had the hardihood to risk the wrath in so often running counter to his express wishes. A third attempt on the part of Diwan Lakhi Mal to ruin the unfortunate Khan, met with better success. He arranged with Sardar Fateh Singh to seize Shah Nawaz, who had been sent to Lahore by his father to offer condolences on the occasion of Maharajah Ranjit Singh's death, and his arrest was actually affected as the unsuspecting youth on his way back to his own country, clad in a dress of honour which had been bestowed on him by Prince Nau Nihal Singh heir apparent to the throne. The Sardar sent his prisoner to Diwan, who kept him in close confinement for over two years, at the same time confiscating the whole of the revenues of Isa Khel. Muhammad Khan again fled to Bannu, and Lakhi Mal managed the property, taking the chiefs share for him, and all he could get besides.

Sarkar-i-Khalsa

Malik Fateh Khan Tiwana 1836 (Contd)

Muhammad Khan had in the meantime lost his good friend Prince Nau Nihal Singh, who on the day his father's funeral was himself killed by the falling of the palace gateway at Lahore as he passed underneath. The Wazir Dhian Singh took up the case and ordered Lakhi Mal to send his prisoner Shah Nawaz to Lahore. He was received with much honour, presented with Khilat and permitted to return to his home in company with Malik Khan Tiwana then about to start on tax collecting expedition in Marwat country. Fateh Khan's orders were to reinstate the chief of Isa Khel on his way to Bannu. But the Diwan refused to recognise the Malik's authority, and Fateh Khan returned to Lahore without having put Ahmed Khan in possession. Thither too returned wretched Shah Nawaz to sit at the Wazir's door and cry for justice. The murder of Wazir Dhian Singh was indirectly the means of Ahmed Khan's restoration, though after considerable period. Malik Fateh Khan was at Lahore when Maharajah Sher Singh met with his death, and he was suspected of having joined in the conspiracy for Wazir's removal. He managed to get away in the confusion and took refuge in the Fort of Jhandu Khel, and on the Kurram, where also was his friend Ahmed Khan, outlawed under the orders of the Diwan. The Wazarat at Lahore had devolved upon Raja Hira Singh after his father's murder; but he in turn was assassinated by Sardar Jawahir Singh, uncle of Maharajah Dalip Singh, who speedily removed Lakhi Mal from the Derah governorship and restored Fateh Khan to his favour. But Muhammad Khan's trials were not yet over. Sardar Jawahir Singh who was would have helped him, was murdered at the instigation of his sister the Rani Jindan, by her paramour Lal Singh who assumed the Wazarat, and handed over the Dera Province to Lakhi Mal's son Daulat Rai. He was removed shortly afterwards by Sir Henry Lawrence, to whom Captain Edwards had furnished a full report on his father's iniquities, of which Isa Khel troubles were but a sample. The new governor lost no time in restoring Muhammad Khan to his patrimony, which he enjoyed without further worry for the remainder of his life. Captain Edwards had championed his cause throughout, and old chief proved his gratitude shortly afterwards by aiding him during the Second Anglo-Sikh war, and doing his best to hold the Sikhs in check. His son Muhammad Alam was in the citadel of Fort Dalipgarh with Malik Fateh Khan Tiwana when the latter was killed in attempting to cut his way out. Muhammad Alam was taken prisoner and carried away across the Indus by the Sikhs, who did not release him until after the battle of Gujrat.

Sarkar-i-Khalsa

Fatah Khan 1836
Genera Hari Singh Nalwa dashed into the heart of his territory attacked Panjar and defeated Fatah Khan. He destroyed the chief's village and compelled him to sign a document of submission and payment of a tribute. Soon afterwards Fatah Khan began to repent of his act of submission, and towards the close of 1836 again raised the standard of revolt. He made number of incursions into Chach, an extensive plain east of River Indus. Maharajah Ranjit Singh despatched Raja Gulab Singh with a Lahore force consisting of three battalions of Najib Infantry, a thousand horse and twelve pieces of Artillery under Illahi Buksh. On the approach of the Lahore force, the Yusafzais fled into the mountains. Nevertheless Gulab Singh continued his operations. There was nothing to eat in the upper regions. Hunger forced the followers of Fatah Khan to return to the plains to find their hearths and homes reduced to ashes. Starving they came to the camp of the Lahore force, holding a few blades of grass in their mouths. This implied that they were their cows and must be saved. They were all blown from the guns a dozen at a time. Gulab Singh collected great amount of money and few horses. He left a garrison of 300 men at Jahangira and returned to Jammu.

Jamrud 1837
General Hari Singh Nalwa's energetic measures, particularly the chain of forts that he was making, gave the Afghans reason to believe that he was contemplating an invasion of their country. Dost Muhammad decided to isolate the garrisons, and ultimately defeat them. The first on the list was Jamrud, which were the most advanced outpost and the weakest link in the Lahore chain of fortresses. One detachment was sent to prevent Lehna Singh Sandhawalia for leaving the fort. General Hari Singh Nalwa's illness immobilised the garrison at Peshawar. Jamrud was invested by twenty-five thousand Afghans and Pathans equipped with eighteen heavy guns. Maha Singh had only six hundred men and a few light guns in the fort. Within few hours the besieger's artillery reduced the walls of Jamrud to rubble. Maha Singh's men dug themselves into trenches and for four days kept the Afghans and Pathans at bay. Maha Singh sent a desperate appeal for help to Peshawar. Nalwa rose from his sick bed and made his way to Jamrud. On Nalwa's approach enemy raised the siege of Jamrud and took up positions in the valley of Khyber which would ensure escape in the event of defeat. Nalwa drew up his troops in battle formation and waited for the enemy, who outnumbered him three to one, to attack. For seven days the armies faced each other.

Sarkar-i-Khalsa

Jamrud 1837 (Contd)
When Nalwa realised that the Afghans and the Pathans had no desire for battle, he ordered the troops to advance. The engagement took place on April 30TH, 1837. The Lahore troops drove the enemy before them. Dost Mohammad's son, Muhammad Akhar Khan, who was watching the Afghan debacle from an escarpment, noticed Nalwa well ahead of the bulk of his army. Akbar Khan swooped down on the advance column and poured led into Nalwa's howdah. Nalwa was mortally wounded. He ordered his officers to keep his death a secret until the enemy had been driven beyond the mouth of the Khyber. For the Afghans the killing of General Hari Singh Nalwa turned the defeat at Jamrud into a victory. Much as Dost Muhammad tried to claim the battle of Jamrud as an Afghan victory, nothing could stop the stench of eleven thousand Afghan and Pathan corpses strewn about the Khyber from reaching the nostrils of the tribesmen in the neighbouring hills and valleys. The Lahore Kingdoms standards still fluttered on Bala Hissar, Shabkadr, and the battered walls of Jamrud. And now the ghost of the valiant General Hari Singh Nalwa haunted the rocky defiles, spreading terror among the people. He was the noblest and the most gallant of the Sikh generals of his time, the very embodiment of honour, chivalry and courage. His position at the Court was high and he was idol of the Sikhs.

Dhund Tribe 1837
Maharajah Gulab Singh in 1837 almost exterminated the Dhund Tribe. Their country had been made over to Gulab Singh, when he had reduced Yusafzai to something like order; he marched with twenty thousand men, regulars and irregulars, to crush the revolt in the Murree and Hazara Hills.
Under the leadership of Shamas Khan, the whole country had risen, and all the hill forts of Jammu Rajas had fallen into their hands. Very soon Gulab Singh's promise and his bribes brought disunion into the hostile camp. He marched into the hills, burning the crops and the villages as he advanced, and offering a reward a rupee for the head of every man, woman or child connected with insurgents. The wretched people, divided amongst themselves, and confounded by this display of ferocity in their enemy, made little resistance. At length Gulab Singh ordered the women to be spared and kept as prisoners with the army, and there was soon to be seen following each division a troop, of half clothed starving females, driven like cattle by day and at night penned in thorn enclosure and exposed to the utmost brutality of the soldiery, with the exception of a few of the handsomest reserved for Gulab Singh's Zenana were sold as slaves.

Sarkar-i-Khalsa

Ahmad Khan 1838
In 1825, Ahmad Khan succeeded to the Chieftainship Isa Khel. A Sanad was given him 1836 confirming his possession, but required payment of seven-eighths of the collections, thus leaving little for the maintainace of the chief and his family. Ahmad Khan demurred in subscribing to the terms; and was reported to the Lahore Government as dangerous rebel. A force was sent to eject him. Resistance would have been fruitless. He fled to Kot Chanda in the Khattak hills, and thence to Bannu, where he was received by Sher Mast Khan, of the Jhandu Khel. He died afterwards in exile. Fortunately for the family, Prince Nau Nihal Singh had received kindness at the hands of Ahmad Khan, and refused to support the policy of crushing the clan out. He insisted on appointing Mohammad Khan, brother of the deceased Ahmad Khan, to the full rights and possession of villages of the Chieftainship.

Tripartite Treaty 1838
May 1838, Sir William Macnaghten was deputed to Lahore to engage the Maharajah in a treaty which aimed at the revival of the defunct Sikh Afghan agreement of 1833. The treaty was signed by Ranjit Singh on 26TH June 1838. It confirmed control of the Sikh kingdom, in perpetuity, over the former Afghan possessions of Kashmir, Attock, Hazara, Peshawar and its dependencies up to the Khaibar, Bannu, Tonk, Kalabagh and other dependent Waziri districts, the Derajat and the rich and fertile province of Multan. Shah Shuja` agreed to abide by the settlement made by the British and the Sikh. Shah Shuja` surrendered to joint Anglo-Sikh authority control of the foreign relations of Afghanistan. The Lahore Government bound itself, to maintain a Muhammadan auxiliary force for the Shah`s aid. Finally, Herat was to be independent, and, at Kabul, Shah Shuja` was required to live a British envoy. It has been said that the real purpose of the British in working out the tripartite treaty was to thwart Sikh designs on Sindh.

Colonel Shaikh Basawan 1838
In 1838 when under the Tripartite Treaty he was given command of the Muslim contingent (6,146 men and 140 pieces of artillery) to escort Shahzada Taimur to Kabul across the Khaibar. Shaikh Basawan accomplished the task efficiently, occupying Ali Masjid on 29 July 1839 and reaching Kabul in time to participate in the victory parade there on behalf of the Khalsa army. Lord Auckland expressed "high satisfaction" with the conduct of Colonel Shaik Basawan, to whom he sent a sword "in testimony of his gallantry and determination."

Sarkar-i-Khalsa

Lahore forces in 1839:

Commander-in-Chief
Maharajah Ranjit Singh

Ghorchurras (21,239)
Original Dehras
2ND Generation Dehras (4 Dehras)
3RD Generation Dehras (5 Dehras)
4TH Generation Dehras (4 Dehras)

Regular Cavalry (4,664)
8 Rajman

Irregular Cavalry
Rajman Bute Khan
Rajman Pir Daulat Khan
Rajman Haidar Shah, Mianwali
Rajman Khudayar Khan Tiwana
Rajman Qadir Khan
Rajman Shamsuddin Khan
Rajman Fateh Shah
Rajman Baz Khan
Rajman Karam Illahi
Rajman Mohammad Ali Khan
Rajman Maqsud Ali Khan
Rajman Mohammad Yar Khan
Rajman Mohammad Khan
Rajman Fatehdinn Khan Kasuria
Rajman Maqsud Ali Khan
Rajman Mohammad Ali Khan
Rajman Allah Yar Khan
Rajman Jalal Khan Bhatti
Rajman Mian Ghallu Khan
Rajman Jamiat Khan
Rajman Jalal Khan Bhatti
Rajman Khuda Yar Khan Tiwana
Rajman Charag Ali

Regular Infantry 30,000)
7 Brigades

Irregular Infantry (9,000)
Paltan Khuda Baksh
Paltan Bahadur Khan
Paltan Misri Khan Rohilla
Paltan Waris Khan
Paltan Pir Bakhsh
Paltan Karim Baksh
Paltan Haidar Shah
Paltan Yasin Khan

Artillery (4,490)
Horse Artillery Aspi
Derah Illahi Baksh
Derah Mazhar Ali Beg

Jinsi Trains
4 Batteries of Jinsi
Derah Illahi Baksh
Derah Sayyid Imam Shah.
Derah Sultan Mahmud Khan

Zambreks (500)
Derah Abdul Rahim.
Derah Khair 'Ali Khan
Derah Mohammad Shah

Garrison Infantry
Personal Guards
Constabulary

Jagirdari (27,000)
Feudal Horse (11,800)
Feudal Infantry, 30 Bns.

Sarkar-i-Khalsa

Death of Maharajah Ranjit Singh 1839
Maharajah Ranjit Singh died on 27TH June 1839. He rose from the status of a petty chieftain of a few villages and by welding together the rude Barons of the Sikh Confederacy became a King of an Empire extending from Tibet to the deserts of Sindh and from the Khyber Pass to the Satluj. His Army was one of the most powerful at that time in Asia. He was a benevolent King. The kingdom under Maharajah Ranjit Singh was the most peaceful time Punjabis had ever seen. This period of 40 years was Golden era of Punjab. Muslims, Hindus and Sikh reaffirmed their Punjabi roots. Several schools were opened, which were open to all Punjabi population. Punjabi Muslims who from centuries had looked westwards towards Afghanis and Persians and had been betrayed by them were now leading Punjabi armies of Sarkar-i- Khalsa. Ranjit Singh's legacy was such that he created a secular kingdom with equality for all. The spirit of stern religious discipline and sacrifice which had supported Sikhs through a critical period of their history and led them to power and glory was not dimmed in the pomp and splendour of his sovereignty. Ranjit Singh's death on June 27TH, 1839, left a deep hiatus. During his reign, there were no outbursts of communal fanaticism, no forced conversions, and no attempts at bloody revenge, no language tensions, no second class citizens, no repression, no bloodshed, no executions and no tortures. Punishments were humane There was no capital punishment which even the modern governments have not been able to abolish. It was not awarded even when there was an attempt on the life of He bore no rancour for his Muslim predecessors who were responsible for the persecution of the Sikh Gurus and had unleashed a reign of terror on the Sikh community. Being of a tolerant disposition, the Maharajah made Muslims part of his government, and they manned the key component his army. The Lahore forces lost a leader who had, by commanding personality, foresight and skill, become their *beau ideal* and secured them the status of sovereign people.

Army of Indus 1839
In December 1838 the British launched an invasion of Afghanistan from India with the aim of overthrowing the Afghan ruler, Amir Dost Mohammad Khan, and replacing him with the supposedly pro-British former ruler, Shah Shuja. The Lahore army under the command of Colonel Shaikh Basawan was to force the Khyber Pass and approach Kabul from the east.

Sarkar-i-Khalsa

Army of Indus 1839 (Contd)
British army under the command of Sir John Keane was to go through Sindh to Khandhar, Ghazni, and join the Maharajah's troops at Kabul. At the invasion of Afghanistan when Maharajah Ranjit Singh died, Prince Naunihal Singh, honoured the tripartite treaty and ordered Colonel Shaikh Basawan to Afghanistan. Colonel Shaikh Bassawan's Najib Battalions of 6,140 men with 16 guns and 140 pieces of Artillery forced the Khyber passes, suffering heavy casualties, and occupied Ali Masjid. Meantime Kabul had fallen to the British. Colonel Sheikh Basawan carried the Lahore banner at the victory parade in Kabul. Lord Auckland, the British Governor General of India, expressed "high satisfaction" with the conduct of Colonel Shaikh Basawan, to whom he sent a sword "in testimony of his gallantry and determination." The Army of the Indus, numbering between 24,000 and 28,000 including families of soldiers, military and political pundits, suffered a series of defeats at the hands of rebel Afghan tribesmen. The main British Indian and Sikh force occupying Kabul, having endured harsh winters as well, was almost completely annihilated while retreating in January 1842. At first light on 6 January Elphinstone's column began to slowly move out of Kabul leaving Shuja Shah Durrani and his followers to their fate. As Akbar Khan had guaranteed safety to all concerned, the sick, wounded and infirm were also left behind. However once the rearguard finally left the cantonments, Afghans quickly moved in and began firing at the retreating troops from the walls while setting fire to the garrison buildings, killing all those left behind.

Colonel Shaikh Basawan 1839
Colonel Shaikh Basawan was a ranked Muslim officer at Maharajah Ranjit Singh`s court, started his career as an assistant to Misr Beli Ram, who had entered the Maharajah`s service in 1809 and who in 1816 had become superintendent of the to shakhana or treasury. Basawan by dint of hard work gradually rose in rank and status and had been made a colonel of the Lahore forces army by 1838 when under the Tripartite Treaty he was given command of the Muslim contingent (6,146 strong Infantry some Cavalry and 140 pieces of artillery) to escort Shahzada Taimur to Kabul across the Khaibar. He crossed the formidable Khyber Pass, which even the British dare not cross at the peak of their power, occupying Ali Masjid on 29TH July 1839, and planted Maharajah Ranjit Singh's flag at the fort of Kabul. Shaikh Basawan accomplished the task efficiently, in time to participate in the victory parade there on behalf of the Lahore army. *Colonel Shaikh Basawan and the Lahore force he commanded believed to have perished at the retreat from Kabul.*

Sarkar-i-Khalsa

Army of Maharajah Ranjit Singh 1839
Army of Maharajah Ranjit Singh, a formidable military machine that helped the Maharajah carve out an extensive kingdom and maintain it amid hostile and ambitious neighbours, was itself the creation of his own genius. His inheritance was but a scanty force which, in the manner of the Sikh Misaldari days, comprised almost solely horsemen, without any regular training or organization. Everyone brought his own horse and whatever weapon he could afford or acquire. What held these troopers together was their personal loyalty to the leader. The tactics followed were those of the guerrilla warfare. The system had stood the Khalsa in good stead during the turbulent and anarchic eighteenth century, but was unsuited to the needs of the changed times and to Ranjit Singh's ambition to establish a secure rule. Early in his career, he had watched how the British troops with their systematic training and their discipline, had vanquished Indian forces vastly superior in numbers. He had also realized how crucial in warfare was a well drilled infantry as well as artillery. In 1802, soon after his occupation of Amritsar, he engaged some deserters from the army of the East India Company to train his own platoons of infantry. He even sent some of his own men to Ludhiana to study the British methods of training and tactics. As Sikhs generally looked down upon infantry service, he recruited Poorbias, as soldiers of fortune from Gangetic plain were called, Punjabi Muslims and Afghans and, later, Gurkhas as well. These troops were soon tested during the short campaign against Ahmad Khan Sial of Jhang and the Zamindars of Uchch during the winter of 1803-04. Their success and the fact that the Maharajah himself regularly saw them train made the infantry an enviable service and Sikhs too started joining its ranks in large numbers. Ranjit Singh gave equal importance to artillery which had, till his time, been limited to the use of Zambooraks or swivels only. He increased the number of guns. The casting of guns of larger calibre as well as the manufacture of ammunition was undertaken on a large scale. The reorganization and training of cavalry, however, waited until the induction into Sikh service of European officers. Ranjit Singh gave them employment after considerable initial hesitation and elaborates verification. He charged them with the raising of a special corps of regular army, the Fauji Khas or Faujia'in. Lahina Singh Majithia continued to head the armament workshops, and Dr John Martin Honigberger, a Hungarian physician, was entrusted with the mixing of gunpowder. There was a rapid increase in the strength of the army during the years following 1822.

Sarkar-i-Khalsa

Army of Maharajah Ranjit Singh 1839 (Contd)

Fauji Hajat or garrison infantry to guard important forts, and a 4000strong crack brigade of Akalis or Niharigs. Infantry thus became the central force, with cavalry and artillery as supporting arms. It was organized into battalions of about 900 men each. A battalion, commanded by a commandant, assisted by an adjutant and a major, was the standard administrative and manoeuvring unit. Its administrative staff included, besides the usual camp followers and tradesmen, a mushier clerk, a mutsaddi or accountant, and a graiiittii or priest and scripture reader. A battalion had eight companies of 100 men each, further divided into sections of 25 men each. Similarly, regular cavalry was organized in rissalah, regiments, subdivided into turps or troops, and artillery into deras and batteries. Artillery was further classified according to its mode of traction, which was generally determined by the size of the guns. In 1804, this arm had been bifurcated into Topkhana Kalan, heavy artillery and Topkhana Khurd, light artillery. Zamburaks or swivels, usually carried on camels, were attached to infantry units. Horse drawn artillery was introduced in 1810. During the same year, a special artillery corps, known as topkhanaikhas or topkhanaimubarak, was formed as the royal reserve under Ghaus Muhammad Khan, and popularly known as Mian Ghausa. In 1827, General Court reorganized the artillery into three wings. Topkhana Jinsi, literally personal artillery (reserve), was a mixed corps with batteries of gavi, bullock-driven, Aspi, horse-driven, fill, elephant-driven, guns and the Aobobs or howitzers. Topkhana Aspi or horse-driven artillery consisted of batteries for attachment to divisions of irregular army.

Zamburaks or camel swivels and ghubaras or mortars were organized into deras or camps subdivided into batteries. Batteries were subdivided into sections of two guns each, with provision for even a single gun functioning as a subunit. The entire field army was divided into faujia'in or regular army, irregular army and Jagirdari Fauj or feudal levees. Faujia'in, with five infantry battalions, three cavalry regiments and 34 guns under General Ilahi Bakhsh, formed the hard core troops. Fauji Beqava'id forming a larger bulk consisted of deras of Ghorchurras, or irregular cavalry grouped into divisions, each under one of the many distinguished generals such as Hari Singh Nalva. Each Derah comprised several smaller groups, composed of members of a clan or their close relations commanded by heads of respective clans known as Misldars. Darahs of Jagirdari Fauj, or feudal levees, were similarly organized forming part of one or the other division.

Sarkar-i-Khalsa

Army of Maharajah Ranjit Singh 1839 (Contd)

Artillery formed a single central corps from which attachments were made to the divisions, depending upon the requirements of a particular campaign. Nominal overall command of a particular expedition was vested in one of the princes royal. Ranjit Singh himself was the supreme commander. He also led some expeditions personally. The crack brigade of Akalis under their famous leader, Phula Singh, was virtually an autonomous formation pressed into service when needed by the Maharajah through his personal influence and tact. Standard deployment at the commencement of a battle was guns in the centre and slightly forward of the rest of the force, infantry a little behind and also covering the flanks of artillery, and cavalry on the extreme flanks. The battle usually commenced with artillery barrage. Regular troops wore distinctive uniforms prescribed for each arm. Cavalrymen were dressed in red jackets (French grey for lancers), long blue trousers with a red stripe, and crimson turbans. Woollen jackets were used during winter. The regiments were armed with varying combinations of weapons sword/sabres and carbines and matchlocks or lances. Infantry was clad in scarlet jacket/coat, white trousers with black belts and pouches. Different regiments were distinguished by the colour of their headdress white, red, green or yellow. The Gurkhas had green jackets and black caps. Postins or fur coats, or padded jackets were used during winter. The gunners wore white trousers and black waistcoats with cross belts. Officers were not bound by rules of uniform. They used gaudy dresses of bright coloured silks each dressing differently. The Ghorchurras or the irregular cavalry had no uniform laid down for them; yet they turned out remarkably well, as testified by Baron Hugel, a Prussian noble, who visited Maharajah Ranjit Singh in 1836 and inspected a cavalry parade. "I never beheld," he wrote of a troop of Ghorchurras, neither "a finer nor a more remarkably striking body of men. Each one was dressed differently and yet so much in the same fashion that they all looked in perfect keeping." Recruitment to the army was on a purely voluntary basis. There was no class composition on the basis of religion or nationality, nor was there a prescribed age limit for enrolment or retirement. Physical fitness and loyalty to the State were the essential conditions. However, the clannish basis of the Misls in the Fauji Beqava`id ensured solidarity in the lower rungs of military administration. Similarly, bravery in the field and efficiency in the performance of duty were the only considerations for promotion and reward, which were also extended to the sons of those who died in action.

Sarkar-i-Khalsa

Army of Maharajah Ranjit Singh 1839 (Contd)

A well defined system of reward and punishment was enforced to maintain discipline and morale. The system of fasli or six monthly payment, or payment through jagirs was later replaced by regular monthly payment in cash. Rates of pay ranged between Rs 4, 00,500 for a general, Rs 1,725 for an infantry soldier and Rs 2,226 for a horseman per month. Allowances were sanctioned from out of the religious charities fund to those permanently disabled on active service or to the dependants of those killed in action. Distinguished service in peace or war was also recognized through the award of civil and military titles, bestowal of khill`ats or robes of honour and grant of jagirs or landed estates. There were three grades of khill`at marked by the number, variety and quality of the garments, ornaments and weapons comprising each of them. Military titles were high sounding Persian expressions, which the recipients and their bards and ushers could use before their names, such as Hizbari Jang (the lion of battle), Zafar Jang Bahadur (victorious, brave in war) Samsam uddaulah (sharp sword of the State), Shuja` uddaulah (valour of the State), Tahavurpanah (asylum of bravery), and so on. For military officers, the title of Sardar was considered one of considerable distinction. Towards the end of his reign Ranjit Singh instituted an Order of Merit named KaukabiIqbaliPanjab (Star of the Prosperity of the Punjab). It was a gold medal, 2.25 inches across with five large and five small pointed branches issuing outwards alternately from a roundish centre bearing a likeness of the Maharajah in bust on one side, and his name on the other. It was meant to be worn round the neck suspended on a gold and scarlet riband passing through a ring on top of the semi globular head of the star. The kaukabwas was of three different classes representing the three grades of the Order, distinguished by the size and quality of the inset precious stones. Star of the first class, meant to be awarded only to members of the royal family and very few distinguished chiefs and nobles for their proven devotion and fidelity to the person of Maharajah and his House, was ornamented with a single large diamond. The Order of the second grade was bestowed upon loyal courtiers, governors of provinces, generals and ambassadors in recognition of political services. It had a diamond (of smaller size) and an emerald on it. The Order of the third grade, having a single emerald, was awarded to military officers of the rank of colonel, major or captain for bravery, resourcefulness, alertness and faithfulness; to civil servants for distinguished administrative ability and honesty; and to others enjoying greater confidence of the sovereign. The kaukabs was, accompanied by appropriate khillats and titles for the awardees.

Sarkar-i-Khalsa

Lahore Durbar 1839
Lahore Durbar i.e. the Sikh Court at Lahore denoted the government of Maharajah Ranjit Singh and his successors. However, the Persian chroniclers refer to this government as Sarkar Khalsa ji, and the term "Lahore Durbar" is not used even in British records until about the death of Maharajah Ranjit Singh. The composition of the Lahore Durbar was highly diversified. In the direction of all State affairs, political, foreign and domestic, it was completely subservient to the will of the Maharajah. Highly personalized, the Lahore Durbar was a creation of the Maharajah, a devout Sikh; he in theory at least publicly proclaimed that he was "the drum of the Khalsa" and that his government was based on the ideals of the Khalsa or the commonwealth of Guru Gobind Singh, but in actual practice it was totally secular. It comprised councillors, ministers, and advisers of all denominations Hindus, Sikhs, Muslims and Christians. The Jammu brothers were all Brahmans. The Faqir brothers were Muslims. The Lahore nobility presented a very picturesque aspect. The Jatt Sikh of the ruling class with his commanding figure and his handsome beard and turban was the adornment of the court which excelled in oriental pageantry and splendour. Personally, the Maharajah was not given to ostentation. He was usually dressed in simple white, wore no ornaments but a single string of pearls and, on special occasions, the celebrated Kohi Nur diamond on his arm. "My sword," he once confined to Baron Charles Hugel, "procures me all the distinction I desire; I am quite indifferent to external pomp." But he liked to be surrounded by magnificently robed ministers and fine looking Sardars majestically accoutred and armed. "The dresses and jewels of the Rajah's court were the most superb that can be conceived," observes H.E. Fane. "The whole scene can only be compared to a gala night at the opera." Golden pillars covered three parts of the Durbar hall; rich shawl carpets embroidered with gold and silver and inset with gems covered the floor. Behind the Maharajah invariably stood the Raja Kalan Dhian Singh; all others ministers, officials, courtiers and Sardars stood with folded hands and lowered eyes at places according to their ranks and status. Yellow and green were court colours and most of the officials were clothed in yellow garments of Kashmir silks or woollens. There being no rigid classification or gradation of rank, the status of courtiers was normally determined by the degree of trust reposed in them by the Maharajah. Titles conferred upon officials were usually honorific's, but many favoured Sardars held them along with lucrative jagirs.

Sarkar-i-Khalsa

Lahore Durbar 1839 (Contd)

The Lahore Durbar treated all foreign visitors with decorum and hospitality. Strict protocol was observed according to the status of the visitor. The visitors were on arrival met by protocol officers especially appointed, their lodgings were fixed according to their status, and funds in cash and kind were provided for their entertainment. The magnificence of the Lahore Durbar was unmatched on diplomatic and ceremonial occasions. Full regalia and military might of the Durbar were then on display. The Lahore Durbar transacted State business in the buildings inside the Lahore Fort called the Musamman Burj. A public court was held in the morning till noon in the Diwan-i-Am or the Hall of Audience, attended by princes, ministers, nobles and civil and military officers. The Maharajah sat cross-legged on a golden chair, clad in plain clothes. High civil and military appointments were made; reports from the provincial satraps and Kardars were read out and royal orders given orally to be transcribed for final approval; tributes and nazarana were accepted and supplicants dismissed gracefully with khill'ats (robes) and cash awards. When on tour or on expedition, business was conducted by the Maharajah on horseback or under the shade of a tree. He dictated orders to the provincial governors while inspecting troops or fighting a battle.

Court factions 1839

In his lifetime, Maharajah Ranjit Singh, there were three groups of Individuals whom he had given power to pursue different matter of state. One group of Dogra Hindus led by Dhian Singh Dogra, he got his brothers inducted in different departments in the government. Soon Dogras had all the administration of state. The Dogras became immensely rich in territory and connections. Dhian Singh's possessions extended from Satluj to Kashmir; his soldier brother Raja Gulab Singh the master of Jammu. The third brother Raja Suchet Singh was the ruler of Ramnagar. Neither a soldier nor a statesman, but immensely rich both in treasure and intrigue, he was one of the principal chiefs at Lahore Durbar. Then the other group was led Azizuddin brothers. This group led departments like foreign affairs, medicine and science under Sarkar Khalsa. Third group was comprised of Sikh noblemen from all over Punjab. This group was mostly involve in defence of state, based their political opportunism on religious fanaticism.

Sarkar-i-Khalsa

The Lahore Army 1839
This efficient machinery worked well under Maharajah Ranjit Singh and Punjab was on its way to prosperity. The balancing factor between the rival factions was the Lahore army, which was totally separated from state affairs. Its strength though not staggering in numbers, was quite formidable. Maharajah Ranjit had built up this army with consummate skill. Part of it was modelled upon European pattern. Maharajah Ranjit Singh was the master of this colossal machine; the British did not dare attacked Punjab as long as Ranjit Singh lived. In fact the British were forced to sign series treaties of friendship with the Sarkar-i-Khalsa. Maharajah Ranjit Singh had bequeathed the Army to his unwarlike son, who had no power to control it.

Maharajah Kharak Singh 1839
Frail in constitution, Kharak Singh ascended the throne in June 1839 on the death of his father. On the death of his father he was proclaimed Maharajah and installed on the throne at Lahore Fort on 1ST September 1839. The Austrian physician Johann Martin Honigberger who was present at court, described his coronation as a dark day for the Punjab, and referred to the Maharajah as a blockhead who twice a day deprived himself of his senses.

Anglo-Sikh Treaty 1840
The treaty between the Sikh and British governments, signed in the time of Maharajah Kharak Singh on 27TH June 1840. The treaty provides a schedule of rates of duties on the mercantile boats, viz. on boats not exceeding 250 mounds of freight, 50 rupees; on boats exceeding 250 mounds but not exceeding 500 mounds, 100 rupees; and on all boats above 500 mounds, 150 rupees. Grain, wood and limestone were declared to be free of duty while duty was payable on every other commodity according to the measurement of the boat.

Maharajah Kharak Singh 1840
Raja Dhian Singh had previously resisted attempts to allow Kharak training in state craft, and on 8TH October 1839 he instigated his removal from the throne with Nau Nihal Singh becoming de facto ruler. Kharak Singh was poisoned with white lead and mercury. Within six months he was bedridden, and eleven months after the poisoning he died on 5TH November 1840 in Lahore, from a lonely and disgraceful existence.

Sarkar-i-Khalsa

Maharajah Nau Nihal Singh 1840

Upon Maharajah Kharak Singh's death, Nau Nihal Singh was in line to become Emperor. Naunihal Singh came back to Lahore to fulfil his obligation to cremate the body of his father Maharajah Kharak Singh. On the same day when the party was returning from cremation ground, a large block of concrete from Archway fell on top of Naunihal Singh. It is said that he was not hurt bad and was able to walk himself but still Gulab Singh Dogra insisted on getting a *Palki*. Two days later Dhian Singh Dogra declared that Naunihal Singh had died due to complications of his injury. Even Naunihal Singh's mother and wife were not allowed to meet him after injury. English doctor that operated on Naunihal Singh testified to British author McAuliffe that initially Naunihal Singh did have some injury on head and he applied bandages but next day when he went to see Naunihal Singh his head was totally crushed and bandages were changed, he was not eating. Dhian Singh Dogra now proclaimed other son of Ranjit Singh named Sher Singh as Maharajah of Punjab

Maharani Chand Kaur 1840

Maharani Chand Kaur was married to Prince Kharak Singh in February 1812. After the death in most tragic circum stances of her husband, then Maharajah of the Punjab, as well as other son, Kanwar Nau Nihal Singh, in November 1840, she staked her claim to the throne of Lahore. Sher Singh, winning support of a rival group at the court and of a section of the army, marched upon Lahore. A compromise was, however, arrived at between the two factions by whom Chand Kaur became regent and Raja Dhian Singh principal minister of the State. The truce, however, did not last long.

In January 1841, Dhian Singh Dogra, openly supported claims of Sher Singh who was proclaimed by the army, also changing sides, sovereign of the Punjab. Chand Kaur was pensioned off with an annual jagir, and her Sandhanwalia's supporters fled across the Sutlej into British territory. Chand Kaur retired gracefully to her late son's palace inside the city of Lahore. In July 1841, Nau Nihal Singh's widow. Sahib Kaur delivered a stillborn son. This ended whatever hopes Chand Kaur had of resurrecting her claims. But courtly intrigue had not ceased. Dhian Singh replaced the maidservants of the Dowager Maharani with hill women from his own country. The latter tried to kill her by poisoning her food and eventually finished her off on 11TH June 1842, smashing her head with wooden pikes from the kitchen. Dhian Singh however had had their tongues cut off to prevent them divulging the plot. In the end, they were executed under his own orders.

Sarkar -i- Khalsa

Langar Khan 1841
Maharajah Sher Singh ordered him, with two hundred horsemen, to accompany the camp of General McGaskil through the Punjab during the Afghan War, and in July 1841, commanding the same force; he went with Major H. Lawrence as far as Charbagh in Langhman. After the assassination of Maharajah Sher Singh, Langar Khan was sent by Raja Hira Singh against Fateh Khan Tiwana, who was ravaging the country between the Chenab and the Indus; but the expedition had not much success, and it was not till the death of Hira Singh that Fateh Khan submitted and came to Lahore, where he offered his services to Jawahir Singh, the new Wazir.

Commander Sultan Mahmud Khan 1841
On the accession of Maharajah Sher Singh he was reinstated and his son Sultan Ahmad Ali Khan was made a Colonel. In 1843, both father and son were engaged in the assault on the Fort of Lahore which had been taken possession of by the Sandhanvalia after the murder of Sher Singh; and, for their services on this occasion, they received additional jagirs from the Dogra Raja Hira Singh. Sultan Mahmud was then sent in command of the artillery to Hazara where he remained until 1848 when both he and his son were moved to the Derajat.

Maharajah Sher Singh 1841
He became Maharajah on 27TH January 1841. He was the half brother of Nau Nihal Singh's father, Maharajah Kharak Singh. He was proclaimed Maharajah by his Wazir (prime minister) Dhian Singh Dogra; he won the throne after a protracted siege of the Lahore Fort which was held by the Royal family. The Dogras, like puppet masters, pulled the strings of others to bring about the death of Sher Singh. Sher Singh was killed as he reached for a new shotgun held by Ajit Singh Sandhawalia, who pulled the trigger. Sher Singh only had time to utter, "What treachery."

Ajit Singh Sandhawalia 1841
On 15TH September 1843, as Maharajah Sher Singh was inspecting troops in the Baradari of Shah Bilawal, Ajit Singh shot him dead with an English rifle which he cunningly pretended to present to the Maharajah for inspection. As the Maharajah fell, Ajit Singh drew his sword and severed his head. Later Ajit Singh killed Dhian Singh on the spot. Hira Singh, son of Dhian Singh, and his uncle, Suchet Singh, aroused a section of the army, and with crack battalions, they besieged the Fort on 16TH September 1843, and in the resultant action both Ajit Singh and Lahina Singh were slain.

Sarkar -i- Khalsa

Raja Azimullah Khan 1841
Raja Azimullah Khan was the head of the family, which was held by them in sovereignty upto the year 1841. On a suspicion of attempting the life of Raja Gulab Singh, Rahimullah Khan was sent prisoner to Gobindgarh fort and his lands taken over by Lahore. He was shortly afterwards set at liberty; but his country remained with Raja Gulab Singh and formed part of the territory confirmed to him under the treaty of March, 1846. Faizullah, son of Rahimullah, took active part in conjunction with Nawab Imamuddin Khan, the Governor of Kashmir, in resisting surrender of possession to then Maharajah Gulab Singh. But his efforts were fruitless. He was exiled in Rehlu in Kangra, where his descendents now live as foreigners, never having been heartily received by the indigenous Rajput princes.

Mirza Ghulam Murtaza 1841
During the time of Nau Nihal Singh, Ghulam Murtaza was continually employed on active service. In 1841 he was sent to Mandi and Kulu and in 1843 to Peshawar in command of an infantry regiment. He distinguished himself in Hazara at the time of insurrection there.

Khairuddin Khan 1844
Maharajah Dalip Singh for compensation of this loss of Mamdot Jagir gave to Khairuddin Khan in 1844, six villages near Kasur. During the later part of Anglo-Sikh war he fought on the side of the British, crossing the river with his whole family and joining the camp after the battle of Ferozeshah. During the retrenchments that followed the deposition of Raja Lal Singh his Jagir was reduced and shortly afterwards two more villages were taken away. At the time of the Multan outbreak, Khairuddin Khan was at Dera Ismail Khan, under the orders of Captain Taylor. He was sent to Bannu to relieve Fateh Khan Tiwana, who was besieged in Dalipgarh; but Fateh Khan was slain and the fort reduced before he reached it. He was afterwards sent from Isakhel with two hundred horse and five hundred foot into the Pindigheb country to harass Sardar Gaur Singh the rebel Kardar of Sardar Chattar Singh, and to encourage the Attock garrison. He performed the duty most satisfactorily. Sardar Gaur Singh was routed in two or three encounters, and was forced to fly the country; and while the Lahore Army on the left bank of the Jhelum, Khairuddin held his ground to the north of the Salt Range. He died in 1866.

Sarkar -i- Khalsa

The Army Panches 1844
The assignation of Sher Singh and the subsequent murder of Dhian Singh Dogra led to the virtual transfer of all power into the hands of the Army. The virtual collapse of the civil authority had allowed the Army to assume new status, and became an executive sovereign of the state. They ruled through the congregation of the Panchayats, the five selected members from each Unit. The Panchayats in the several corps began to correspond and act in concert. Its successful campaigns in the north and south during 1841-44 had made it conscious of its strength. To the common Sikh solder the assumption of power of the State by the Army appeared as defensive measure against national disintegration and threat from foreign invasion. The transform of power to the Army appealed to him as he understood no politics and transformed him as a soldier of the people. Thus was transformed the Army of Maharajah Ranjit Singh. No political or religious leader guided its destiny and it sought guidance from the Panches. They faced a corrupt government, the Sardars and the Sovereign, who were seeking British interference to safeguard their estates and privileges. The Lahore forces proceeded to punish the traitors. The aversion of the Sikh Army for all foreigners was unmistakable and positive, and expelled the foreigners from the state. The European officers of the Lahore Army, felt insecure and left their posts, and despatched intelligence to the British on state of affairs in the Punjab, The Durbar at Lahore and the leading Sardars frantically sought British intervention for the destruction of the Lahore Army. At the insistence of the Durbar, Lal Singh and Tej Singh were appointed to lead the Lahore forces.

The British 1844
After the fall of Delhi, the British had a standoff against Maharajah Ranjit Singh. However, they checked the expansion of the Sikh Kingdom by taking the Sikh Cis Satluj territories under their protection. They also checked the state's expansion towards Sindh and the sea, by taking the Amirs of Sindh under their protection. The Kingdom Lahore under the leadership of Maharajah Ranjit Singh stood firm against its powerful neighbour, British India. It was an independent nation forming Britain's buffer state against Russia. After the death of Maharajah Ranjit Singh, they had made no secret about the destruction of the Kingdom of Lahore and annexation of the Punjab to the British Empire. With the turmoil in the Punjab, and their under estimation of the fighting qualities of the Punjabi soldier, the British started massing their armies; the largest force ever assembled in India, on the Kingdom's borders.

First Anglo-Sikh war

Lahore Army in 1845:-

Commander-in-Chief Sardar Tej Singh
Wazir, Raja Lal Singh

Ghorchurras (21,239)
Original Dehras
2ND Generation Dehras (4 Dehras)
3RD Generation Dehras (5 Dehras)
4TH Generation Dehras (4 Dehras)
6 New Dehras

The Fauj-i-Ain (Regular Army) 22 brigades
    62 Infantry Battalions, 49,000 Soldiers
    13 Cavalry Regiments, 7,800 Troopers
    32 Artillery Batteries

The Fauj-i-Khas
    4 Infantry Battalions (Sikhs)
    2 Cavalry Rajman
    Shahddilah Risala (Cavalry Squadron)
    Artillery of General Illahi Baksh
    1 (32 Guns, Sikh & Muslim)
    2 12 Guns Horse Artillery
    3 22 Field Guns under Sikander Khan and Fateh Khan

Diwan Jodha Ram's Brigade
    4 Infantry Paltans
    1 Cavalry Rajman
    10 Guns Horse Artillery under Boland Khan
    8 Heavy Field Guns under Rustam Beg

General Kahn Singh's Briagde (Sikh & Muslim)
    4 Infantry Paltans
    10 Guns Horse Artillery

General Mehtab Singh Majithia's Brigade
    4 Infantry Paltans (Sikh)
    1 Cavalry Rajman (Mixed)
    12 Guns Horse Artillery (Sikh & Muslim)

First Anglo Sikh war

Lahore Army 1845: (Contd)

Commander-in-Chief Sardar Tej Singh
Wazir, Raja Lal Singh

General Tej Singh's Brigade
    4 Infantry Paltans
    1 Cavalry Rajman
    10 Guns Horse Artillery`

General Gulab Singhs Pahavindhia's Brigade
    3 Infantry Paltans (Muslim)
    14 Light Artillery Pieces (Sikh & Muslim)

Raja Suchet Singh's Brigade (Dogra & Muslim)
    2 Infantry Paltans
    1 Cavalry Rajman
    10 Heavy Garrison Guns
    4 Horse Artillery Guns

General Gulab Singh Calcluttawala's Brigade (Sikhs)
    4 Infantry Paltans
    1 Cavalry Rajman
    16 Horse Artillery Guns

General Jawala Singh's Brigade
    2 Infantry Paltans (Sikhs)
    4 Guns Horse Artillery (Sikhs & Muslims

General Lehna Singh Majithia's Brigade
    2 Infantry Paltans (Sikhs)
    2 Heavy Garrison Guns
    3 Field Guns
    10 Guns Horse Artillery (Sikhs)

General Bishan Singh's Brigade (Muslims & Some Sikhs)
    2 Infantry Paltans
    3 Horse Artillery Guns

General Gurdit Singh Majithia's Brigade
    3 Infantry Paltans (Sikhs)
    8 Artillery Guns

First Anglo Sikh war
Lahore Army 1845 (Contd)

Cololen John Holmes Brigade
    1 Infantry Paltan
    10 Horse Artillery Guns

General Dhonkel's Brigade
    2 Infantry Paltans (Dogras)

General Courtaland's Brigade
    2 Infantry Paltans (1 Sikhs & 1 Dogra)
    10 Horse Artillery Guns (Sikh & Muslims)

Sardar Nihal Singh Ahluwalia's Brigade
    1 Infantry Paltans (Sikh & Dogras)
    11 Heavy Field Guns
    4 Horse Artillery Guns

Diwan Sawan Mull's Brigade (Mainly Muslims & some Sikhs)
    3 Infantry Paltans
    40 Heavy Garrison Guns
    6 Horse Artillery Guns

Raja Hira Singh's Brigade
    2 Infantry Paltans
    I Cavalry Rajman
    3 Heavy Garrison Guns
    3 Heavy Field Guns

Raja Partap Singh's Brigade
    3 Infantry Paltans (Sikh)

Raja Gulab Singh's Brigade (Sikh & Dogra)
    3 Infantry Paltans
    40 Heavy Garrison Guns
    15 Horse Artillery Guns

Sheikh Imam-ud-din's Brigade
    3 Infantry Paltans
    4 Horse Artillery Guns

First Anglo Sikh war

Lahore Army 1845 (Contd):

Sheikh Ghulam Mohi-ud-Din's Brigade
    1 Infantry Paltan (Sikh)
    8 Heavy Field Guns (Muslim & Sikh)
    6 Horse Artillery Guns (Muslim & Sikh)

State and Independent Artillery
    Commandant Bhag Singh, 6 Horse Artillery Guns (Sikh & Muslim)
    Commandant Shiv Prasad, 8 Horse Artillery Guns (Sikh & Muslim)
    Missar Lal Singh, 10 Horse Artillery Guns (Sikh & Muslim)
    Sardar Kishen Singh, 2 Heavy Garrison Guns
    General Kishen Singh, 22 Horse Artillery Guns (Sikh & Muslim)
    Sardar Sham Singh Attari, 10 Heavy Field Guns (Sikh & Muslim)
    Mian Prithi Singh, 56 Heavy Field Guns (Muslim)
    General Mewa Singh, 10 Heavy Field Guns & 10 Guns Horse Artillery (Sikh & Muslim)
    Colonel Amir Chand, 10 Heavy Field Guns (Muslim)
    (Artillery of Lahore) Commandant Mal Mistry, 10 Horse Artillery Guns (Muslim & Dogra)
    (Artillery of Amritsar) Commandant Sukhu Singh, 20 Heavy Field Guns & 12 Heavy Garrison Guns (Sikh & Muslim)
    (Artillery of Peshawar), 10 Heavy Garrison Guns (Muslim & Dogra)
    Miscellaneous, 50 Heavy Garrison Guns (Sikh & Muslim)

Total Strength of Fauj-i- Ain as listed abov stands at:
    Infantry 60 Battalions of 600 soldiers' each-36,000
    Cavalry 8 Regiments of 600 soldiers each-4,800
    Artillery 384 Guns used in the field (not Zambrooraks)
    Horse Artillery-228 Guns
    Heavy Field Guns-156 Guns
    Heavy Garrison Guns-171 (Not used the field!)

First Anglo Sikh war

British Army in 1845:

Commander-in-Chief
General Sir Hugh Gough

Aide-de-Camp
Captain H.B. Edwards

Governor General of India
Lt. General Sir Henry Hardinge

Aids –de-Camp
Brevet Major W.R. Harries
Brevet Captain G.E. Hillier
Lt. John Munro

Adjutant General
Sir James Lumley
Lt. Colonel M. Bar

Deputy Adjutant General
Major Patrick Grant

Quartermaster General
General Sir Harry Smith
Major General Sir R. H. Sale

Deputy Quartermaster General
Lt. Col. Garden

1ST Infantry Division
Major General Sir Harry Smith

Deputy Assistant Adjutant General
Captain E. Lugard

1ST Brigade
Brigadier Samuel Bolton CB
31ST Foot Regiment
24TH BNI Regiment
47TH BNI Regiment

2ND Brigade
Brigadier Hugh Wheeler
HM 50TH Foot Regiment
42ND BNI Regiment
48TH BNI Regiment

2ND Infantry Division
Major General Sir W.R. Gilbert

Assistant Quartermaster General
Major R. Codrington

1ST Brigade
2ND BNI Regiment
45TH BNI Regiment

2ND Brigade
16TH BNI Regiment

3RD Infantry Division
Major General Sir John McCaskil

1ST Brigade
Brigadier Newton Wallace
HM 9TH Foot Regiment
HM 80TH Foot Regiment
26TH BNI Regiment
73RD BNI Regiment

Cavalry Division
Major General Sir J. Thackwell
Brigadier M. White

Assistant Adjutant General
Captain Tritton
Brigade Major T.L. Harrington

1ST Brigade
Brigadier W. Marctier
9TH B. Irregular Cavalry Regiment
4TH BLC (Lancer) Regiment

2ND Brigade
Brigadier J.B. Gough
Governor General's Bodyguard
5TH Bengal Cavalry Regiment

First Anglo Sikh war

British Army in 1845 (Contd)

Commander-in-Chief
General Sir Hugh Gough

3RD Brigade
Brigadier M. White
HM 3RD light Dragoons Regiment
4TH Bengal Light Cavalry(Lancers)

Army Artillery
1ST Brigade BHA
Brigadier George (Bully) Brooks

533 Troops, Bengal Horse Artillery
Brevet Major Frederick Brind

European Troops (BHA)
Captain Francis Dashwood

European Troops (BHA)
Brevet Major Elliot Darcy Todd

European Troops (BHA)
Captain G.H. Swinley

Native Troop (BHA)
Captain Hubert Garbet

1ST Division
Brevet Major J.T. Lane

European Troops (BHA)
Lt. G. Moir

1ST Troop, 1ST Brigade (BHA)
Captain Francis Dashwood

2ND Troop, 1ST Brigade (BHA)
Major Elliot Darcy Todd

3RD Troop, 1ST Brigade (BHA)
Captain G.H. Swinley

1ST Troop, 3RD Brigade (BHA)
Brevet Major Frederick Brind

1ST Div, 2ND Troop, 3RD Brigade
Lt. G. Moir

4TH (Native) Troop, 3RD Brigade
Captain Hubert Garbet

2ND Field Batteries
Captain R. Horsfod

7TH Heavy Field Battery
Captain Jasper Thrower

9TH Heavy Field Battery
Captain R. Horsfod

3RD Company, 4TH Battalion, Bengal Artillery
Captain R. Horsfod

2ND Company, 6TH Battalion, Bengal Artillery
Captain R. Horsfod

First Anglo-Sikh War

Lahore Army 1845
The morale of the Lahore Army was extremely high. The Lahore soldier was extremely brave and had always carried everything before him. Neither of the two principal Generals, Lal Singh and Tej Singh, were Sikhs, but Brahmins, and were not committed to the cause for which they were fighting. A powerful, well-trained, and confident Lahore Army prepared for War under the leadership of a Commander in Chief under orders from a Vizier, and watched from the sidelines by a powerful and clever Chieftain. All three men dedicated to the defeat of the Army they led, and secretly informing their opponents of that fact! The Lahore Army decided to be the first in the field and crossed the Satluj on 12TH December 1845.

Lahore Forces at the battle of Mudki 1845:

Commander-in-Chief Sardar Tej Singh
Wazir, Raja Lal Singh

3,500 Cavalry,
2,000 Infantry
20 guns

British Forces at the battle of Mudki 1845:-

Commander-in-Chief
General Sir Hugh Gough

Sir Harry Smiths Division
HM 31ST Foot
24TH Native Infantry
27TH Native Infantry

Major Generals Division
45TH Native Infantry
2ND Grenadiers
16TH Grenadiers

Sir John McCaskill's Division
HM 9TH Foot
HM 80TH Foot
26TH Native Infantry
73RD Native Infantry

Brigadier Wheeler's Division
HM 50TH Foot
42ND Native Infantry
48TH Native Infantry

Sir Hugh Gough
Sir Hugh Gough, commander of the British armies in the first and second Sikh wars, was born on 3RD November 1779, at Wood town, Limerick, Ireland. He joined British army service in 1793 and served at the Cape of Good Hope, and in the peninsular wars under the Duke of Wellington. He came to India in 1837, and, after serving in the army in various capacities, became the Commander in Chief in 1843.

First Anglo-Sikh War

Sir Harry Smiths

Sir Harry Smiths, divisional commander of the British armies in the first Sikh war, was born on 28TH June 1787 at Whittlesey, Cambridgeshire, England. He joined British army service in 8TH May 1805 and served at South America, and in the peninsular wars under the Duke of Wellington. He went on serve in the United States of America and the Cape of Good Hope, where he commanded a force in the Sixth Xhosa War of 1834-36. He came to India in 1840, where he here he took part in the Gwalior campaign and the First Anglo-Sikh War and in command of a division under Sir Hugh Gough.

Sir John McCaskil

Sir John McCaskil was a veteran of Indian campaigns since 1806, Sir John McCaskil Mudki he was in his sixties, renowned for his part in the retaking of Kabul after the debacle of the First Afghan War, and proud of his reputation for being in front when leading his men into battle. He served as a divisional Commander during the First Anglo-Sikh under Sir Hugh Gough.

Shamasuddin Khan 1845

Kasur was conquered and taken possession of by Maharajah Ranjit Singh in 1807. Shamasuddin Khan was also for many years a servant of the Mamdot Chief, and attendant Lahore Court as his vakil; and for some fault he was summarily dismissed, and became afterwards the confidential agent of Raja Lal Singh. The position he held at the time of the Satluj Campaign, and was the medium of communication between Raja Lal Singh and the British officers. On the 12TH December 1845, when the Lahore army was crossing the Satluj, Raja Lal Singh sent Shamasuddin Khan to Captain Nicholson at Ferozepore to assure him that both he and the Maharani were the friends of the British; that he would keep his force back two days from joining the regulars; and he had marched that day back to Asal, and the next day would march to Harike. To this Nicholson that he would report the matter. The next day Raja Lal Singh proposed delaying the army under the pretence of making a bridge at Harike and discovering fords. On 16TH December, Nicholson, hearing that the Governor-General and Commander-in-Chief were approaching by way of Mudki, sent for Shamasuddin Khan, and said if the Raja had the influence he asserted he would act and not talk, and that his good intentions would be seen his marching as he proposed.

First Anglo-Sikh War

Shamasuddin Khan 1845 (Contd)

On the 18TH Shamasuddin Khan came and reported that the Raja had marched to Ferozeshah, and Nicholson gave him a letter to Major Broadfoot, which it is believed, was delivered to that officer as the troops were going into action at Ferozeshah on the afternoon of 21ST, as it was found in his pocket when his body was brought it in on the 22ND. On the 19TH December, the day after the battle of Mudki, Raja Lal Singh sent a messenger to Major Broadfoot to express his desire to be of any service; but the Major considered that the only object of the Raja was to ascertain the effect of the action of the previous day, and sent him with the guard beyond pickets. Nothing more was heard of the Raja till two days before the battle of Sabraon. He had been hidden in a dry ditch during the battle of Ferozeshah, but gave on that he was wounded, and retired to Amritsar, where according to popular report; he concealed himself in an oven from the fury of the soldiers who swore to murder him. But through the remonstrations of the Maharani he joined the army about the middle of January; and on the 8TH February he sends Shamasuddin Khan to Major H. Lawrence with the plan of the entrenchments and a detailed account of the number and disposition of the Lahore troops. After the first Anglo-Sikh war when Major Lawrence was appointed Resident at Lahore, Shamasuddin Khan was made agent of the Durbar, to communicate its wishes and sentiments to the Resident. In 1848 he did good service, and a donation was granted to him and after annexation when his Jagir was resumed, he received a life pension.

Battle of Mudki 1845

As soon as Lal Singh crossed the Satluj, he waited for instructions from Captain Nicholson. Lal Singh followed the instructions and split the Lahore forces Army in two parts. The smaller force under Tej Singh was sent to threaten but not attack Ferozepore. Lal Singh marched the main force and entrenched it near the village of Ferozeshah. He then took a detachment from the main force of 3,500 Cavalry, 2,000 Infantry and 20 guns and advanced to confront the British force of 12,000 men with 48 guns and four troops of horse Artillery. They sighted the British forces on 18TH December 1845, near the village of Mudki, and attacked immediately. As soon as the attack started, Lal Singh promptly deserted his men and retreated to the camp at Ferozeshah. When Lal Singh had fled the battlefield early, there was no other commander giving orders, whereas on the British side there were battle hardened experienced military commanders.

First Anglo-Sikh War

Battle of Mudki 1845 (Contd)

Although the irregular cavalry, the Ghorchurras, were the elite of the Lahore Army, and individually very skilled, they were comparatively ineffective against the disciplined British and Bengal units. The leaderless Ghorchurras finally broke and withdrew from the battlefield and left the infantry and the gunners to fight the battle on their own. The British and Bengal infantry advanced. In the gathering darkness and the clouds of smoke and dust, the advance quickly became disordered. Soon the superiority of the Lahore Army over the Sepoys became apparent. The Sepoys showed marked reluctance to throw themselves against the half-hidden enemy, of who little could be seen in the deepening dusk, but the red flashes of their muskets. The Sepoys were panic-stricken and firing there muskets in the air to their right and left. The English officers tried unsuccessfully to get them to follow them. General Wheeler's Brigade was so terrified at the sight of the Sikh Cavalry, it formed squares, and would not obey orders to reform and advance. Although outnumbered five to one, the Sikh Fauj-i-Ain (regulars) resisted desperately. What remained of the infantry was firing as rapidly as it was possible. Their sharpshooters had climbed trees to pick off British officers and any one exercising any semblance of command d as they fought their way and made their back to Ferozeshah. The Muslim gunners continued to serve their guns, oblivions of the fact that the British and guns and infantry were now concentrating on them, and kept firing volleys of grapeshot until they were overrun. The gunners refused to leave their guns and died where they fought serving them. In the fierce encounter, the Lahore troops took on the numerous enemies in grim hand-to-hand fighting, in which the men could not have fought in more gallant manner than they did. The British cheers were intermingled by the 'Jaikaras' of Sikh troops and 'Allah ho Akbar' of the Muslim gunners and the infantry battle was fought virtually blind from start to finish. By the time the British infantry reached the guns, it was already dark. Having lost almost half of their force and fifteen guns, the leaderless troops withdrew back to the main force at Ferozeshah. The British had lost 872 dead and wounded. The dead included Quartermaster-General Sir Robert Sale, Sir John McGaskil and Brigadier Bolton. The British were shaken by the fighting qualities of the Lahore troops, the likes of which they had never encountered in India. The Commander in Chief Lord Gough, warned Gen Lahore troops, but evades the Lahore troops and joins the main force. The British licked their wounds and frantically waited for reinforcements to arrive from Ambala, Meerut and Delhi.

First Anglo-Sikh War

Commander Fateh Khan
At the battle of Mudki, General Illahi Baksh commanded the artillery of Fauj-e-Khas, with his sons, Commander Sikander Khan and Commander Fateh Khan, commanded the horse artillery and field guns. Commander Fateh Khan, although outnumbered, valiantly lost his life in defence of the guns at Mudki.

The Lahore forces at the battle of Ferozeshah 1845:

Raja Lal Singh's wing:
Fauj-i-Ain,

Fauj-i-Khas Brigade
4 Paltans Infantry (3,159)
3 Rajman Cavalry (1,438)

Artillery General Illahi Buksh
Aspi (12 Guns & 360 Men)
Jinsi (12 Guns & 360 Men)
Balder (Engineer Company)

Mehtab Singh's Brigade
4 Infantry Paltans (3,380)
1 Cavalry Rajman (490)

Artillery:
Aspi (12 Guns & 360 Men)
Jinsi (13 Guns & 390 Men
Belder (Engineer Company)

Bahadur Singh's Brigade
4 Infantry Paltans (3,764)
Artillery:
Aspi (11 Guns & 330 Men)
Belder (Engineer Company)

Ghorchurras Cavalry
Ardalian Derah (2,866)
Mohd. Shah's Swivels (73)

Derah Khas
Ghorchurras (2,089)

Naulakha Kalan Derah
Ghorchurras (2,096)
Abdul Ramin's Swiles (127)

Naulakha Khurd Derah
Ghorchurras (2,096)

Pindiwala Derah
Ghorchurras (1,060)

Raja Lal Singh's Derah
Ghorchurras (1,039)

Jagirdari 6 Derah (2,455)
Regular Army Artillery
Howitzer Derah
Jinsi (15 Guns & 360 Men)
Makhi Khan's Battery Derah
Jinsi (15 Guns & 360 Men

First Anglo-Sikh War

The British forces at the battle of Ferozeshah 1845:-

Commander-in-Chief
General Sir Hugh Gough

Aides –de-Camp
Captain Sackville West
Lt. F.P. Haines

Governor General of India
Lt. General Sir Henry Hardinge

Aides –de-Camp
Captain Sackville West
Lt. F.P. Haines

Governor General of India
Lt. General Sir Henry Hardinge

Military Secretary
Brevet Major A.W.F. Somerset

Assistant Military Secretary
Captain William Hoer

Aides –de-Camp
Lt.Col. Wood
Major W.R. Harries
Lt. John Munro
Lt. Peel

Deputy Adjutant General
Major Patrick Grant

Judge Advocate General
Lt.Col. Birch

Military Board
Colonel Benson

Assistant Adjutant General
Captain JR Lumley

Quarter Master General's Dept
Captain Abbot
Captain Mills
Lt. Arthur Beecher

1ST *Infantry Division*
Major General Sir Harry Smith

Aide-de-Camp
Lt. E.A. Holditch

Deputy Assistant Adjutant General
Captain E. Lugard

Deputy Assistant Quarter Master General
Lt. A.J. Galloway

1ST Brigade
Brigadier George Hicks

Brigade Major
Captain J. Garvock
HM 31ST Foot, Major Spence
24TH BNI, Major Griffin
47TH BNI, Captain Pott

2ND Brigade
Brigadier Thomas Ryan

Brigade Major
Captain Pringle O'Hanlon
HM 50TH Foot, Lt. Col. Petit
42ND Bengal Native Infantry
48TH BNI , Captain Palmer

2ND *Infantry Division*
Major General Sir WR Gilbert

Aides-de-Camp
Captain H. Houghton
Lt. FM Gilbert

Political Agent
Major George Broadfoot

First Anglo-Sikh War

The British forces at the battle of Ferozeshah 1845 (Contd)

Deputy Assistant Judge Advocate General
Captain G. Carr

Deputy Assistant Quartermaster General
Lt. TS Lawson +

1ST (3RD) Brigade
Brigadier James McLaren, CB
1ST Bengal European Light Inf.
26TH Bengal Native Infantry
45TH Bengal Native Infantry

2ND (4TH) Brigade
Brigadier Charles Cyril Taylor

Brigade Major
Captain JO Lucas
HM 29TH Foot
HM 80TH Foot
41ST Bengal Native Infantry

3RD Infantry Division
Brigadier Newton Wallace

Deputy Assistant Adjutant General
Captain JR Pond

Brigade Major (6TH Brigade)
Brevet Captain P Garden

Lt. Col. A Beresford Taylor
HM 9TH Foot
2ND Bombay Native Infantry
16TH Bombay Native Infantry
73RD Bengal Native Infantry Regt.

4TH Infantry Division
Major General Sir John Littler

Aides-de-Camp
Lt. Harvey
Lt. Fullerton

Deputy Assistant Adjutant General
Major P Innes

Deputy Assistant Quartermaster General
Captain John Francis Edgerton

Commissariat Department
Captain WJ Thomson

Political Officers
Captain Nicholson
Col. Van Cortland (ex-Sikh Army)

Chief of Artillery
Lt.Col. Edward Huthwait

1ST (7TH) Brigade
Brigadier Thomas Reid

Brigade Major
Captain CPJ Burnett
HM 2ND Foot- Major Short
12TH BNI-Lt. Col. Luis Bruce
14TH BNI - Lt. Col. Gardner

2ND (8TH) Brigade
Brigadier Thomas Ashburnham
33RD BNI-Captain Sandeman
44TH BNI-Major Wake
54TH BNI- Major Osborn

First Anglo-Sikh War

The British forces at the battle of Ferozeshah 1845 (Contd)

Divisional Artillery
3RD Brigade BHA
Lt. Col. Edward Huthwait
Bengal Horse Artillery
European Troop
Captain Campbell
Native Troop
Captain EF Day
1ST Brigade , BHA
5TH Native Troop
3RD Troop,3RD Brigade, BHA
Bengal Field Artillery
Heavy Field Battery
Lt. AG Austen
19TH Light Field Battery
Captain J Fordyce ,manned by:
2ND Company, 7TH Battalion, BA
4TH Company, 6TH Battalion, BA
Bengal Sappers and Miners
Lt. Goodwin

Garrison of Firozepur
Lt. Col. Wilkinson
29TH Bengal Native Infantry
Lt. Col. Carnegy
63RD Bengal Native Infantry
Lt. Col. Wilkinson
6TH Heavy Field Battery
Lt. JS Tulloh
Reserve Heavy Garrison Battery
Lt. Angelo

A detachment of Bengal Sapper and Miners

Cavalry Division
Major General Sir Joseph Thackwell
Brigadier D. Herriot

Deputy Assistant Quartermaster General
Captain CF Havelock

1ST Brigade
Brigadier JB Gough

Governor Genera's Bodyguard
5TH BLC

2ND Brigade
Brigadier Herriot

3RD BLC
8TH Irregular Horse
Brevet Captain Beecher

3RD Brigade
Brigadier White

3RD Light Dragoon
4TH BLC

First Anglo-Sikh War

Battle of Ferozeshah 1845
Artillery on both sides opened fire, and the British immediately found themselves outgunned in both numbers and firepower by 24, 32 and 36-pounders against British horse artillery's 6-pounders. The British guns were quickly moved forward, and littler began to advance ahead of the rest of the army. Littler's Bengalis and the 62ND Foot, hungry and footsore as they were after their march from Ferozepore, closed to within 150 yards of the Durbars entrenchments in the face of savage fire. They were about to launch a final charge when they were blasted with a hail of grapeshot. Seven officers and 97 men fell dead and another 200 were wounded. Seeing this happen to the British regiment, the Bengali regiments collapsed and General Littler had to pull them back to reorganize. At this point, the battle was going in favour of the Lahore forces. Their triumphant 'Jaikaras' and shouts of 'Allah ho Akbar' rang out above the sound of battle. They had repulsed littler, and were winning the artillery battle. Moral was high and they intended doing the same to the other divisions. On the right, where Gough had placed himself, the 29TH Foot and 80TH Foot charged forward in the face of murderous fire, crossed the entrenchments, captured the guns on their front, and broke through into the Durbars camp. There, a group of Akalis in chain armour fought with great valour until British bayonets killed them all. The Muslim gunners, wielding tulwar, fought to the last man. In the centre, the 3RD Division met with such devastating fire that their left fell back. But Smith threw in a brigade from the reserve and restored the situation. The 50TH Foot was attacked by the pride of the Lahore force's four battalions. The 50TH beat them back in a hand-to-hand fight and captured their guns. Smith now charged with his reserve division and, joined by troops who had lost contact with their own units, burst into Ferozeshah. The Lahore troops refused to surrender; they fought until they were slaughtered. As night was falling, the 3RD Light Dragoons charged through the centre of the Lahore forces position, creating more havoc. Then a huge explosion lit up the position as a Lahore forces powder magazine went up in flames. Fires quickly spread, setting off more explosions as the flames reached stocks of powder and ammunition. Smith pushed on to an area of the Lahore forces camp about half a mile to the north of the village. There he rallied many soldiers who had lost contact with their units in a semicircle on the 50TH Foot. He now had about 3,000 troops in all.

First Anglo-Sikh War

Battle of Ferozeshah 1845 (Contd)

When the moon rose just after midnight, Smith's isolated force was revealed to the Lahore forces, who closed in and opened fire on them. Casualties were heavy among the British troops, including many who were killed or wounded without waking up while they slept an exhausted sleep. His losses mounting, Smith decided that he could not hold the position. He made a feint attack and fought his way out under cover of the smoke and dust. Guided by the dead from his original line of advance, Smith brought his force safely to the rear. During the cold night, Gough decided to reform his mixed-up divisions and retire. All units withdrew from Ferozeshah, picking up the wounded and returning to their original positions before the attack. Despite their heavy losses, the Lahore forces immediately reoccupied the entrenchments the Anglo-Bengalis had taken at fearful cost and opened fire again. The night of December 21ST was one of gloom for the British soldiers, who were close to annihilation. The Sikhs had practically recovered the whole of their entrenched camp; exhausted and decimated British divisions bivouacked without cohesion over a wide area. The situation was so critical that Hardinge packed up his papers and valuables for dispatch to the rear, including a sword that had belonged to Napoleon and had been given to him by Wellington at Waterloo. At daybreak Gough lined up his forces for another assault on Ferozeshah. His infantry, in the centre, was supported by heavy guns and a rocket battery and on both flanks by horse artillery and cavalry. Gough placed himself at the head of the right of the line, with Hardinge at the head of the left. The British artillery opened fire and the army lunged forward. British and Bengali soldiers moved forward in ragged lines, with the horse guns thundering ahead of them. The Lahore gunners battered them and picked off the ammunition wagons. Undaunted, the British forces fought their way into Ferozeshah, driving the British and Bengali soldiers moved forward in ragged lines, with the horse guns thundering ahead of them. Lahore forces gunners battered them and picked off the ammunition wagons. Undaunted, the British forces fought their way into Ferozeshah, driving the Lahore forces before them and sweeping irresistibly through the Lahore force's camp, bayoneting all enemies in their path. At the far end of the camp the attack halted and the troops, displaying captured Lahore forces standards, presented arms and cheered as Gough and Hardinge rode along the ranks. The ferocity of the fighting became the stuff of legend.

First Anglo-Sikh War

Battle of Ferozeshah 1845 (Contd)

Captain Joseph Cunningham, an East India Company political agent, wrote that "guns were dismounted and their ammunition was blown into the air. Squadrons were checked in mid career. Battalion after battalion was hurled back with shattered ranks. The obstinacy of the contest threw the English into confusion. Men of all regiments and arms were mixed together. Generals were doubtful of their own success, and colonels knew not what had become of the regiments they commanded or of the army of which they formed a part." But they had taken Ferozeshah and captured 73 cannons and a huge booty of ammunition, cattle, and grain. The troops were so parched with thirst that they drank from wells choked with enemy corpses and from earthenware pots of water the Lahore forces had used for washing wounds. Many were so exhausted that they lay down where they were. Two hours after the end of the battle, when the British troops were assembling around their standards, Tej Singh's 20,000-strong force from Ferozepore suddenly appeared, a tide of cavalry with heavy squadrons with tulwar in the centre, lancers on the flanks, and massed ranks of infantry behind them. Fewer than 10,000 Britons and Bengalis—exhausted, starving, and almost out of ammunition—fixed bayonets and awaited the onslaught. If the British lost the battle, the road would be open to Meerut, Delhi, and Calcutta. Now, at the height of the crisis, he ordered the commanders of most of the cavalry and horse artillery regiments, in the name of the governor-general, to fall back on Ferozepore. Some of them immediately began to do so. The other was an order from Gough to Brigadier General Michael White to charge the Lahore cavalry that was advancing on Gough's right. White got the timing of his charge exactly right. Forcing their blown horses forward into a charge, the Dragoons, Lancers, and Irregulars struck the enemy flank as they moved from the gallop to the charge, throwing them off course, breaking their momentum, and driving them into blundering confusion. The British horsemen charged in among the Lahore forces with lances and sabres flashing in the sun. While Lahore forces guns continued their bombardment, what was left of the British and Bengali cavalry began leaving the battlefield following Lumley's order (in Harding's name) to retire on Ferozepore. The Lahore forces guns stopped firing and the great mass of Lahore infantry began marching on the exhausted, battered, and bloody ranks of the British and Bengali infantry. "The fate of India," one observer remarked, "trembles in the balance."

First Anglo-Sikh War

Battle of Ferozeshah 1845 (Contd)

Suddenly, to the utter surprise of the British, the Lahore forces advance halted and voices could be heard shouting orders. The British and Bengalis watched in dumbfounded silence as the Lahore forces ranks turned around in clouds of dust and 20,000 of the best native troops in India turned their backs on an almost helpless enemy and marched off the battlefield. "India has been saved by a miracle," Major Henry Havelock muttered in awe. The British were secretly assured that although Ferozepore would be an easy victory for the Lahore forces, it would not be attacked. Tej Singh maintained his watch on Ferozepore while Lal Singh and a detachment of his force moved south from Ferozeshah to meet the British divisions advancing from Ambala on Mudki. On the final day of the Battle of Ferozeshah, when Tej Singh and his Lahore forces arrived on the battlefield from Ferozepore, he refused to attack the British although urged to do so by his commanders who were sure they could defeat the British. He did little more than send out skirmishers, delaying a full assault until Lal Singh's forces were driven back and the British and Bengali line had time to reform and range themselves around their colours. And when the British cavalry regiments and horse guns began leaving the battlefield under orders from the deranged Captain Lumley, instead of it being a sign for Tej Singh to attack the remaining enemy troops, it gave him the excuse he needed to stop the attack. He convinced his commanders that the British planned to drive around them to attack them on the flanks and at the rear. Unaware that the exhausted British and Bengali troops were down to their last shot and shell, his subordinates agreed with him. The attack was called off and the Lahore forces left the field, making their way back to the Satluj. British losses were high—215 officers and men killed and 655 wounded at Mudki and another 2,415 killed or wounded at Ferozeshah. Lahore forces losses were about the same as the British at Mudki, and an estimated 5,000 more fell at Ferozeshah. Hardinge shuddered: "Another such victory and we are lost." The Lahore forces and the Bengal Army were left facing each other across the Satluj, battered and bleeding, while reinforcements and supplies were rushed in for the next battle. Although not decisive, Ferozeshah would prove to be one of the bloodiest battles of the century in the Far East.

(At the conclusion of the war the British rewarded Tej Singh by making him a Raja of Sialkot).

First Anglo-Sikh War

The Lahore forces at battle of Aliwal 1846:

Commander-i-Chief:
Ranjodh Singh Majithia

Fauj-i-Ain (Regulars)

Jodh Ram's Brigade (4627)
Rup Singh's Infantry Paltan (936)
Bhagat Singh's Infantry Paltan (901)
Jiwand Singh's Infantry Paltan (870)
Gobind Cavalry Rajman
Baland Khan's Aspi (12 Guns & 360 Men)
Rustam Beg's Jinsi (6 Guns & 180 Men)
Balder (Engineer) Company

Ranjodh Singh's Brigade (1360)
1ST Sirdar Infantry Paltan (500)
2ND Sirdar Infantry Paltan (500)
Jinsi (12 Howitzers & 360 Men)
Ghorchurras Khas Derah
Ghorchurras (1600)
Jay Singh's Swivels (76)
Fateh Singh Jogis Derah
Ghorchurras (1600)

Ghorchurras (995)
Gurmukh Singh Lamba's Derah
Imam-ud-Din's Derah
Ghorchurras (993)
Jawahar Singh's Derah
Ghorchurras (960)
Mul Raj's Derah
Ghorchurras (921)

Jagirdari Light Cavalry Regiments
Raja of Ladwa's Sowar Regiment (960)

State Army Artillery
Munbarak Khan's Artillery Brigade
1ST Jinsi (12 Guns & 360 Men)
2ND Jinsi (9 Guns & 270 Men)
Mortar Derah
Aspi (4 Heavy Mortars & 120 Men)
Independent Derah
Jinsi (12 Guns & 360 Men)

First Anglo-Sikh War

The British forces at battle of Aliwal 1846:

General Officer Commanding
Major General Sir Harry Smith

Aides-de-Camp
Lt. Holditch
Lt. H. Tombs

Assistant Adjutant General
Captain E. Lugard

Deputy Assistant Adjutant General
Lt. Plowden

Engineering Staff
Lt. Strachey
Lt. Baird Smith

Commissariat General's Dept.
Captain Mainwaring
Captain Williamson
Captain Jack

The Shekawati Infantry
Major H. Foster

Principal Medical Officer
Doctor Murray

Political Officers
Major Mackeson
Captain Cunningham
Lt. Lake

1ST Infantry Division
Major General Sir Harry Smith
Brigadier Hugh Wheeler, CB

Deputy Assistant Quartermaster General
Lt. AS. Galloway

1ST Brigade
Brigadier George Hicks

Brigade Majors
Captain O'Hanlon
Captain Palmer

HM 31ST Foot Regiment
Lt. Col. Spence

24TH Bengal Native Regiment
Major Bird

47TH Bengal Native Regiment
Captain Corfield

2ND Brigade
Brigadier Wheeler

Brigade Major
Captain Garvock

HM 50TH Foot Regiment
Lt. Col. Ryan

48TH Bengal Native Regiment
Captain Troup

Sirmoor Gurkha Battalion
Captain Fisher

3RD Brigade
Brigadier Archibald Wilson

Brigade Major
Captain Loftie

HM 53 Foot Regiment
Lt. Col. Philips

First Anglo-Sikh War
The British forces at battle of Aliwal 1846 (Contd)

4TH Brigade
Brigadier G. Gody

Brigade Major
Lt. Vanteren

36TH Bengal Native Regiment
Captain Fleming

Nusiri Gurkha Battalion
Brigadier Nickolas Penny

2 Field Batteries
2 8in Howitzers

Cavalry Division
Brigadier Charles Robert Cureton

Deputy Assistant Quartermaster General
Captain Waugh

1ST Cavalry Brigade
Brigadier McDowell

Brigade Major
Lt. Pattison

Governor General's Bodyguard

30TH Bengal Infantry Regiment

1ST BLC

5TH BLC

The Shekawati Cavalry

4TH Bengal Irregular Cavalry
Captain Hill

3 Batteries Horse Artillery
Major Laurenson

HM 16TH Lancers Regiment
Major J. Rowland Smith

3RD BLC Regiment
Major Angelo

2ND Cavalry Brigade
Brigadier Stedman

Battle of Aliwal 1846
Following the Battle of Ferozeshah, Tej Singh withdrew his Lahore army across the Satluj River, while General Sir Hugh Gough formed his force on the south bank and awaited reinforcements. Seeing this inactivity on the part of the British and Bengali army, Tej Singh detached Ranjodh Singh with 8,000 troops and 70 guns to march east along the river and cross, so as to menace the British base at Ludhiana, as a large slow column of supplies with the British siege train was coming up from the east. Gough dispatched General Sir Harry Smith with a brigade of infantry, cavalry and guns, to clear the Lahore army away from his line of communication and prevent the Lahore army from taking Ludhiana. Smith captured two small forts occupied by the Lahore army and moved on towards Ludhiana. Ahead of him, Ranjodh Singh Majithia with Raja Ajit Singh of Ladwa was following much the same route, but with little apparent urgency.

First Anglo-Sikh War

Battle of Aliwal 1846 (Contd)

Gough reinforced Smith with HM 16TH Lancers and another battery of guns, and ordered him to march to Jagraon, on the more southerly road, where he was to take under his command HM 53RD Foot. He was then to march to Ludhiana, where he would find Colonel Godby with four native regiments, including two battalions of Gurkhas and four guns. Ranjodh Singh, being still on the riverside road leading to Ludhiana, stopped and dispersed his army across the countryside. Smith sent word to Godby, to join him at the village of Suneth for a joint assault on the Lahore army. Smith left his baggage under guard at Jagraon, and, in the early hours of 21ST January 1846, marched out to join Godby. While on the march, word reached Smith that further Lahore forces had come up, giving Ranjodh Singh around 10,000 troops and 40 guns, and that the Lahore army were marching to cut the route from Jagraon to Ludhiana at Baddowal. In the light of the strength of Ranjodh Singh's army, Smith resolved to march around it and on to Ludhiana, which he managed to achieve, even though the Lahore forces had the benefit of being on the road. The British and Bengali infantry reached Ludhiana in a state of exhaustion, many of the foot soldiers carried by the cavalrymen on their horses. Smith found that Godby was still at Ludhiana. After a day's rest for his troops, Smith marched out to attack Ranjodh Singh at Baddowal, but found that the Lahore army had left to return to the Satluj, where more troops were crossing the river to join them. Smith received further reinforcements from Gough, and, now having 12,000 men and 32 guns, marched north in pursuit of Ranjodh Singh. The reinforcement that had crossed the Satluj to join the Lahore army included the crack regiment of Infantry. With this addition, Ranjodh Singh was poised to take the offensive, when Smith's army came up with him in his fortified position between the villages of Aliwal and Bhundri, his back to the River Satluj. Smith formed his army, with the cavalry in the rear and the infantry of two brigades, Wheeler's and Wilson's, in the first line, supported by two further brigades, Godby's and Hick's, in the second, and continued his advance. At a range of 600 yards, the Lahore artillery opened fire along the length of their position, causing Smith to halt and consider what move to make next. Smith directed Godby and Hicks to move out from the second line, storm Aliwal on the right and then attack the Lahore line in enfilade. These two brigades took Aliwal and turned towards the centre, at which, Ranjodh Singh brought up a body of cavalry to restore his collapsing flank.

First Anglo-Sikh War

Battle of Aliwal 1846 (Contd)

Brigade Cureton launched Brigadier Stedman's cavalry brigade, comprising 5th Bengal Light Cavalry, the Bodyguard, 1st Bengal Light Cavalry, 4th Bengal Irregular Cavalry and the Shekawati Cavalry, in a series of charges against the Lahore horsemen, driving them back from Aliwal, and leaving Godby free to advance beyond the line, towards their camp on the bank of the Satluj, at the point where the fords gave Ranjodh Singh's army the only escape route across the river. Under the pressure of this attack, the line swung back along the river bank, pivoting on the village of Bhundri. A force of cavalry emerged into the plain beyond Bhundri to threaten the British and Bengali flank. Brigadier Cureton ordered Captain Bere's squadron of HM 16th Queen's Lancers and the 3rd Bengal Light Cavalry to drive this force back. It is said, but with little authority, that the 3rd did not press home their attack, unlike Bere's lancers, who charged the Lahore horsemen with great violence and hunted them to the bank of the Satluj. Returning from their charge, Bere's squadron encountered the regiment of infantry, which formed to receive cavalry; the formation being a triangle, rather than a square. Again, the squadron charged home, despite receiving a devastating volley, and broke up the Lahore infantry. Two horse artillery guns, acting in support of the wing, unlimbered and opened fire on the remains of the Lahore regiment, completing its ruin. Meanwhile, the right wing of the 16th Lancers, commanded by Major Smyth, charged another battalion of Lahore infantry and a battery of guns, Smith beginning the attack with three rousing cheers for the Queen. In this charge, many of the soldiers and officers became casualties. General Smith met the squadrons of the 16th Lancers, fighting back through the Lahore line, and called out 'Well done 16th'. Smith ordered the survivors of the right wing to join Bere's squadrons and the whole regiment delivered a last devastating charge, capturing the village of Bhundri and driving the garrison to the river bank. HM 53ft Foot came up behind the cavalry, and cleared Bhundri of the remaining determined pockets of Lahore forces. While the cavalry fights were raging on the flanks, the British and Bengali infantry regiments, supported by artillery, pressed over the fortifications, forcing the Lahore troops back to the Satluj; a large force being driven out of a nullah by the 30th Bengal Native Infantry into the path of a barrage of grape from 12 guns.

First Anglo-Sikh War

Battle of Aliwal 1846 (Contd)
As the Lahore regiments took to the fords to escape across the Satluj, a battery of nine Lahore guns unlimbered on the river bank to cover the retreat, firing only one salvo before being overrun by the pursuing British and Bengali troops. Ranjodh Singh attempted to bring some of his guns back across the river, but only two reached the far bank, two more being abandoned in the stream and a further two sunk irretrievably in quicksand. On the far bank, Ranjodh Singh formed a new line but his troops were quickly dispersed by artillery fire. General Sir Harry Smith's army suffered 589 casualties. The casualties were spread evenly through all the units, provoking the admiration of the Duke of Wellington for Smith's use of all arms of his army. The only exception was HM 16TH Lancers which suffered 144 casualties. The Sikhs admitted to 2,000 killed and lost all their 67 guns, camp equipment and baggage. Ranjodh Singh Majithia cannot have known of the Lahore Durbar's conspiracy to decimate its own army. Knowledge of this decision was restricted to Maharani Jindan Kaur, the C-in-C Tej Singh, and the Wazir Lal Singh. It was Ranjodh Singh's timidly that forced him to act in the manner he did. He was not an experienced or even a well known Sikh general, and had not taken part in any previous battle. Why he was given the important task of cutting the British supply lines is not known. Perhaps his appointment fitted with the larger game plan, to put a timid general in command without an adequate force to carry on his orders. He opted of attacking Harry Smith when he was at Baddowal, when Smith was at his most venerable with an exhausted army. At the battle of Aliwal, after being reinforced twice, Harry Smith's army was superior both in strength and composition.

Many commentators referred to Smith's victory as the "Battle without a mistake. The victory at Aliwal removed the threat to the British rear. Smith, awarded a baronetcy for his generalship, soon moved to rejoin Gough

'I have gained one of the most glorious battles ever fought in India ... Never was victory more complete, and never was one fought under more happy circumstances, literally with the pomp of a field day; and right well did all behave.'
General Sir Harry Smith after the Battle of Aliwal,

First Anglo-Sikh War

The Lahore forces at battle of Sabraon 1846:

Commander-i-Chief: Raja Tej Singh
Second –in- Command Raja Lal Singh

Fauj-Ain (Regulars
S. S . Sandhanwalia's Brigade
4 Infantry Paltans
Ram Rajman (Cavalry)
Aspi (9 Guns)
Belder (Engineer) Company

Rattan Singh Mann's Brigade
4 Infantry Paltans
Hazoori Rajman (Cavalry)
Aspi (12 Guns)
Jinsi (9 Guns)
Belder (Engineer) Company

Kahn Singh Mann's Brigade
4 Infantry Paltans
1 Rajman (Cavalry)
Aspi (11 Guns)
Jinsi (9 Guns)
Belder (Engineer) Company

Mewas Singh's Brigade
5 Infantry Paltans
Aspi (9 Guns)
1ST Jinsi (9 Guns)
2ND Jinsi (9 Guns
Belder (Engineer) Company

Fauji-i-Khas Brigade
4 Infantry Paltans
3 Rajman (Cavalry)
4 Infantry Paltans
Belder (Engineer) Company

Mehtab Singh's Brigade
4 Infantry Paltans
Lancer Rajman (Cavalry)
Belder (Engineer) Company

Bahdur Singh's Brigade
4 Infantry Paltans
Akal Rajman (Cavalry)
Belder (Engineer) Company

Jiwan Singh Toshakhani's Brigade
2 Infantry Paltans
Aspi (12 Guns & 360 Men)
Jinsi (9 Guns & 270 Men)

Ghorchurras Cavalry Brigade
18 Ghorchurras
Abdur Ramin's Zambooks
Jalal Din's Zambooks

State Artillery
Topkhana of Sultan Mahmood
Bakhtawar Khan's Battery
Bukshi Khan's Battery
Jawahir Mall's Artillery
Ishwar Khan's Jinsi
Imam Shah's Jinsi

Ali Khans Artillery Brigade
Huber Khan's Battery
General Illahi Baksh's Brigade
Mixed Horse &Field Guns
Howitzer Darahs
3 Howitzer Darahs

First Anglo-Sikh War

The British forces at the battle of Sabraon 1846:

Commander-in-Chief
General Sir Hugh Gough

Military Secretaries
Captain Haines
Captain Sackville West

Persian Interpreter
Lt. Col. Henry Havelock, CB

Personal Medical Officer
Assistant Surgeon Stephens

Aides-de-Camp
Lt. Bogot
Lt. Edwards
Lord James Brown

Governor General of India
Lt. General Sir Henry Hardinge

Personal Staff

Military Board
Col. Benson

Military Secretary
Lt. Col. Wood

Political Agent
Major Lawrence

Secretary to Government (political)
Currie Esq,

Private Secretary
Hardinge Sqr.

Assistant Political Agents
Captain Mills
Captain Cunningham
Cust Esq.

Judge Advocate General

Assistant Adjutant General
Major Patrick Grant

Deputy Assistant Adjutant General
Captain Anson
Captain Tucker

Assistant Commissary General
Major Thompson

Deputy Commissary General
General
Major Curtis
Lt. Col. Birch

Field Surgeon
J. Steele

Aides-de-Camp
Captain Grant
Lord Arthur Hay
Captain Peel
Captain Hardinge

Personal Surgeon
Dr. Walker
Army Staff

Acting Quartermaster General
Lt. Col. JB. Gough

Assistant Quartermaster General
Lt. Col. Garden

Deputy *Quartermaster General*
Lt. Col. Drummond

First Anglo-Sikh War

The British forces at the battle of Sabraon 1846 (Contd)

Commander-in-Chief
General Sir Hugh Gough

Foreign Military Observers
Prince Waldemer of Prussia
Count Oriole
Count Grueben

Postmaster
Lt. Sandy

Superintending Surgeon
Dr. MacLeod

Deputy Assistant Quartermaster General
Lt. Arthur Beecher

Acting Adjutant General
Lt. Col. Bar

1ST Infantry Division
Major General Sir Harry Smith

Deputy Assistant Adjutant General
Lt. Galloway

ADC
Lt. Holditch

1ST Infantry Brigade
Brigadier George Hicks

Brigade Majors
Captain Coomb
Lt. Robert Hay

HM 50TH Foot
Brevet Lt. Col. Thomas Ryan

42ND Bengal Native Infantry
Major Polwhele

2ND Infantry Brigade
Brigadier Nicholas Penny

Brigade Major
Captain Garvock

HM 31ST Foot
Captain Corfield

Nasiri Gurkha Battalion
Captain O'Brian

2ND Infantry Division
Major General Sir WR Gilbert

Assistant Adjutant General
Captain Houghton

Deputy Assistant Quartermaster General
Lt. TS. Rawson

ADC
Lt. MacDonald Gilbert

3RD Infantry Brigade
Brigadier Charles Cyril Taylor

Brigade Major
Captain AG Ward

HM 29TH Foot
Captain Stepney

41ST Bengal Native Infantry
Major Sibbald

68TH Bengal Native Infantry
Brevet Major Marshall

First Anglo-Sikh War

The British forces at the battle of Sabraon 1846 (Contd)

Commander-in-Chief
General Sir Hugh Gough

4TH Infantry Brigade
Brigadier James McLaren

Brigade Major
Lt. Jones

1ST Bengal European Light Infantry
Major Burrell

Sirmoor Ghurkhas
Captain Fisher

16TH Native Infantry
Bervet Major Graves

3RD Infantry Division
Major General Sir R. Henry Dick

Deputy Assistant Adjutant General
Captain JR Pond

Deputy Assistant Quartermaster General
Lt. JS Paton

ADC
Lt. R. Bates

5TH Infantry Brigade
Brigadier Thomas Ashburnham

Brigade Major
Captain JL Taylor

HM 9TH Foot
Lt. Col. Davis

HM 62ND Foot
Major Short

26TH Bengal Native Infantry
Major Hanscombe

6TH Infantry Brigade
Brigadier Wilkinson

Brigade Major
Captain Gordon

HM 80TH Foot
Lt. Col. Bunbury

33RD Bengal Native Infantry
Captain Sandman

63RD Bengal Native Infantry

7TH Infantry Brigade
Brigadier Stacy
Brigadier Orchard

Brigade Major
Lt. Dunsford

HM 10TH Foot
Lt. Col. Franks

HM 53RD Foot
Lt. Col. Philips

43RD Bengal Native Infantry
Brevet Lt. Col. Nash

59TH Bengal Native Infantry
Brevet Lt. Col. Thompson

4TH Infantry Division
Major General Sir John Grey

8TH BLC

45TH Bengal Native Infantry
Captain Short

41ST Bengal Native Infantry

First Anglo-Sikh War

The British forces at the battle of Sabraon 1846 (Contd)

Commander-in-Chief
General Sir Hugh Gough

59TH Bengal Native Infantry
Lt. Col. Thompson

Brigadier Wheeler
(To hold Ludhiana)

48TH Bengal Native Infantry

Major General Sir John Littler
(To hold Firozepur City)

Cavalry Division
Major General Sir J, Thackwell

Deputy Assistant
Captain J. Tritton

Deputy Assistant Quartermaster
Captain CF Havelock
ADC
Lt. TJ. Francis

1ST Cavalry Brigade
Brigadier T. Scott

Brigade Major
Captain Houghton

HM 3RD Light Dragoons
Lt. Col. Michael White

8TH Bengal Irregular Horse

9TH Bengal Irregular Horse
Captain Christie

2ND Cavalry Brigade
Brigadier Alexander Campbell

Brigade Major
Captain Spottiwoodi

HM 9TH Lancer
Lt. Col. Fullerton

2ND Bengal Irregular Cavalry
Captain Leeson

2 Troops HA

4TH Cavalry Brigade
Brigadier Charles Robert Cueton

Brigade Major
Lt. Pattison

HM 16TH Lancers
Captain Pearson

3RD BLC
Major Angelo

4TH Bengal Irregular Cavalry

5TH BLC
Army Artillery
Commander 2ND Brigade, BHA
Brigadier GE Gowan

Deputy Assistant Adjutant General
Captain E. Christie

Deputy Assistant Quartermaster General
Lt. Maxwell

Commissaries of Ordnance
Captain Pillans
Captain Warner

Bengal Horse Artillery
Brigadier E. Biddulph

First Anglo-Sikh War

The British forces at the battle of Sabraon 1846 (Contd)

Commander-in-Chief
General Sir Hugh Gough

2ND *Company* 6TH *Battalion Bengal Artillery*

4TH *Company* 6TH *Battalion Bengal Artillery*

Brigade Major
Captain Austen

Troop, BHA
Lt. Col. Lane

Troop BHA
Captain Day

Troop BHA
Lt. Col. Alexander

Troop BHA
Captain Hubert Garbett

Troop BHA
Captain Swinly

Troop BHA
Captain Turton

Troop BHA
Major Cambell

Troop BHA
Captain Waller

Troop BHA
Major Frederick Brind

Troop BHA
Major Grant

Horse Artillery Troops
1ST Troop, 2ND BHA
3RD Troop, 2ND BHA
2ND Troop, 3RD BHA
3RD Troop, 3RD BHA

Bengal Foot Artillery
Brigadier Deniss

Brigade Major
1ST Lt. E Kaye

Special Purpose Batteries
Brigadier George 'Bully' Brooke

Brigade Major
Captain Murray Mackenzie

Superintendence
Brigadier Biddulph

Mortar Battery
Lt. Col. Wood

18 Pounder Battery
Major Laurenson

2ND *Company,* 2ND *Battalion*
Lt. Angelo

3RD *Company,* 3RD *Battalion*
Captain Master

4TH *Company,* 3RD *Battalion*
Captain Anderson

2ND *Company,* 4TH *Battalion*
Lt. Counternay

First Anglo-Sikh War

The British forces at the battle of Sabraon 1846 (Contd)

Commander-in-Chief
General Sir Hugh Gough

Howitzer Battery
Brigadier Dennis

8 Howitzer Troop
Lt. Col. Edward Huthwait

Independent Artillery Units

Rocket Troop
Lt. Col. Geddes

12 Pounder Elephant Battery
Captain Day

Heavy Field Battery
Major Grant

9 Heavy Field Battery
Captain Horsfod

19 Light Field Battery
Captain Fordyce

Engineers
Brigadier Smith

Bengal Sappers & Miners
Major Riley

Bridge, Park and Train
Major Abbot

Observer
Brigadier Irvine

Brigade Major
Major Charles Napier

The Governor Generals Escort

The Governors Generals Bodyguard
Captain Quin

Detached Troops
73RD Bengal Native Infantry
4TH Bengal Native Infantry
5TH Bengal Native Infantry

First Anglo-Sikh War

Battle of Sabraon 1846
Following the battle of Aliwal the Lahore army encampments south the River Satluj had been abandoned. The army had withdrawn north of the river, except for a defensive enclave that had been maintained south of the river at Sabraon. Sabraon, across the Satluj towards Lahore, with well-built high defensive embankments with entrenchments on top, were thrown across the front, linking with the river Satluj at both ends. A bridge of boats connected both shores. The opposite rear bank was higher than the front bank and was being prepared as a position for the heavy guns, so they could cover an attack from any direction. At Lahore, Gulab Singh on his arrival was appointed Wazir. At the same time, Gulab Singh opened communications with the British, making the following requests: to confirm him and his family forever in possessions of their present estates and lands, and leave in possession of all the territories under his rule which included Kashmir, contenting themselves with a tribute of four annas in every rupee of revenue. Hardinge was quite prepared to negotiate with the Lahore Durbar while Gulab Singh represented it, since he believed that the summer fast approaching, it would be more prudent to resolve the position through negotiations. Negotiations with Gulab Singh were opened. It was made clear to him, provided the Lahore forces were disbanded, or greatly reduced in strength. Sikh sovereignty in Lahore would still be acknowledged. Gulab Singh then ordered the Lahore forces at Sabraon to withdraw north across the Satluj into Lahore territory. His order caused much uncertainty and low morale, and it was not obeyed. So Gulab Singh let the British know he could not control the Lahore forces. It was, therefore, agreed that the Lahore forces should be attacked and beaten by the British, who would the cross the Satluj and advance on Lahore without opposition, the Lahore forces being refused additional arms, was ordered to stay where it was at Sabraon, more or less disowned by its own government. A few days later what was said to be plans of the British defences around Sabraon found their way into the hands of Major Lawrence. It was under such circumstances of discreet policy and shameless treason that the battle of Sabraon was fought. Hearts to dare and hands to excute were numerous, but there was no mind to guide the animate the whole: each inferior commander defended his front according to his skill and means.

First Anglo-Sikh War

Battle of Sabraon 1846 (Contd)

In their defensive position, the Lahore regular units and artillery were massed in centre along with Mehtab Singh Majithia, who had earlier commanded his brigade with distinction at Ferozeshah. Sardar Sham Singh Attari commanded the left flank and Colonel Mouton, who also commanded the irregular cavalry on the right. Tej Singh was in overall command and was positioned within the defensive perimeter, between the second and third line of entrenchments. Lal Singh commanded the major part of the cavalry across the river on the north bank. The position allowed the army no room to manoeuvre, and should they have to retreat, the river behind them was danger, despite the boat bridge.

The defences were based on eight brigades of the regular army. Of these, three were below strength, -the Fauj-i-Khas, Mehtab Singh Majithia's and Bahadur Singh's brigades- having taken part in the battle of Ferozeshah, where Bahadur Singh had been killed. None of them had their complement of guns with them, having lost them at Ferozeshah. The total strength within the Sabraon defended sector was put at 20,000 men, of which 15,000 were combatants and 67 guns, all Aspi or Jinsi.

The artillery detachment of the Fauj-i-Khas, under General Illahi Baksh, had lost its guns at Ferozeshah. As he was detached from his parent brigade, the Fauj-i-Khas at Sabraon, and is listed under the army artillery, he was probably commanding a detachment of heavy artillery on the north bank under Lal Singh. The total number of guns deployed in the battle, both north and south of the river, was reported to be 103, of which 36, mostly heavy calibre, belonged to the Lahore army artillery, which were deployed in the north bank. On 8th February 1846, Major General Smith re-joined the main army, and Major General Sir Hugh Gough prepared to drive the Sikhs back across the Sutlej River with his complete force. He decided to make the main thrust against the Lahore forces right, commanded by Colonel Moulton, because he considered it the weakest point of the defensive position. Most of the heavy guns were assigned to bombard these western defences, with the assault to be delivered by General Dick's division, on the left opposite Moulton. Gilbert's division would menace the southern section of the defences, opposite Mehtab Singh Majithia, while Harry Smith threatened the eastern, facing Sham Singh Attari. Scott's cavalry brigade supported Dick, while Campbell supported Smith. Brigadier Cureton took his brigade upstream to create a diversion. The lighter guns were spread around the Lahore position, concentrated particularly at the south-east corner.

First Anglo-Sikh War

Battle of Sabraon 1846 (Contd)

Early on 10TH February 1846, the British and Bengali regiments got under arms as silently as possible, but no action could be begun due to a dense mist, which lasted until around 6 a.m. As the mist dispersed, the artillery opened fire on the Lahore army lines at 6.30 a.m. The bombardment was a failure. The heavy batteries, short of gunners, were forced to borrow soldiers from the field batteries, many of whom had no experience of serving the larger guns. Due to the recent arrival of the siege train and the lack of time for preparation, insufficient ammunition had been brought up to the gun positions, which were themselves too far back. By around 8.30 a.m. the gun ammunition had run out, with little damage inflicted on the Lahore positions. Gough's reaction to this anti-climax was characteristic: "Thank God." He said. "Now I'll be at them with the bayonet" and ordered Dick to attack with his infantry. It was at this point that a series of messages arrived from Hardinge urging Gough to abandon the attack. Gough ignored these pleas and ordered Dick forward. At 9 a.m. on 10TH February 1846, Dick's division went into the attack, led by Stacey's brigade with HM 10TH Foot on the right and 43RD and 59TH Bengal Native Infantry and HM 53RD Foot in line. Horse and Field Artillery batteries galloped forward on the flanks and opened a covering barrage. The Lahore troops and guns opened a heavy fire in response, but Stacey's regiments stormed the ditch and wall, driving the defenders from their positions. The Lahore troops rallied and counter-attacked Stacey's brigade. Many of HM 53RD fell to an enfilading the Lahore battery firing from the north bank, but the line pressed on and stormed the right with bayonets, pushing the gunners back to their inner line of trenches. At this point, HM 10TH also suffered from a Lahore battery, which had swung its guns around and opened fire on them. Gough ordered Gilbert and Smith to launch feint attacks, to draw off the Lahore troops from the western face of the entrenchments. These feints had little effect, the Lahore troops in overwhelming numbers driving Dick's brigades out of the positions they had taken. Sir Robert Dick was killed with a bullet to the head; Stacey's brigade was finally dislodged and fell back. Gough's first attack had failed. With the collapse of the assault on the western face of the entrenchments, Gough ordered Gilbert and Smith to convert their feints into full attacks on the southern and eastern sections of the Lahore position. They were halted by high, well built ramparts. On the Lahore forces extreme left, Brigadier Penny's 1ST Brigade led Harry Smith's division followed by Hick's 2ND Brigade met the same fate.

First Anglo-Sikh War

Battle of Sabraon 1846 (Contd)
Unable to cross the formidable height of the ramparts, the brigade fell back exhausted and retired through Hick's brigade, which was now moving into the attack. Once again, unable to cross the high ramparts and being under continuous fire from above, this attack failed too, and Hick's brigade also fell back and took cover in a dry gulley close by in order to reorganise. While in this position, they witnessed the Lahore tops coming off the ramparts and dispatching their wounded with their tulwars. Anger at the killing of their wounded comrades gave fresh impetus to Hick's brigade. Backed by HM 31ST of Penny's brigade which had joined them, it launched its attack and this time the troops scaled the ramparts by standing on each other's shoulders. Shouting their battle cry they stormed the position, pushing the enemy back and establishing a foothold. In the centre, Gilbert's division began its advance in response to Gough's order. In the counter attack the Lahore troops, having repulsed Dick's division led by Stacy's brigade, now turned on Gilbert's division and McLaren' brigade. Watching their move, Gough shouted, 'Good God, they will be annihilated.' The Lahore forces centre under Mehtab Singh Majithia was the strongest, and as the Bengal European Regiment found them confronted by the massive walls, which in the distance had appeared less formidable, they found these works too high to escalade without ladders. To retire again was to encounter the storm of fire through which they had just passed, to remain in their present position was annihilation, therefore the regiment, was forced to seek shelter under cover of the bank of the dry river which it had left but a short time before. Meanwhile, Hick's brigade had entered into Sham Singh Atari's defences, but was hard put to hold on. Sir Robert Dick had been killed, and however, hard pressed to hold the centre and left, the Lahore forces had thinned their right, after the repulse of Stacey's first attack, to strengthen their centre and left, which was being attacked. Dick's division now attacked again, secured a foothold and entered the Lahore again, secured a foothold and entered the Lahore forces position, cutting down the gunners. Giblet's division was again attacked the left of centre, but again was repulsed. General Gilbert was wounded and so was the brigade commander Brigadier McLaren. A third attempt was made, and this time the troops, standing once again on each other's shoulders, secured a foothold, enlarged it and assaulted the guns, bayoneting the gunners and spiking the guns. Gilbert's second brigade commander, Brigadier Taylor, was also shot in the head and killed.

First Anglo-Sikh War

Battle of Sabraon 1846 (Contd)

All three divisions had now secured a foothold in the Lahore forces position and before the Lahore forces could consolidate and renew their counterattacks, Gough ordered General Thackwell's and his cavalry division to sweep the entire defensive perimeter silencing the guns. The Engineers created a gap on the Lahore forces right and General Thakwell personally led the 3RD Dragoons through a single file. They galloped along the Lahore gun positions, cutting down the gunners and infantry who were attempting to form squares. Just then a Lahore battery changed direction and opened grape on the Dragoons bringing them to a halt until the 4TH and 5TH Bengal Cavalry Regiments joined them. Jointly they charged and silenced the battery. Yet once again, an outer battery, which still manned its guns, turned those inwards and opened fire on the Dragoons. At this moment the Lahore Commander-in-Chief, Tej Singh was once again deserting his command. He crossed the boat of bridges to the north bank and to safety, damaging the central span, either by mistake or intent, leaving his command to their fate. Sham Singh Attari, the commander of the left who was opposing Harry Smith's 1ST Division and was in his first battle, realized the desperate situation they were now in. He had volunteered to be part of Tej Singh's army after their defeat at Mudki, Ferozeshah and Aliwal, and left his village of Attari, having taken a vow in his Gurdwara, along with the followers of his feudal levy, to either return victorious from Sabraon or die in the attempt. He now came forward on the ramparts with a white robe (the colour of sacrifice) over his clothes, calling to his troops to rally round him. There followed a hand-to-hand battle, the bayonet against the sword until Sham Singh fell mortally wounded and died on the ramparts. There his body lay alongside those of his men until it was taken back to Attari the following day, 53 other men from his village who had taken vow with him were also cremated at the same site. As the fighting penetrated deeper into the Lahore forces defences, the British guns and men were able to pour through the gaps now prepared by the Engineers. Object to these increasingly successful attacks, the Sikh line began to collapse, the soldiers making for the river crossings to escape. Unfortunately, this was not possible. During the night, heavy rainfall in the mountains had caused the Sutlej River to rise by seven foot, flooding all the fords.

First Anglo-Sikh War

Battle of Sabraon 1846 (Contd)

The retreating Lahore Army attempted to cross by the swollen fords, or crowded onto the southern section of the bridge, which began to collapse, throwing the soldiers into the torrential river. Many were drowned, while Gough's guns bombarded the struggling masses. At some time around midday the battle came to an end. The Lahore Army lost their great general Sham Singh Attari, and Sardars Gulab Singh Koopta, Heeera Singh Topee and Kishan Singh, and commander of the artillery general Mubaruck Ally. The cost of the First Sikh War to the British was 105 officers killed and 315 wounded. Those included 3 major generals, Sir Robert Sale, Sir John McGaskil and Sir Robert Dick and Brigadier Wallace. The wounded included Major General Gilbert and 3 brigadiers, Taylor, White and McLaren.

General Sham Singh Attariwala

Sham Singh Attariwala was a general of the Sikh Empire. He was born in the 1790s in the house of well known Sikh farmers in the town of Attari, in the Majha region of Panjab, India. Asa child he was educated in Grumukhi and Persian. When Ranjit Singh became the Maharajah of Punjab, he got Attariwala services at his disposal. Maharajah Ranjit Singh knowing his qualities and fighting abilities made him a 'Jathedar' of 5000 horsemen. He participated actively in many campaigns, notably in the, Battle of Attock, Battle of Multan, Battle of Peshawar, and the 1819 Kashmir expedition. At the outbreak of the first Anglo Sikh war, Sham Singh was at Kakrala, south of the Sikh frontier, for the wedding of his second son, Kahn Singh. As he heard the news, he rushed back to the Punjab. Sham Singh immediately repaired to Lahore. He chided the commanders, Misr Tej Singh and Misr Lal Singh, who had fled the field, and himself crossed the Sutlej swearing an oath on the Guru Granth Sahib that he would lay down his life rather than return in defeat. The battle was joined at Sabraon on 10 February 1846. Dressed in white and riding his white steed, the grey bearded Sardar Sham Singh moved from column to column calling upon his men to fight to the last. As the battle was in a critical stage, Sham Singh, rushed into the thick of the battle. He made a desperate charge along with his fifty men against the advancing enemy. Within minutes he was overpowered and he fell to the ground dead. In the evening as the battle was over, his servants swam from across the river to recover the body. On 12TH February 1846, Sham Singh was cremated outside his village. A Samadhi raised on the site now honours his memory.

First Anglo-Sikh War

Raja Raheem Ullah Khan 1846
Mirza Reheem Ullah Khan rendered service to the British Government during the First Afghan War by sending his son Yahiya Khan, under Maharajah Ranjit Singh's orders, with a force of about one thousand men to keep the road open between Peshawar and Ali Masjid. 1819 Maharajah Ranjit Singh while conquering Kashmir also captured Rajouri, where he appointed Mirza Reheem Ullah Khan as Raja of Rajouri in place of Raja Agar Khan. Raja Raheem Ullah Khan remained as Rajouri ruler upto 1846, under the control of Khalsa Durbar of Lahore. On 15th March, 1846, Jammu, Kashmir and Ladakh were sold by the British to Raja Gulab Singh of Jammu and Kashmir.

Frontier 1846
When Lieutenant Edwards marched down the Frontier in 1846 to attack Dera Ghazi Khan, the Lagharis naturally sided with the Sikhs, while the Khosas and Gurchanis went over to Lieutenant Edwards. Jalal Khan joined Mul Raj in the Sindh Sagar Doab, and five hundred of his tribesmen assembled under Longa Mal, the Kardar at Dera Ghazi Khan. They were defeated by the Khosas under Ghulam Haidar Khan and Kaura Khan, and suffered heavy losses. After the occupation of Dera Ghazi Khan by Lieutenant Edwards, at the conclusion of the First Anglo-Sikh war, Jalal Khan came over to him with eighty men

Mitha Khan 1846
Lieutenant Edwards tried to win him over but without success. He then sent a party of horsemen to Mitha Khan, and called him to assist in expelling Chatan Mal. He went to his drum the village, raised the country, and despatched a short message to Chatan Mal, that if he did not wish to be besieged, the sooner he vacated Mangrotha the better. The governor took the hint and fled in haste with his garrison, leaving the fort to Lieutenant Edwards's men. Mitha Khan continued to hold Mangrotha for some time, and was the medium through whom Assad Khan Nutkaul endured to negotiate with Lieutenant Edwards. He ultimately joined Lieutenant Edwards, and when peace was declared he was confirmed in all his holdings.

Ismail Khan 1846
In 1847, after the establishment of the British Agency at Lahore, the District Came under its charge and in 1848 Ismail Khan of Jhang rendered important services against the rebel-chiefs, for which he received a small pension.

First Anglo-Sikh War

Colonel Imam Shah 1846
Imam Shah was of Persian descent and a grandson of Qamaruddin, an officer in the army of Nadir Shah. Imam Shah seeking his fortune left for Lucknow, where he lived for some time with an old retired officer of Artillery, Bahadur Khan, who taught the lad all he knew about Artillery. In the Punjab he met Sardar Jodh Singh, who induced him to enter his service as Jamadar of Artillery. Next year Sardar Jodh Singh died: and Imam Shah then entered the army of Maharajah Ranjit Singh, and fought in many battles as Colonel of Artillery. He served throughout the reign of Maharajah Ranjit Singh. He was killed in action on 10TH February 1846 at Sabraon during the first Anglo-Sikh war.

Commandant Mian Imam Bakhsh 1846
Mian Imam Bakhsh joined the armed forces of Maharajah Ranjit Singh and soon rose to be a cavalry commandant. He received the Jagirs of Chimiari and Kotla Muhammad Qaim in Ajanala of Amritsar district. Mian Imam Bakhsh, under the command of Kharak Singh, held Gobindgarh Fort and refused to surrender to the British even after the British victory was complete. He was taken prisoner and shot.

Umed Singh 1846
In 1846, during the first Anglo-Sikh War, Umed Singh, of Jaswan he joined the Sikhs, against the British. His palaces were plundered and razed to the ground, and his territory annexed. He was stripped of his title and exiled to Almora, where he died a year later.

Nawab Ghulam Ali Khan 1846
Ghulam Muhiddin was the rightful successor to the principally of Kunjpura, in Karnal district, northwest of Delhi. On the death of Ghulam Muhiddin in 1841, the cheifship reverted to Nawab Ghulam Ali Khan. In 1843, the Nawab had an opportunity of proving his loyalty to the British, by furnishing a party of 50 Sowars in suppressing the disturbances at Kaithal. The men of his contingent remained at the disposition of Sir Henry Lawrence for two months, and their services were duly acknowledged in a letter of thanks to the Nawab. He was again forward in assisting during the First Anglo-Sikh war with carriage and supplies.

First Anglo-Sikh War

Sikh Regular Army & Feudal Forces which did not take part during the First Anglo-Sikh War.

Fauj-e-Ain (Regulars)

Arjan Singh's Brigade (4,288)
1ST Infantry Paltan (847)
2ND Infantry Paltan (847)
3RD Infantry Paltan (847)
4TH Infantry Paltan (847)

Artillery
Aspi (360) (12 guns)

Court's Brigade (4,292)
Chattar Singh Attari in Command
1ST Infantry Paltan (848)
2ND Infantry Paltan (848)
3RD Infantry Paltan (848)
4TH Infantry Paltan (848)
Cavalry Rajman (540)
Artillery
Aspi (12 guns) (360)

Dhian Singh's Brigade (5738)
Hara Singh in Command
1ST Jasrota Infantry Paltan (833)
2ND Jasrota Infantry Paltan (833)
3RD Jasrota Infantry Paltan (833)
4TH Jasrota Infantry Paltan (833)
5TH Jasrota Infantry Paltan (833)
6TH Jasrota Infantry Paltan (833)
Jagirdari Sowar Regiment (500)
Artillery Jasrota Aspi 8 guns (240)

Raja Gulab Singh's Division (10,430)
1ST Nowshera Infantry Paltan (600)
2ND Nowshera Infantry Paltan (600)

Raja Gulab Singh's Division (Cont)
1ST Jammu Infantry Paltan (600)
2ND Jammu Infantry Paltan (600)
3RD Jammu Infantry Paltan (600)
4TH Jammu Infantry Paltan (600)
5TH Jammu Infantry Paltan (600)
6TH Jammu Infantry Paltan (600)
7TH Jammu Infantry Paltan (600)
8TH Jammu Infantry Paltan (600)

Cavalry Brigade
1ST Jagirdari Sowar Regiment (750)
2ND Jagirdari Sowar Regiment (569)
3RD Jagirdari Sowar Regiment (672)
4TH Jagirdari Sowar Regiment (759)
Jai Singh's Zambruks (76)

Suchet Singh's Brigade (4,816)
1ST Infantry Paltan (979)
2ND Infantry Paltan (979)
3RD Infantry Paltan (979)
4TH Infantry Paltan (979)
Cavalry Rajman (540)
Artillery
Aspi (12 guns) (360)

Artillery Brigade
Nowshera Aspi (10 guns) (300)
1ST Jammu Aspi (12 guns) (360)
2ND Jammu Aspi (12 guns) (360)
1ST Jammu Jinsi (12 guns) (360)
2ND Jammu Jinsi (12 guns) (360)

First Anglo-Sikh War

Sikh Regular Army & Feudal Forces which did not take part during the First Anglo-Sikh War. (Contd)

Gulab Singh's Pouvinda's Brigade
1ST Infantry Paltan (866)
2ND Infantry Paltan (866)
3RD Infantry Paltan (866)
4TH Infantry Paltan (866)
Artillery
Aspi (12 guns) (360)

Sardar Ahluwalia's Brigade
1ST Kapurthala Infantry Paltan (600)
2ND Kapurthala Infantry Paltan (600)
1ST Jagirdari Sowar Regiment (676)
2ND Jagirdari Sowar Regiment (676)
Artillery
Kapurthala Aspi (12 guns) (360)

Raja Suchet Singh's Brigade
1ST Samba Infantry Paltan (600)
2ND Samba Infantry Paltan (600)
3RD Samba Infantry Paltan (600)
4TH Samba Infantry Paltan (600)
Jagirdari Sowar Regiment (400)
Artillery
Samba Aspi (8 guns) (240)

Fauj-e-Gair
Ghorchurras Cavalry
Attariwala Derah
Derah Khas
Derah Kalan
Ramgarhia Derah
Fyshushashi's Zambruks (101)

The Aftermath of First Anglo-Sikh War 1846
In the Treaty of Lahore on 9 March 1846, the Sikhs were made to surrender the valuable region (the Jullundur Doab) between the Beas River and Sutlej River. The Lahore Durbar was also required to pay an indemnity of 15 million rupees. Because it could not readily raise this sum, it ceded Kashmir, Hazarah and all the forts, territories, rights and interests in the hill countries situated between the Rivers Beas and Indus to the East India Company, as equivalent to ten million of rupees.[14] In a later separate arrangement (the Treaty of Amritsar), the Raja of Jammu, Gulab Singh, purchased Kashmir from the East India Company for a payment of 7.5 million rupees and was granted the title Maharajah of Jammu and Kashmir. Maharajah Duleep Singh remained ruler of the Punjab and at first his mother, Maharani Jindan Kaur, remained as Regent. However, the Durbar later requested that the British presence remain until the Maharajah attained the age of 16. The British consented to this and on 16 December 1846, The Maharani to be awarded a pension and be replaced by a British resident in Lahore supported by a Council of Regency, with agents in other cities and regions. This effectively gave the East India Company control of the government. Although the Sikh Army was weakened by the war, resentment at British interference in the government led to the Second Anglo-Sikh War within three years.

Second Anglo-Sikh War

Multan 1848

Multan had been captured and incorporated into the Sikh Empire of Ranjit Singh in 1818. In 1845, it was ruled by a Hindu vassal, Diwan Mulraj. At the conclusion of First Anglo-Sikh War, Mulraj was nominally subject to the Sikh Durbar and the East India Company. Early in 1848, the newly appointed Commissioner in the Punjab, Sir Frederick Currie, demanded that Mulraj pay duties and taxes previously paid to the central Durbar of the Sikh Empire and now in arrears. Mulraj could not pay and abdicated in favour of his son. Currie nevertheless decided to impose a compliant Sikh ruler, Sardar Khan Singh, who was to be accompanied by a British Political Agent, Patrick Vans Agnew. On 19TH April, Mulraj conducted Khan Singh and the two British officers to the citadel and handed over the keys, with no sign of hostility. As the two officers began to ride out of the citadel, a soldier from Mulraj's army attacked Vans Agnew. Both officers were wounded, and they retired to a Mosque outside the city, where Anderson wrote a plea for help. During the night, most of Vans Agnew's escort left. Next morning, the mob pushed General Khan Singh aside and hacked the two British officers to death. Nihang then presented Vans Agnew's head to General Khan Singh and told him to take it back to Currie. Mulraj had probably not been a party to the conspiracy among his own troops. He nevertheless regarded himself as committed to rebellion by their actions.

Lieutenant Herbert Edwards

Lieutenant Herbert Edwards intercepted the second copy of Vans Agnew's letter to Currie, and immediately began to concentrate troops. The common soldier felt humiliate and joined the revolt in Multan. In early June, Edwards began to lead an army against Multan. They were engaged by Mulraj's artillery and forced to take cover for several hours. Mulraj's infantry and cavalry began to advance but Edwards was reinforced by two regiments of the Sikh Khalsa Army under Colonel Van Cortland, an Anglo-Indian soldier of fortune. Van Cortland's artillery caused heavy losses among the Multani troops and Edwards's Pashtuns counter-attacked. Mulraj's forces retreated to Multan, having suffered 500 casualties and lost six guns.

Second Anglo-Sikh War

Sher Singh Attariwala 1848
Currie at last ordered a comparatively small force from under General Whish to begin the siege of Multan. Currie decided to reinforce them and Edwards with a substantial detachment of the Khalsa under Sher Singh Attariwala. Despite warnings, Currie nevertheless ordered a detachment from Chattar Singh's army under his second in command, Jundial Singh, to reinforce Sher Singh. This allowed Jundial Singh and other officers to influence Sher Singh Attariwala and spread disaffection among his regiments. Mul Raj was reinforced by several other regiments of the Sikh Khalsa Army. The common Sikh soldier felt humiliate and joined the revolt in Multan. On 14TH September, Sher Singh Attariwala openly rebelled against the East India Company.

Chatar Singh Attariwala 1849
Chatar Singh rose into political prominence in 1843, after the assassination of Maharajah Sher Singh, and his daughter Tej Kaur was betrothed to Maharajah Duleep Singh. Chatar Singh Attariwala was appointed governor of Peshawar in August 1846. He was then transferred to Hazara, where as the governor of the province he came into conflict with the overbearing Assistant British Resident, Captain James Abbott. James Abbott had been continually reporting to the Resident at Lahore that discontent prevailed among the Sikh troops stationed at Hazara. Resident Frederick Currie issued orders which amounted to Chatar Singh`s virtual dismissal and the confiscation of his jagirs which drove him to open defiance. The Hazara revolt now escalated into hostilities between the British and the Sikhs. The Sikh contingents at Bannu, Kohat, Tonk, Peshawar and Attock revolted and joined him.

The Siege of Multan 1848
Late in November, General Whish was reinforced by a substantial force from the East India Company's Bombay Army. General Whish's combined force amounted to 32,000, of which 15,000 were from the British Army. He also had 150 pieces of artillery, many of which were heavy guns or mortars. Inside the city, Mulraj commanded 12,000 troops, with 54 guns and 12 mortars. On 27TH December, General Whish ordered four columns of troops to attack the suburbs. Mulraj's forces were driven back into the city, and Whish's force set up batteries 500 yards from the city walls. Under cover of their fire, breaching batteries were set up only 80 yards from the walls, and created two breaches in them while causing great damage in the city. On 30TH December, the main magazine in the citadel exploded, killing 800 of the defenders.

Second Anglo-Sikh War

The Siege of Multan (Contd)

Mulraj nevertheless maintained his fire and sent a defiant message to General Whish, stating that he still had enough powder to last a year. He attempted to mount a sortie against the besiegers on 31ST December but this was driven back. General Whish ordered a general assault on 2ND January 1849. The attackers successfully scaled the breaches, and the battle became a bloody house-to-house fight in the city, in which many defenders and civilians were killed indiscriminately. General Whish ordered the civilians to be herded into the main square; he may have intended to spare them from further fighting but the action of corralling them was also accompanied by further casualties. With the fall of the city, only the already-scarred citadel remained, but it held out for another fortnight against heavy bombardment. On 18TH January, Whish's sappers exploded three mines under its walls, causing heavy losses and destroying large sections of its walls. Mulraj offered to surrender if his life was spared, but General Whish insisted on unconditional surrender, and on 22ND January, Mulraj gave himself up, with 550 men. The British gained vast quantities of loot. Mulraj's treasury was worth three million pounds, a huge sum for the time. There was also much looting in the town, by both British and Indian soldiers. With the fall of Multan, Whish's army was able to reinforce the main Bengal Army force under Sir Hugh Gough. Mulraj was placed on trial for the murders of Vans Agnew and Anderson. He was cleared of premeditated murder, but was found guilty of being an accessory after the fact, in that he had rewarded the murderers and openly used the deaths as pretext for rebellion. Mulraj was sentenced to death, but the sentence was commuted to exile for life.

Second Anglo-Sikh War

The British Army of the Punjab, 1848:

Commander-in-Chief
Sir Lord Gough

Second-in- Command
General Sir Joseph Thackwell

1ST Infantry Division
Major General Whish

1ST Brigade
Brigadier Markham

2ND Brigade
Brigadier Harvey

3RD Brigade
Brigadier Dundas

2ND Infantry Division
Major General Sir Walter Gilbert

1ST Brigade
Brigadier Mountain

2ND Brigade
Brigadier Godby

3RD Division
General Sir Joseph Thackwell

1ST Brigade
Brigadier Pennycuick

2ND Brigade
Brigadier Pope

3RD Brigade
Brigadier Salter

1ST Cavalry Division
Brigadier Cureton

1ST Brigade
Brigadier Michael White

2ND Brigade
Brigadier Pope

3RD Brigade
Brigadier Salter

Bengal Artillery
Brigadier Tennant

Horse Artillery
Brigadier Brooke
Col. Brind
Col. Grant

6TH Troop
Lt. Col. Lane
Major Christie
Huish Warner

Foot Artillery
Brigadier Hathwait

3 Field Batteries
Major Dawes
Captain Kinelsied

1ST Bombay Field Battery

Heavy Batteries
Major Horsford

Second Anglo-Sikh War

Battle of Ramnagar 1848
The British commander in chief, Lord Sir Hugh Gough crossed the Ravi on 16 November 1848, with 24,000 men and 65 guns. In the early hours of the morning of 22 November, Gough ordered a force of cavalry and horse artillery, with a single infantry brigade, to move to the Chenab crossing near Ramnagar apparently intending to capture the position by surprise. The Sikhs occupied strong positions on both banks of the river and on an island in mid-stream. The river was only a narrow stream, but the wide bed it occupied during the monsoon season was treacherous soft sand, in which cavalry and artillery could become bogged down. At dawn, the British force assembled opposite the fords. The 3rd Light Dragoons and 8th Bengal Light Cavalry drove some Sikhs back across the river from positions on the east bank. At this point, hitherto concealed Sikh batteries opened fire. The British cavalry had difficulty extricating themselves from the soft ground. Gough's horse artillery was outgunned and forced to retire. The brigade commander, Sir Colin Campbell, called up troops to retrieve the gun but was over-ruled by Gough. Sher Singh sent 3,000 horsemen across the fords to take advantage of the British check. Gough ordered the main body of his cavalry (the 14th Light Dragoons and the 5th Bengal Light Cavalry) to attack them. These drove back the Sikh horsemen but as they pursued them down the river bank, they were hit by heavy artillery fire. The Sikh cavalry also turned about and hit the 5th Light Cavalry, causing heavy casualties. The Commanding Officer of the 14th Light Dragoons, Colonel William Havelock, led another charge, apparently without orders. He and his leading troopers were surrounded and cut down. After a third charge failed, Brigadier Charles Robert Cureton, the commander of the cavalry division to which the troops belonged, galloped up and ordered a retreat. He himself was then killed by musket fire. Official British casualties, including Brigadier General Cureton, were 26 killed or missing, 59 wounded. This may have referred to the 14th Light Dragoons only. Sher Singh had skilfully used every advantage of ground and preparation. Although the Sikh forces had been driven from their vulnerable positions on the east bank of the Chenab, their main positions were intact, they had undoubtedly repulsed a British attack, and the morale of Sher Singh's army was boosted. On the British side, several shortcomings were obvious. There had been little reconnaissance or other attempts to gain information on the Sikh dispositions. Gough and Havelock had both ordered foolish or reckless charges. The action at Ramnagar was a signal defeat for the British.

Second Anglo-Sikh War

Sadulpur 1848

For about a week after the British reverse at Ramnagar, the two armies faced each other across the river. Lord Gough waited impatiently till his heavy guns came up. On 30TH November, he detached a force under Major General Sir Joseph Thakwell to make its way across the river and take the Lahore army in the flank. In the meantime, he pushed British batteries and breastwork to the bank of the river and opened up a cannonade upon Sher Singh's front in order to divert his attention from the flank movement intended by Thakwell. At the sometime, another brigade of infantry under Brigadier Godby was detached from the main army and ordered to ford the river six miles from Ramnagar and give support to Thackwell's force. Across the river, at a principal ford about two miles from the town of Ramnagar, Sher Singh's entire force, 12,000 men and 28 guns lay strongly entrenched. As the numerous fords were vigilantly guarded by the Lahore forces, Thackwell's force had to move 22 miles up the river to Wazirabad, where on 2ND December it made the crossing. Godby's brigade had crossed the river 16 miles below, and so Thakwell hastily marched southwards. At mid day on 3RD December, he arrived at Sadulpur, barely four miles from the Lahore forces encampment. Here he halted; giving well-earned rest to his men who were in the state of complete exhaustion from five days continues the March. The Lahore forces realised the danger was imminent. Sporadic artillery fire from the British guns on the Ramnagar embankment had continued on their centre. Two British columns had successfully crossed the river and threatened their flanks and rear. Sooner than expected, heavy Lahore forces artillery opened upon Thackwell's position, while their cavalry barred the passage of Godby's force. Thackwell's instructions were not to engage the enemy till Godby's brigade had joined up with him. For some time the British guns remained silent; they opened up tardily and the desultory fire continued for two hours on both sides. But Godby could not form junction in time, with the result that Thakwell could neither attack the enemy's flank nor the rear. As the dusk fell the guns on both sides became silent; and as the darkness enveloped Sadulpur, entire Lahore army crossed over to the left bank of the river Jhelum. Sher Singh's action thus nullified the British manoeuvre; it also made possible for Chatter Singh's force to join him later. British general claimed a victory without a battle. But the news of the ineffective action was received by Lord Dalhousie on 7TH December at Ambala, and scoffed at the Commander-in-Chief's suggestion of firing a salute for the victory at Sadulpur.

Second Anglo-Sikh War

Battle of Chillianwalla 1849

On 6TH December Gough ordered Thakwell to form a standing camp at a place called Helan. On 18TH December Gough crossed the Chenab across a bridge of boats laid at Ramnagar and joined Thakwell at Helan. Soon it became clear through reports that the main Lahore Army had not been dispersed but firmly entrenched at Rasul on the bank of river Jhelum. Meanwhile Gough since he had already exceeded his instructions did not attempt any major movement towards Sher Singh's position at Rasul. The country between Helan and Rasul was a sandy waterless plain interspersed by patches of thick jungle. Meanwhile a column of the Bombay Army had finally reinforced General Whish at Multan on 22ND December taking his force up to 15,000 regular troops apart from some 20,000 irregulars. Multan's siege was resumed and the fort was assaulted beginning from 27TH December. The city and suburbs were captured by 1st January and the Citadel captured by 22ND January. The British losses were 210 killed and 910 wounded 29. Gough received news about arrival of Bombay column at Multan and the city's capture on 6th January. On 7TH January Dalhousie who was now at Lahore wrote to Gough that now that Multan had been captured, he would be rejoiced to hear of a similar blow being struck at the Sikhs upon the Jhelum. Dalhousie's despatches to Gough were however non-committal; thus he urged him to fight..." If sure of a big success at small cost ".... "If he should deem himself strong enough," Dalhousie's vaguely worded despatch was enough for Gough to once again start the job begun at Ramnagar on 22ND November. Gough was under pressure to attack, but no explicit orders were given to him by Dalhousie. Finally the news of the fall of the strategic fortress of Attock on river Indus received on 10TH January acted as a catalyst. Fall of Attock meant that all Lahore troops investing Attock and the Afghans could now easily reinforce Sher Singh at Rasul. Major Mackeson the political officer at Gough's camp also urged Gough to attack following the news of fall of Attock. Finally on 11TH Gough resolved to attack Sher Singh. His plan of attack was to advance to Dinga and from their march straight to Rasul and turn the enemy's left. Despite having ample cavalry British intelligence about the Lahore f Lahore forces position extended from Rasul situated on a line of ridges parallel to river Jhelum to the vicinity of Mung a village 5 miles south west of Rasul and again very close to river Jhelum. Rasul was situated on a dominating height but immediately south of it was a plain intersected by dry channels and a belt of trees and thorny scrub.

Second Anglo-Sikh War

Battle of Chillianwalla 1849 (Contd)

The Lahore forces had entrenched the whole position but there was a wide gap between their left at Rasul and their centre and right, which extended till Mung. Gough he could muster 12,000 men and 66 guns to attack the Lahore forces position at Rasul. The information which he had about the Lahore forces position was vague i.e. that it extended from the village of Rasul on the left till Lakhna Walla 6 miles to the south and facing east in a concave line with the broad fast flowing Jhelum river to the rear. Fortescue who exaggerated the odds as a matter of habit placed the Sikh strength at 30, 000[33]. Malleson who was dismissed by Fortescue as "pseudo historical" "inaccurate" "slovenly" and "untrustworthy" estimated the Lahore Army's strength at Chillianwalla to be in the neighbourhood of 23,000[35]. British historians do not agree on what was General Gough's exact plan for 13TH January. Gough and Innes who wrote their book primarily to defend Gough stated that it was Gough's intention to march from Dinga to Chillianwalla, drive in the Lahore outposts and launch the attack on the main Lahore forces position on 14TH January after detailed reconnaissance was carried out on the 13TH January.[36] Fortescue states that on the evening of 12TH January Gough summoned his generals and gave them orders for the fateful morrow. However Fortescue does not elaborate at all i.e. what were those orders for the fateful morrow! On 12TH January Gough advanced 11 miles north to Dinga and encamped there. On 13TH January he left two regiments of Native infantry, two of Irregular cavalry and 2 guns to escort and protect his baggage train which was to follow him and began his advance at about 7 A.M towards Rasul. Goughs' army covered a front of a mile and half while in marching order. All the brigades marched in column with one cavalry brigade on each flank and the European regiments leading the advance of each brigade. The heavy guns were in the centre and the other horse and field batteries in the gaps between the four infantry brigades. After marching for five miles he halted at a place from where a track branched to the village of Chillianwalla which was westwards off the road from Dinga to Rasul. Gough's intention was to carry out a reconnaissance. Engineers were sent forward with cavalry to check whether the road was practicable for the heavy guns or not. Once this was confirmed, the march was resumed. Soon however some Lahore Army deserters who were mostly Muslim arrived and informed the British through the political agent Major Mackeson that the Lahore forces were occupying the villages of Mujianwala and Chillianwalla on the left of the British in strength.

Second Anglo-Sikh War

Battle of Chillianwalla 1849 (Contd)

It was probably at this juncture that Gough changed his earlier plan of advancing till Rasul and then taking the Lahore Army position by rolling up their left flank downwards. Gough ordered some heavy guns and infantry to dislodge the reported strong Lahore forces screen position at Chillianwalla. This was successfully done since the Lahore forces did not offered only token resistance instead of exploiting the dominating position of the mound over which Chillianwalla was located and quickly withdrew into the thick jungle west of Chillianwalla. Gough now personally rode to the village of Chillianwalla while the British troops who had cleared Chillianwalla were deployed 500 yards west of Chillianwalla facing west ,to carry out personal reconnaissance and assess the situation himself. There was a thick jungle in front but Gough observed the Lahore forces positions parts of which were visible to understand that the Lahore forces had swung their right and centre forward leaving their entrenchment and were now deployed some 4000 yards west of Chillianwalla with the jungle in between masking their front and Chillianwalla. In response to the discovery of the Sikh positions so close to Chillianwalla, Gough extended his brigades into deployed formation .By the time Gough completed his reconnaissance it was two o clocks in the afternoon and Gough decided to attack the Sikh position on the next day. Because of the proximity of the Lahore Army it was now no longer possible to stick to the old plan of marching to Rasul since this would have exposed the left and rear of the British Army to a Lahore Army's attack from a position which they could barely observe from Chillianwalla. Gough now decided to bivouac on the open ground west of Chillianwalla and to launch his main attack on 14th January. While the British were making preparations to bivouac some Sikh artillery guns opened fire on the British, from the positions hidden by the jungle. The artillery fire was inaccurate and did little damage. Gough however ordered the heavy guns to return fire on the Lahore forces positions which could not be located. Once this was done, some thirty Lahore forces guns from different points in the jungle in front opened fire. Gough suddenly realised that he was too close to the Lahore forces positions and Sher Singh had full intention of fighting on 13TH January. It is necessary to examine the Lahore forces Army's plan in order to understand the developments till 2 p.m. on 13TH January. The Lahore forces position at Rasul was not an ideal one in terms of cohesiveness or frontage.

Second Anglo-Sikh War

Battle of Chillianwalla 1849 (Contd)

With 23,000 men they were occupying a concave shape position extending over six miles with large gaps in between there left and their centre and right. The entrenched Lahore forces position extended with the left resting on Rasul and the right on Lakhniwala. All the six miles of this concave position were not held by the Lahore forces and there were gaps in between, the most marked one between the Lahore forces centre and left. The Bannu garrison was deployed at Lakhniwala, approximately a regiment of cavalry and four infantry battalions, with eleven guns. A mile to the north were Lal Singh's two regiments of cavalry and ten infantry battalions and 17 guns deployed around Chak Fateh Shah, a further one mile north there was Sher Singh at Laliani with one regiment of cavalry, nine infantry battalions and some irregulars placed at 4,000 horse and 20 guns. The position from north of Laliani till Rasul was held by irregular levies. There is no independent and reliable Sikh account of the battle, therefore we have relied on the above mentioned description based on Fortescue's narrative which is true as far as general deployment is concerned but highly exaggerated as far as the numbers are concerned, since Fortescue suffered from the usual Victorian malady of magnifying the odds. Fortescue40 placed the total number of Lahore Army at Chillianwalla at 30,000. A line of small ridges with thick vegetation in shape of trees and thorny bushes and scrub covered the entire Lahore forces front with small gaps right from Lakhniwala to Rasul. Rasul itself was located on a very dominating ridge. The ridge on which the Lahore forces position was based sloped gently towards the eastern plain from which Gough's army was expected to attack, but had abrupt slopes towards its northern side which lay south of river Jhelum. From Lakhniwala till Lulianee this ridge followed a roughly north south alignment, but beyond Lulianee it changed direction to an east west alignment, also gradually increasing in height till Rasul which was the highest point being roughly 90 feet higher than the adjacent plain to the south of Rasul. Durand who participated in the battle described the Sikh initial defensive position as, "It was evident that the enemy occupied a position too extended for his numbers". Sher Singh's original intention seems to have been to force the British to attack a well entrenched position under conditions of extremely limited fields of fire and observation due to the thick jungle in front, which ensured that British artillery, could not effectively pound and soften up the Sikhs before the main infantry attack.

Second Anglo-Sikh War

Battle of Chillianwalla 1849 (Contd)

Another important strong point of his position was the fact that the left flank was protected by river Jhelum while the right flank was refused by virtue of being inclined backwards towards Mung. It appears that Sher Singh decided on 12TH January to slightly change his plan when he received news of Goughs advance Sher Singh now decided to bring his right and centre forward, ahead of the entrenchment's and give battle to the British under more disadvantageous circumstances, rather than passively waiting for them, while they marched without being opposed till Rasul and from there roll up the whole Lahore forces position by attacking in oblique order. It appears that keeping in view the line of British advance Sher Singh decided to swing his right and centre forward and force the British to attack through thick jungle country rather than allowing them to skirt round the jungle and threaten him from his right flank. This decision of Sher Singh stands out as the most brilliant tactical decision of the entire Second Sikh War. The British possessed superiority in artillery in terms of calibre of guns. Most of the 60 pieces of Sher Singh were of small calibre, while Gough had 12 heavy guns and howitzers (8 eighteen pounders and 4 eight inch howitzers), 17 nine pounders, 25 six pounders, and a number of horse artillery guns, in all. The British artillery was organised into two heavy batteries of four 18 pounders and, two 8 inch howitzer each, three field batteries, and six horse artillery batteries, 66 guns in all. The overall artillery commander was Brigadier Tennant and under him Brigadier Brooke commanded the Horse artillery brigade while Brigadier Huthwait commanded the Foot Artillery. Once Gough ordered general deployment for battle at about two-o clock the artillery was deployed as following. The heavy gun batteries i.e. two batteries of four 18 Pounders each and two batteries of two 8 inch howitzers each, under Majors Shakespeare and Ludlow with Major Hereford as the overall Heavy artillery commander, thus a total of 20 heavy guns, were all deployed in the centre of the British line. Three Troops of Horse Artillery (Colonel Brand) of six 6 Pounder guns each and two field batteries (Lieutenants Walker and Robertson) of 9 pounders under Major Mowatt were attached to the left attacking division i.e. Campbells. The left attacking division i.e. Major General Sir Gilberts was supported by three troops of Horse Artillery (Colonel Grant) and one Field Battery of 9 Pounders under Major Dawes. The British army was as earlier stated, divided into two infantry divisions.

Second Anglo-Sikh War

Battle of Chillianwalla 1849 (Contd)

Both the infantry divisions were supported by one cavalry brigade each on the outer flanks i.e. 1ST Cavalry of Brigadier White on the left flank and 2ND Cavalry Brigade of Brigadier Pope on the right flank. Campbell's division consisted of Brigadier Pennycuick's Brigade and Brigadier Hoggan's Brigade. Major General Gilbert's division consisted of Brigadier Mountain's Brigade and Brigadier Godby's Brigade. Brigadier Penny's Brigade originally under Brigadier General Campbell was the army reserve with two infantry battalions' i.e. 15TH and 69TH Bengal Native Infantry. The 20TH Bengal Native Infantry along with 3RD and 9TH Bengal Native Irregular Cavalry along with three field guns was designated as baggage guard, with Brigadier Hearsay as baggage guard commander. We have earlier discussed that Gough ordered his army to form up for battle at 2 o'clock. By 3 o'clock Gough's army was formed up to attack. Four infantry brigades each comprising two native and one British infantry battalion commenced their advance towards the Lahore forces position east of the thick jungle around three o' clock. The jungle consisted of trees interspersed with thick undergrowth and extremely thorny trees and bushes sometimes referred to as "Musket" in the Punjabi Shikari (Hunting) terminology. The closest European equivalent to this term is brushwood. Malleson states that Gough was a "thorough believer in the bayonet and looking upon guns as instruments which it was perhaps necessary to use but which interfered with real fighting, he, wild with excitement ordered his infantry to advance and charge the enemy's batteries". The reader may note that the Lahore forces position was at least 1760 yards from the British army and there was dense forest in between! We will now precede brigade wise and briefly discuss the battle. Firstly we will deal with Brigadier General Campbell's Division. Campbell was a Royal British Army officer born in 1792. He had seen action under Wellington in the Peninsular War and in 1849 had some 42 years of service behind him. Son of a Glasgow carpenter Campbell was helped getting into the class-conscious British army through the help of a rich relative. Campbell became, as was the norm at that time a colonel after some 30 years service. He was described by many contemporaries as "extremely brave" and "thorough" but "utterly devoid of dash" and "too cautious" and "too selfish for any place" as is mostly the case with men with humble origins who progress upwards slowly mastering all the red tapism and bureaucratic obstacles in armies!

Second Anglo-Sikh War

Battle of Chillianwalla 1849 (Contd)

Campbell like Gough was a firm believer in the power of the bayonet! Campbell's prime responsibility was to command and co-ordinate the function of both his brigades. However keeping in view the adverse terrain he decided to accompany his left brigade i.e. Hoggan's brigade in the attack while ordering Pennycuick's the right brigade commander to lead the attack on his own. Gough and Innes well summed up Campbell's decision as following, "He abrogated the duties of a divisional commander to discharge with splendid success those of a brigadier"! However before the attack commenced Campbell rode to Pennycuick's brigade and after briefing Pennycuick's about the attack rode on to HM 24TH Foot, the British unit of Pennycuick's brigade and gave them the following orders, "There must be no firing, and the work has to be done with the bayonet". HM 24TH Foot 1000 bayonets strong had newly arrived in India. The unit was thus highly enthusiastic but highly inexperienced in the British Indian way of warfare! By some oversight or due to an out of proportion sense of excitement, once HM 24TH Foot commenced its advance, it did so without loading its muskets!49 through some confusion the artillery designated to provide fire support to Pennycuick's trotted to the left. Pennycuick's advanced rapidly towards the Lahore forces position, HM 24TH Foot doing so more rapidly, full of enthusiasm to bayonet the accursed natives, that thin red line tipped with steel, as the British infantry at that time was known! The Lahore artillery whose overall commander was Illahi Baksh a Punjabi Muslim functioned admirably and as soon as 24 Foot came within round shot range of 800 yards, it was effectively engaged by Lahore artillery, and men starting falling. At 100 yards the Lahore infantry engaged the unit with musket fire, but the unit advanced stoically without firing back, their muskets unloaded, determined to do the work with the bayonet as ordered by Campbell. 24TH Foot was the first to emerge in open ground west of the jungle outstripping both the native units of Pennycuick's brigade i.e. the 25TH and 45TH NI on the right and left flanks respectively. To add further bad luck to 24TH Foot's fate right across its axis of advance was a large water pond between the Lahore forces position and the British unit. 24TH Foot thus had to break formation to cross the pond bypassing it from left and right while some braver souls attempted to wade through it. At this moment the Lahore artillery played havoc with 24TH Foot causing inflicting great slaughter. 24TH Foot did reach the Lahore guns but the punishment inflicted was too severe.

Second Anglo-Sikh War

Battle of Chillianwalla 1849 (Contd)

As close quarter fighting started 24TH Foot soon lost many officers including its commanding officer. The unit had not loaded its muskets and had advanced too fast thus reaching the Lahore forces position unsupported by both native units. Beveridge states that the unit advanced at a double time pace because of a misunderstanding on part of two officers leading the brigade , however this view is not substantiated by either Fortescue or Gough and Innes .The native units advancing more carefully, while preserving their energy for the final assault under the more experienced British officers of the East India Company's private army did finally attack the Lahore forces position, a few minutes after 24TH Foot's attack, suffering many casualties in the process but by this time HM 24TH Foot was close to the breaking point The Lahore forces counterattacked and the 24TH Foot broke up and withdrew in disorder back into the jungle towards Chillianwalla. The native units also withdrew. Pennycuick's, his son Lieutenant Pennycuick's and his brigade major all died in the bloody engagement. In all Pennycuick's brigade lost some 376 men killed and about 417 wounded. The brigade fought well but failed because of sheer tactical ineptitude of HM 24TH Foot in advancing too rapidly and because of its blind obedience to Campbell's instructions regarding use of bayonets apart from lack of artillery support. Pennycuick's brigade's remnants arrived in driblets back to their start line east of the jungle. Campbell's left brigade whom Campbell accompanied fared better. It was well supported by artillery and HM 61 Foot was a better-led and trained unit. The native units on the flanks of HM 61 Foot knew their job and their pace of advance in any case depended on the European unit in the middle. The reader may note that the British always cleverly placed the European unit in the middle so that the thankless and dirty job of looking after the flanks where most of the Enfilading fire came was assigned to the native units! Soon after commencing advance Hoggan's brigade lost touch with Pennycuick's brigade because of the jungle. Once it crossed the jungle it arrived right in front of a gap in the Lahore forces line in between the Lahore forces left flank of their (Lahore forces) right division and the right flank of the Lahore forces centre. Fortescue denies this and states that once Hoggan's brigade appeared out of the jungle there were Lahore troops in front of it. Hoggan's brigade was able to advance thanks to massive concentration of some 29 British artillery pieces i.e. Mowatt's battery on Hoggans right and Colonel Brind's three horse-artillery batteries (troops) on the left.

Second Anglo-Sikh War

Battle of Chillianwalla 1849 (Contd)

These British guns as per Fortescue were able to silence an excellently sited Lahore heavy battery which otherwise was ideally placed to enfilade the advance of the entire brigade. In any case whether there was a gap in front of Hoggan's brigade as Malleson asserts or not as Fortescue would like us to believe Hoggan's brigade successfully advanced onwards and after doing its job in the front wheeled northwards towards Pennycuick's supposed position , while the cavalry brigade along with Colonel Brind's horse artillery troops ably performed the task of flank protection and defeated a Lahore forces attempt to attack Hoggan's brigade's flank from the south by well directed artillery fire and a sharp cavalry charge. However in the process one squadron of HM 3RD Lancers lost contact with the brigade while pursuing the Lahore cavalry. This squadron was in turn counterattacked by Lahore cavalry and in the process lost 23 men killed. This squadron only re joined its parent unit at the end of the days fighting and thus was a major reason why Brigadier White was unable to utilise his brigade more effectively to attack the Lahore forces from the left .Hoggan's brigade now advanced northwards wheeling right and took in the flank the Lahore troops which had defeated Pennycuick's brigade . The Sikhs were outflanked and fought well but Hoggan's brigade evicted them from their position and continued its advance northwards rolling up the Sikhs flank from the south. Hoggan's brigade continued its advance till it finally met Major General Gilbert's left brigade. The reader may note that Hoggan's brigade was successful in joining up with Mountain's brigade i.e. Sir Walter Gilberts left brigade because Mountain's brigade attacked the Sikhs facing Hoggan's brigade from their unguarded north rear. Major General Walter Gilbert commanding the right division consisting of Brigadier White and Mountain's Brigades was a far more experienced man than Campbell or Gough. He had seen action in the First Sikh War and was not only an extremely brave leader of men but also a relatively more sensible man as compared to Gough and Colin Campbell. Walter functioned as an effective divisional commander and coordinated the advance of both his brigade's well. Brigadier Mountain's Brigade encountered stiff Sikh resistance. The 56TH NI its right flanking unit ran into an excellently sited Sikh position and was counterattacked by an overwhelming number of Lahore Army. The unit fought well but was repulsed after losing in the process 8 officers and 322 men killed and wounded.

Second Anglo-Sikh War

Battle of Chillianwalla 1849 (Contd)

The other two units i.e. HM 29TH Foot and the 30TH NI were however more successful and captured the Lahore forces positions opposite Lulianee spiking a large number of Lahore artillery guns and rendering them ineffective. As a result of success of HM 29TH Foot and 30TH NI 56TH NI was rallied and joined the brigade. It may be noted that Mountain's brigade attacked the Lahore forces facing Hoggan's brigade advancing from the south and thus enabled Hoggan's brigade to defeat those Lahore forces. Gilbert's right brigade i.e. Brigade Godby's brigade performed relatively better than Mountain's brigade. The brigade ably supported by artillery successfully cleared Lahore forces positions in its front and drove the Lahore forces close to the river Jhelum opposite the village of Tupai. Godby then halted his brigade in order to reorganise before the final attack driving into the Lahore forces once he was suddenly attacked by the Lahore forces in force from his rear. We have earlier stated that Brigadier Pope's cavalry brigade was tasked to protect the right flank of the army of Punjab. Pope's cavalry brigade consisted of HM 14TH Light Dragoons, HM 9TH Lancers, 1ST Bengal Native Light Cavalry and 6TH Light Cavalry. The European cavalry regiment average strength was approximately 400 Sabres and Native Cavalry Regiment strength was approximately 300 sabres. Brigadier Pope was from 6TH L Light Cavalry and had more than forty years service. He was a brave and dashing officer in his earlier years but was not really physically or mentally fit to command a cavalry brigade in action. The 6TH Bengal Native Light Cavalry the readers may note was one of the most illustrious units of the native cavalry. One of its most illustrious feats was a daring charge at the battle of Sitabldi in the Third Maratha War where it dispersed a Maratha force of about 18,000 men including 3,000 Arab mercenaries. This battle was unique in the sense that there were no British units present and the battle was an all Indian show barring the British officers of the native units. Pope notwithstanding his dash as a young officer was an invalid in 1849, and one who could hardly sit on horseback. As soon as the British advance commenced Pope with the cavalry brigade on the right flank also advanced. Immediately a body of Lahore cavalry emerging from the high ground around Rasul, made a threatening demonstration towards Popes right rear flank. Pope detached a wing (half regiment) each of HM 9TH Lancers and 1ST and 6TH Light Cavalry under the overall command of Colonel Lane to observe them and to act as a flank protection screen.

Second Anglo-Sikh War

Battle of Chillianwalla 1849 (Contd)

Lane deployed his force a little northwards and thus lost visual contact with the remaining British army, because of the intervening strips of jungle. Pope continued his advance westwards with the remaining brigade. Soon another body of Lahore cavalry appeared in front of Pope's axis of advance The Bengal Horse artillery the best branch of the British immediately deployed into action to engage these Lahore forces. However Pope, without thinking of anything decided to charge the Lahore forces, also masking the British artillery's fire in line formation. The result was a weak charge without any depth or artillery support, delivered in words of Gough and Innes without speed or momentum. The Lahore horsemen led by Jawahir Singh Nalwa, the bold and dashing son of Sardar General Hari Singh Nalwa, now realising that poor execution and bad terrain had brought Pope's apology of a cavalry charge to an absolute halt64 now counter charged. Jawahir Singh with his band of horsemen emerged, once again, through the wild Doab jungle, and charged Popes force, in the process of which some Lahore horsemen physically attacked Brigadier Pope, cutting him across the head with his Tulwar, and wounding him. At this critical stage of the battle Pope's brigade which had already halted and was waiting for orders, now became leaderless. An event then occurred which the British historians right from 1849 onwards find hard to explain or account for the HM 14TH Light Dragoon turned about and bolted! The native cavalry also panicked and followed HM 14TH Light Dragoon rearwards, galloping through at top speed through their own horse artillery batteries backwards! Fortescue states that HM 14TH Light Dragoon bolted because Pope gave them a word of command of "Threes Right" which they heard as something like "Threes about" and that's why the unit bolted! There is no doubt that had a native cavalry unit done so Fortescue's verdict may have been much harsher! Jawahir Singh Nalwa pursued Pope's cavalry brigade with great elan, cutting down many British Horse artillerymen including Major Christie, one of the battery commanders, destroying six guns and carrying four guns intact apart from two ammunition wagons and fifty three horses as war trophies! Pope's cavalry brigade from this moment onwards ceased to be a fighting formation! It was rallied with great difficulty by Gough's staff and the regimental Chaplain of HM 14TH Light Dragoon, with his pistol! It was said that Gough recommended the Chaplain to be promoted to the rank of Brevet Bishop, on the battlefield!

Second Anglo-Sikh War

Battle of Chillianwalla 1849 (Contd)

The flight of Pope's brigade resulted in a serious operational imbalance in the British position. Sher Singh Attariwala immediately ordered a counter attack and Lahore infantry and cavalry west of Rasul immediately advanced down from the heights through the open gap encircling Gilbert's division from the rear! It was Pope's good luck that he died soon afterwards from wounds suffered in the battle. We had already left Gilbert discussing Major General Gilbert's action when Gilbert's brigades suddenly found themselves under attack from their rear. Brigadier Godby whose brigade bore the brunt of the Lahore forces counter attack from the rear reacted in a most resolute manner to the sudden Lahore forces threat from his rear! The day was however saved by brilliant handling of artillery by Major Dawes of No 17 Field Battery. Dawes immediately moved his battery to the right flank and brought such an effective fire on the Lahore forces attacking Godby's brigade that the Lahore forces counter attack was broken up. Almost at the same time Godby gave an order of "Right about face" to his brigade and attacked towards the rear scattering the Lahore forces attacking his rear. Mountain's brigade, whose rear was threatened, also counterattacked rearwards and dispersed the Lahore forces threatening his rear. By this time the reader may note Hoggan's brigade had also joined Mountain. At this stage of battle Brigadier Penny's reserve brigade which had been ordered by Gough to take Pennycuick's position after Pennycuick's brigades repulse had entered the jungle, lost its way and moved north-westwards instead of south westwards now suddenly emerged out of the jungle in front of Gilbert's division, now breaking out eastwards and, also played a marginal role in reducing the Lahore forces threat to the rear of Gilbert's division. By now darkness was approaching and Colonel Lane, all throughout unaware of what was happening emerged from the jungle and attacked the retreating Lahore forces, who had attacked Gilbert's rear from his position in the right rear. Gough now decided to withdraw what remained of his demoralised army to Chillianwalla. All the wounded that could be found were carried back to Chillianwalla in the darkness. The casualties that the British suffered were relatively much larger in proportion as compared to any battle that they fought later or earlier at least as far as unit averages were concerned. The total British casualties were 2,357. The British had failed to dislodge the Lahore forces. At the battle of Chillianwalla British failed to defeat their opponents despite having the advantages of weight of numbers, and superior logistics.

Second Anglo-Sikh War

General Makhe Khan 1849
Makhe Khan fought some of the rebel Misls, and was made a general. He participated in most of the battles of the Sikh battles. General Makhe Khan, died fighting against the British at Chillianwalla.

Commander Maddad Khan 1849
One of the sons of General Illahi Baksh, Commander Maddad Khan, was killed during the battle the battle of Chillianwalla.

Battle of Gujrat 1849
Following the carnage of the Battle of Chillianwalla, General Gough's Army of the Punjab camped around the village of Chillianwalla, while for three days, rain poured down. Sher Singh's Sikh Army lay at the village of Rasul, between Chillianwalla and the River Jhelum. The weather cleared, but Gough resolved not to attack the Sikhs until General Whish had joined him with his division, following Whish's capture of the City of Multan. Sher Singh tried to lure Gough into a premature battle, but to no avail. The army of Chattar Singh joined the Sikhs at Rasul. On 25th January 1849, shortage of supplies forced Sher Singh to leave Rasul and March east, to the more fertile country around Gujrat, on the Chenab River. Gough dispatched Lieutenant Hodson with a force of cavalry to Wazirabad, on the far side of the Chenab, to watch for a Lahore forces incursion across the river. On the last day of the march Whish's division joined the Gough's army. On 19TH and 20TH February 1849, Dundas's Bombay brigade and Markham's Bengal brigade marched in, giving Gough his decisive force for the final battle with the Lahore army. The mass of the regular Lahore infantry, with 59 guns, was in line in the two-mile gap between the dry River Dwara on the right and the flowing Katella River on the left. On each flank, the Lahore cavalry continued the line beyond the two river beds, with the Afghan cavalry on the right. The Lahore army had fortified several villages lying in advance of their line. Behind the Lahore army line, the distant Himalayan Mountains gave a dramatic snow tipped backdrop to the forthcoming battle. Gough planned to launch his main attack along the side of the Dwara nullah, while the 1TH and 2ND cavalry brigades pinned the Lahore army's left flank and centre. His infantry brigades would be formed for the attack: from the right, Hervey's, Penny's and Mountain's brigades, with Markham's brigade in support. To the left of Hervey's would be the heavy guns on the bank of the Dada: on the left bank of the dry nullah; Carney's, McLeod's and Dundas's brigades, with Hogan's in support. White's cavalry brigade would cover the left flank.

Second Anglo-Sikh War

Battle of Gujrat 1849 (Contd)

The British, Bengal and Bombay troops fell in for the battle soon after dawn on 21st February 1849. Gough rode down the line, wearing his white 'Fighting Coat', and was cheered vigorously by his men. On the signal, the Army of the Punjab advanced two miles towards the Lahore army positions, halting as the Lahore guns opened fire. Gough ordered his gun batteries forward, with a covering of skirmishers, and a heavy duel opened between the opposing artilleries, the Bengal and Bombay artillery outnumbering the Sikh guns nearly two to one. The decisive point came when the two Bengal horse artillery reserve batteries took several Lahore guns in enfilade and destroyed them. After two and half hours of bombardment the Lahore army fire began to fade. With the slackening gunfire, the Lahore cavalry on Gough's right moved forward towards Hearsay's cavalry division, leading to extensive manoeuvring between the opposing forces. The main British infantry attack began as Penny's and Mountain's brigades, supported by the heavy guns, moved forward towards the centre of the Lahore army line and were received with a heavy fire from the surviving guns. The village of Bara Kalra (Great Kalra) lay in advance of the right of the Lahore army centre. A party of Gough's light troops moved forward to take the apparently empty village, to be met by a storm of shots from the loop holed houses. Gilbert, the divisional commander, dispatched the 2ND Bengal (European) Fusiliers to attack the Lahore army garrison, the regiment pushing through the village in the face of a stubborn resistance. The Lahore forces counter-attacked, pushing the 2ND Fusiliers back through Bara Kalra, until they were halted by blasts of grape shot at close range from Fordyce's troop of Bengal Horse Artillery, which finally cleared the Lahore forces from the village. At the same time, Hervey's brigade attacked the twin village of Chota Kalra (Little Kalra), HM 10TH Foot and 8TH Bengal Native Infantry leading the advance. Again, the resistance was fierce and the fire extremely heavy. Lahore cavalry threatened the right flank of the brigade, forcing the third regiment, 52ND Bengal Native Infantry, to form to the right. Markham's brigade came up, and, with the supporting fire of Mackenzie's and Anderson's batteries of Bengal Horse Artillery, Hervey's battalions took Chota Kalra. On the left bank of the Dawa Nullah, the artillery cleared the row of villages of their Lahore forces garrisons and Campbell's' three brigades advanced unopposed, enabling the guns to move forward and take the main Lahore forces line in enfilade across the Dawa, causing numerous casualties and the general retreat of the Lahore army.

Second Anglo-Sikh War

Battle of Gujrat 1849 (Contd)

On Gough's left, the Lahore cavalry moved forward and round his flank, but were halted by the fire of Duncan's and Hush's batteries of Bengal Horse Artillery. This was followed by a charge delivered by the Scinde Horse and a squadron of HM 9TH Lancers, which drove the Lahore cavalry back. All along the line, the Lahore army formations were collapsing and taking to flight, in striking contrast to their measured withdrawal in all the previous battles of the wars, other than Aliwal. Thackwell's cavalry pursued the Lahore forces beyond Gujrat for twelve miles towards the River Jhelum, halting only when his artillery horses were exhausted and could go no further. Hearsay, with the right flank cavalry brigade, joined the rest of the Cavalry Division beyond Gujrat and continued the chase until nightfall. Pickets were placed on the Chenab River fords, permitting the Lahore soldiers to cross and return to their farms provided they surrendered their weapons. Casualties at the Battle of Gujrat: British and Indian casualties were 96 killed and 750 wounded. The units that suffered most heavily were the 2ND Bengal (European) Fusiliers and the 31ST BNI of Penny's brigade during the attacks on Bara Kalra. Sikh casualties have been estimated at 2,000 killed, wounded and captured. They lost 56 guns. General Gilbert, with a force of infantry, cavalry and guns took up the pursuit the next day, marching fifty miles to the north in three days, halting for three days, and then resuming the advance. On 14TH March, the Attariwala Sardars surrendered their swords to General Gilbert. The Punjab was annexed to the British dominions. Chatar Singh and his sons, Raja Sher Singh and Avtar Singh, were detained by the British in their village. Atari, and then imprisoned at Allahabad from where they were removed to Fort William at Calcutta to prevent them from establishing contact with the exiled Queen Mother, Maharani Jind Kaur. They were released in January 1854. Chatar Singh died in Calcutta on 27 December 1855, and Raja Sher Singh died at Banaras in 1858. "Observers who watched the surrender greatly admired the bearing of the Sikh soldiers, who still carried themselves with pride. They were tired and hungry, but their spirit was in no means broken. It was noticed that many of the older men threw down their Tulwars with a gesture of disgust. The Punjab was annexed to British India and Maharajah Dalip Singh pensioned off to England.

Second Anglo-Sikh War

General Ilahi Bakhsh 1849
Ilahi Bakhsh defected to the British and gave the British valuable information about the Sikh army. The defection of Bakhsh dealt a major blow to the Sikhs, and they capitulated to the British the following month at Gujrat.

Sikander Khan 1849
One of sons of General Illahi Baksh, Sikander Khan succeeded his father as Chief of the Artillery in the Sikh Army and later inherited substantial properties in Lahore.

Bakhshan Khan 1849
When Major Edwards marched to Dera Ghazi Khan in 1848, Sirdar Bijar Khan sent his cousin Bakhshan Khan, with one hundred men to join him. They were present throughout the Siege of Multan and at the conclusion of the Second Anglo-Sikh war, their leader was presented with a pair of gold bracelets and a Khilat.

Chaudhri Sher 1849
A principal family of Alpials is that of the Choudhris of Chakri, and Chaudhri Sher Khan was head. Sher Khan was conspicuous for his support of the British. After the battle of Gujrat, on 21ST February 1849, Captain Nicholson, on his return to the Sindh Sagar Doab, entrusted several duties to him and found him very useful. At the conclusion of Anglo- Sikh wars and at annexation of the Punjab to British India, he was rewarded by the grant of pension and the rent free lands, which he held under the Sikhs, were continued to him and his nephews.

Fazl Dad Khan 1849
The Gakhars tribe is strongly represented in Jhelum by the Askanderal branches, including the houses of Lahir and Bakala and of Domeli or Rohtas; also the Bhagial branch, which has ramified into eight sections scattered over Jhelum Tehsil. The most noteworthy family is that of the Domeli Rajas, headed by Muhammad Khan who joined Nicolson, and did good service receiving a Jagir of the value of one thousand rupees. His nephew Fazl Dad Khan accompanied Raja Sher Singh to Multan in 1848 and joined with him in the rebellion. He had been released from prison by Sir Henry Lawrence shortly before, but still did not prevent him from intriguing against the English. He was employed as the confidential agent between Raja Sher Singh and Maharajah Gulab Singh. His Jagir was resumed for his treacherous conduct; but he was allowed to receive a subsistence allowance.

Second Anglo-Sikh War

Annexation of the Punjab

Proclamation declaring that the kingdom of the Punjab had ceased to be and that all the territories of Maharajah Duleep Singh had become part of the British dominions in India was issued on 29 March 1849 by Governor General Lord Dalhousie. Earlier in the day a Durbar was held in the palace inside the Fort at Lahore by Henry M. Elliot, the foreign secretary, under the orders of the Governor General. It was attended by the minor Maharajah Duleep Singh, seated for the last time on the throne of his father, Maharajah Ranjit Singh, surrounded by the British troops and his helpless Sardars. Amidst deep silence, the proclamation was read out aloud in English, Persian and Hindustani. In the equally deep silence which followed, a paper was handed over by Raja Tej Singh to the Maharajah containing the conditions on which he and his chiefs might assure themselves of generous treatment at the hands of their conquerors. The young Duleep Singh affixed his signatures to the document which deprived him of his crown and kingdom. Immediately after the document granting terms to Maharajah Duleep Singh had been signed, Elliot read out in the Darbadur the Proclamation issued by Lord Dalhousie to justify his policy and action. It was a most artful statement which, inter alia, said that whereas the British had faithfully kept their word and had scrupulously observed every obligation under the treaties made with the Sikhs, the latter had, on their part, grossly and faithlessly violated the agreements. The claim of Lord Dalhousie and his accusations against the Sikh government were not sustainable factually. There was severe criticism in both India and England of his action. Even the British resident at Lahore, Sir Henry Lawrence, described the annexation of the Punjab and the deposition of young Maharajah Duleep Singh as unjust and impolitic. John Sullivan, a member of the Madras Council commenting on the whole transaction in his Are We Bound by Our Treaties, said: This is perhaps the first instance on record in which a guardian has visited his own misdeeds upon his ward. The British Government was the self constituted guardian of the Rajah (Maharajah Duleep Singh), and the regent of his kingdom: a rebellion was provoked by the agents of the guardian; it was acknowledged by the guardian to be a rebellion against the government of his ward, and the guardian punished that Ward by confiscating his dominions.

Annexation of the Punjab 1849

The British governor general, which finally put an end to the sovereignty of the Sikhs over and Maharajah Dalip Singh, was pensioned off to England.

Second Anglo-Sikh War

Haji Khan Mirani 1849

Haji Khan Mirani fought under Major Edwards during the siege of Multan, on the eve of the Second Anglo-Sikh War.

Mustafa Khan

Mustafa Khan commenced his career in Bahawalpur State; he soon became the Sikh governor. On Mal Raj's rebellion, he was successful in bringing over many Multani Pathans to the British side. For his services he received grants of land and a Jagir and the title of Khan Bahadur.

Sher Singh Attariwala 1849

Sher Singh Attariwala provincial governor under Maharajah Duleep Singh of Lahore, was the son of Chatar Singh Attariwala. He was appointed governor of Peshawar in October 1845, and recalled in August 1846 to Lahore where he was nominated a member of the Council of Regency. He was created Raja in November 1847. In April 1848, Raja Sher Singh commanded the Lahore Durbar troops sent out to Multan by the British Resident to quell the rebellion by Diwan Mul Raj. But on hearing of the humiliation his father, Chatar Singh, who was governor of Hazara, had suffered at the hands of Captain James Abbott, the Assistant Resident; Sher Singh left the British camp and went over to Mul Raj along with the Durbar troops. He moved northwards to join his father, Chatar Singh, at Hazara. Sher Singh`s action set into motion a chain of events which set the whole of the Punjab ablaze. He proclaimed himself a Servant of the Khalsa and that of the sovereign, and called upon the people to rise in arms and expel the British from their country. General Sher Singh gave a devastating blow to the British Army at Chillianwalla. Under his command the Sikh Khalsa Army managed to successfully defend its position against a British army at the Battle of Chillianwalla. Both armies retreated after the battle, with both sides claiming victory, although it became clear after the rains subsided that the Sikhs had defeated the British. It was one of the hardest fought battles in the British Army's history. Within the British Army, such was the consternation over the events at Chillianwalla h that, after the disastrous Charge of the Light Brigade, when Lord Lucan remarked *"This is a most serious matter"*, General Airey replied, *"It is nothing to Chillianwalla."* With the establishment of British control, Sher Singh Attariwala was forced into exile from Punjab. The British feared that such a powerful leader could reignite a full-scale war with them. Sher Singh died in exile, at Benares in 1858, away from his Punjabi homeland.

Second Anglo-Sikh War

General Chatar Singh Attariwala 1849

Chatar Singh Attariwala, commander and provincial governor under minor Maharajah Duleep Singh. On the death of his father in that year, Chatar Singh succeeded to the jagirs, then amounting to over a lakh of rupees annually. He devoted most of his time to farming and kept generally aloof from state affairs during the reign of Maharajah Ranjit Singh. His daughter, Tej Kaur, was betrothed to Maharajah Duleep Singh. He was appointed governor of Peshawar in August 1846. Chatar Singh was then transferred to Hazara, where as the governor of the province he came into conflict with the overbearing Assistant British Resident, Captain James Abbott, his assistant and adviser for the demarcation of boundary between the Punjab and Kashmir which had been given away by the British to the Dogra Raja Gulab Singh for his services to them during the first Anglo Sikh war. Since the Multan outbreak in April 1848, James Abbott had been continually reporting to the Resident at Lahore that discontent prevailed among the Sikh troops stationed at Hazara; in September 1848, he alleged that a conspiracy was being hatched by Chatar Singh, its Sikh governor, to subvert British power in the Punjab. He charged him with high treason, and leading the local chiefs and large numbers of Muslim levies he had raised he marched on Haripur to expel the Sikh governor. At this juncture Commodore Canora, an artillery officer in the Fort, who was in secret communication with Captain Abbott, refused to move his battery, and was consequently shot down at Chatar Singh's orders. Under the orders of the British Resident at Lahore this Hazara incident was investigated by Captain Nicholson who in his enquiry report not only exonerated Chatar Singh, but also justified the defensive measures he had taken to save the besieged capital of Hazara from Abbott's Muhammadan mercenaries. Resident Frederick Currie, notwithstanding Nicholson's report, issued orders which amounted to Chatar Singh's virtual dismissal and the confiscation of his jagirs which drove him to open defiance. The Hazara revolt now escalated into hostilities between the British and the Sikhs. After their defeat at Gujrat on 21ST February 1849, Chatar Singh and his sons, Raja Sher Singh and Avtar Singh, were detained by the British in their village. Atari, and then imprisoned at Allahabad from where they were removed to Fort William at Calcutta to prevent them from establishing contact with the exiled Queen Mother, Maharani Jind Kaur. They were released in January 1854. Chatar Singh died in Calcutta on 27TH December 1855.

Second Anglo-Sikh War

Langar Khan 1849
Langar Khan was stationed at Pind Dadan Khan, and at the close of 1847, was sent under Lieutenant Edwards to Bannu. In 1848, he did good service against Bhai Maharaj Singh. For three days and nights from Jandiala to Jhang, Langar Khan with other Muhammadan chiefs, hang on his tracks till being joined by the fresh troops, and they drove the rebel force into the swollen Chenab. Two months afterwards he joined General Whish's camp at Sardar pur, and served during the whole siege of Multan with great credit. On the end of the Anglo-Sikh wars, his personal Jagirs were released in perpetuity, and the pension granted him was resumed at his death.

Fateh Khan Tiwana 1849
In 1846 he was attacked by Daulat Rai and forced to retire to Mitha Tiwana. In the summer of 1846 he was sent to Kashmir in a bid to influence his friend, the rebel governor Imamuddin Khan. Having achieved his mission with success, he later accompanied Major Henry Lawrence to Kashmir. On his return to Lahore he was held to account for financial irregularities in his former government. He was ordered to pay four lakh rupees, and on pleading impecunity, he was held under house arrest by Lawrence. He was then imprisoned at Gobindgarh fort along with his son Fatah Sher Khan. At the start of the Second Anglo-Sikh War, Lieutenant Edwards recommended he be installed as the Governor of Bannu. A Sikh force brought him to bay in the fort of Dalipgarh where he was killed in action.

Bahawal Khan 1849
In 1848 he once more rendered valuable assistance in connection with the Multan Rebellion, which led to the Second Anglo-Sikh War. His army, cop-operating with the Irregular Levies under Lieutenant Edwards, defeated the troops of Mul Raj and hemmed the rebels inside the walls of Multan until the arrival British under General Whish. These services secured him a reward in life pension and in addition a lump sum for the services of his troops.

Mian Khima 1849
Mian Khima, Maharajah Duleep Singh's favourite Muhammadan attendant who had served him since his childhood. He came with the Maharajah to Fatehgarh after the latter was dethroned and exiled from Lahore by the British in 1849.

Second Anglo-Sikh War

Muhammad Ismail Khan 1849
At the conclusion of the first Anglo-Sikh war, in October 1848, Lieutenant Edwards wrote to Muhammad Ismail Khan directing him to raise troops in behalf of the government and collect the revenue of the district. He raised a force and descending the river, attacked and defeated a rebel chief Atta Muhammad, at Nikorara. Afterwards when Sardar Sher Singh Attariwala had passed through Jhang, and had left Des Raj in command of one thousand men there, Muhammad Ismail Khan attacked this detachment several times with varying results. His Jemadar, Pir Kamal of Isa Shah captured at the fort of Taruka another rebel chief. Thus Muhammad Ismail Khan, representative of a long and illustrious line of chiefs, stood out bravely on the side of the government. After the conclusion of Anglo-Sikh war and the annexation of the Punjab to British India, Muhammad Ismail Khan was made Risaldar of the Jhang Mounted Police.

Assad Khan 1849
On the eve of the Second Anglo-Sikh war, when the Multan war broke out, Assad Khan entered into negotians with Lieutenant Edwards, but declared he could not join him, as this would imperil the safety of his family who were at Multan. At that time Haji Muhammad Massu Khan had joined Lieutenant Edwards, and his brother Muhammad Khan was in consequence treacherously killed by the Sikhs at Harand. Later on Assad Khan joined the army of the Nawab of Bahawalpur, then advancing against Mul Raj. After the war he remained with the Nawab, whom he was related by marriage, receiving a pension from the revenues of Bahawalpur.

Khan Muhammad Hayat Khan 1849
In 1848 he raised a force of horse and foot, which Captain Nicholson employed in holding the Margala Pass. His house at Wah was burnt down by the Sikh force under the command of Attar Singh, and he was shortly afterwards killed Fateh Khan, his own brother, who surprised him when taking his noonday siesta in a garden. His son Muhammad Hayat Khan joined Captain Abbot at Nars with a few recruits, and remained with that officer till the close of the Anglo-Sikh wars.

Commandant Muhammad Shah 1849
Muhammad Shah son of Iman Shah, was made a Commandant of Artillery, when eighteen years of age. He fought in the Satluj campaign, and under the Durbar was successively posted at Pind Dadan Khan, Hasan Abdal and Hazara. At the conclusion of the Second Anglo-Sikh in 1849, when the 5TH Punjab Cavalry was first raised Muhammad Shah was appointed to it.

Second Anglo-Sikh War

Khuda Baksh 1849
Khuda Baksh served under the Maharajah Ranjit Singh in all his chief campaigns, Kasur, Multan, Mankera, Kashmir, and Peshawar, and was distinguished for his gallantry. He was several times wounded; and at the battle of Teri, when badly hurt himself, he cut the head of an Afghan with a single blow. The family had a quarrel with Sardar Wasakha Singh, the Kardar of Kadianbad, and their Jagirs with the exception of Kot Jan Baksh, Gajar Gola and two other villages were resumed. They were pensioned off. During the Anglo-Sikh war of 1848, Khuda Baksh remained loyal to the Sikh cause. On the annexation of the Punjab by the British, Gajar Gola was released for the life of Khuda Baksh.

Commandant Sultan Muhammad 1849
On the conclusion of the First Anglo-Sikh war, Lahore Durbar had to part with a large number of guns. It was a pathetic scene at Lahore when the guns were being handed over to the British, 'when gun after gun,' writes an eyewitness, "was being delivered up, the sight was too much for Sultan Mahmood (Sultan Muhammad), the commandant of Artillery. He Shed tears of pity and chagrin, deploring at his downfall. After this, Sultan, Muhammad Khan was sent to Hazara where he remained until 1848, when he along with his son was sent to Derajat. During the Second Anglo-Sikh war, Sultan Muhammad Khan and his son both had fought against the British with the same zeal. The result was that on the conclusion of the second war, both the father and son were removed from the service and all their jagirs were resumed. Sultan Muhammad was given a life pension

Jamaluddin Khan 1849
In 1844 Jamaluddin Khan was fined for the murder of Suba Rai, the Lahore news-writer at his court, who had rendered himself obnoxious to the chief by giving information of the disorder committed in the district. In 1845, before Satluj Campaign, Jamaluddin Khan that if he stood on British side, his possessions would be confirmed to him; yet at the battles of Mudki and Ferozeshah he fought against the British, and in the later battle his cousin Fateh Din Khan was killed. Only towards end of the campaign, where he perceived where the victory would eventually be, he did turn and render some trifling assistance to General Sir John Littler, when the general was threatened by the Sikh Army at Ferozepore. This induced the British government to grant him sovereign powers and to and confirm in his possessions. In 1848 his contingent under his brother Jalaluddin behaved well at Multan and Jamaluddin Khan was granted the title Nawab. He then settled at Macchiwara in the Ferozepore district.

Post-Maharajah Ranjit Singh Period

B Robina Shoeb, Anum Iftikhar and Muhammad Hameed

On his death in 1839, Maharajah Ranjit Singh passed on to his successors a prosperous, peaceful and tolerant Punjab. For 40 years he had ruled the Punjab with a balance of ambition and patience. His ambition expanded the Khalsa Empire from Dera Ghazi Khan to Peshawar and Kashmir and his patience won him the support of the Akali warriors. His foresight kept the British away from the Punjab and his fair conduct earned him the allegiance and loyalty of the Muslim majority in the Punjab. Despite the intricate socio-political history of the two communities, he skilfully handled the relationship between Sikhs and Muslims. He made mistakes, at times bad ones, but he corrected most and learned from them. Yet within a few years of his death, all the hard-earned and cherished victories of the 'Lion of the Punjab' were wasted by his unscrupulous successors, and subsequently the Sikh kingdom fell to the British. In contrast to the reflections of many historians, the present author maintains that the Sikh monarchy founded by Ranjit Singh was 'Napoleonic in the suddenness of its rise, the brilliancy of its success and the completeness of its overthrow'. Numerous factors were responsible for the decline of the Sikh rule in the Punjab. However, the present author identifies three key reasons. First is the disputed succession of Kharak Singh to the throne, which was not accepted or supported by many, including his own wife and son. In fact, Ranjit Singh himself seems to be mainly responsible for this uncertainty around the succession. Despite his being the eldest son, the obvious succession of Kanwar (Prince) Kharak Singh was not formally announced until the Maharajah was on his deathbed. This ambiguity and uncertainty encouraged the ambitions of the Prince's rivals, and Kharak Singh faced serious opposition and intrigues on his accession. From the first day, the Dogra brothers and his own son Naunihal Singh were conspiring against him and weakening his rule. Moreover, Ranjit Singh had done little to train the Prince to run the Khalsa state after his death. Making no significant contribution to the strengthening of the Sikh kingdom, Kharak Singh was no match for the political and administrative wisdom and even physical strength of his father, his rival Sher Singh, his brother or Naunihal Singh, his son. In short, the selection of Kharak Singh as ruler of the Punjab was not a wise decision. The second reason flowed from the first. The dispute around the succession weakened the Sikh hold on the state and resurrected a deeper political issue, the old antagonism between various courtiers, chieftains and families, mainly Sikhs and Hindus who were holding important positions in the kingdom.

Post-Maharajah Ranjit Singh Period (Contd)

The weakening of state authority also gave birth to the third key reason for the fall of the Sikh kingdom: the rise of the army as a major political player in the state. As the intrigues and disputes among various groups intensified, the significance of the army rapidly grew. Every group wished to have the army on its side against the rival group, and consequently the army assumed a pivotal role in deciding both the succession and the fate of the kingdom. This antagonism not only politicized the institution of the army but also badly weakened it. An army, which had been formidable, and a source of pride and strength became a saleable commodity as its members fought only for those who could pay them. This situation hastened the fall of the Sikh Empire. Maharajah Ranjit Singh had delegated power to Muslims, Hindus and Sikhs to discharge state functions; Dhian Singh Dogra led the Hindu group, and the Faqir Brothers the Muslim group. He did not enforce the Khalsa code of conduct on anyone. Dhian Singh Dogra, who was actually a Hindu, was made prime minister of the Khalsa state, and his whole family was eventually involved in state administration. The Faqir Brothers and other Muslims held portfolios of foreign and internal affairs, medicine, science and the army under the Sarkar Khalsa. The Sikh group comprised nobles from all over the Punjab, such as Dhana Singh Malwai, the Majithia brothers, the Sandhawalia brothers, Ahluwalias, Ramgarhias, the Virks of Sheikhupura, and the Bajwas of Narowal. This group was mostly involved in the defence of the state. Sikhs dominated the cavalry, but the artillery was under the command of the Muslims. Ranjit Singh had kept a fine balance among all three groups. His rewards, privileges and promotions were meant only for capable and loyal people; religion, communal or familial affiliations were hardly considered. After the death of Ranjit Singh the Council of Ministers and the nobility of the Durbar were also divided. The Dogra group included Gulab Singh, Dhian Singh, Suchet Singh and Dhian Singh's son Hira Singh, who was a favourite of the Maharajah Ranjit Singh. The other group included the Sikh Sardars Sandhawalia, Attariwala and Majithia. There was another group, not allied to any other, who did not take any part in of the intrigues of the Durbar. The Faqir Brothers were the most prominent among them. They continued their service to the Lahore Durbar as advisors on various matters, especially foreign affairs and medicine. The brothers' influence continued during the reigns of Kharak Singh and Naunihal Singh. Dhian Singh respected them and always consulted them on important state matters. Maharajah Sher Singh assigned Faqir Azizuddin to get help from the British in handling the Sikh army.

Post-Maharajah Ranjit Singh Period (Contd)

Following the death of Sher Singh, Faqir Azizuddin stopped taking an active part in the politics of the Punjab, due largely to his poor health. His eldest son, Faqir Shahdin, worked as Wakil (ambassador) in Firozepur until his death in 1842. Faqir Chiraghdin, another son, replaced his brother in the post and continued even during the British period. Faqir Azizuddin's brother, Faqir Imamuddin, was governor of the fort of Gobindgarh. He continued as such until his death in 1844. His son Tajuddin replaced him as governor of Gobindgarh and continued until his death in 1846.8 Faqir Nuruddin, the third brother, was also a trusted courtier of the Lahore Durbar. Understanding the significance of the British power, he and Faqir Azizuddin always strove to maintain amiable relations between the British and the Sikh Empire. The Sikh army respected him greatly, and when Rani Jindan sent him with Diwan Dina Nath and Sardar Attar Singh to negotiate with the army, he was the only one who the army did not insult. He was also an important member of the council established to administer the Punjab under the regency of Maharajah Dalip Singh in 1846. He was a wise person and worked for the welfare of the state. His son, Faqir Zahiruddin, was the teacher of Dalip Singh. Similarly the Jagirdar of Mamdot, Jamaluddin Khan, who hailed from the ruling family of Kasur, fought for the Sikhs against the British during the war of Mudki. The British approached him to help them against the Sikh army and also promised to reward him well, but he refused. His cousin Fatah-ud-Din also fought for the Sikhs and gave his life. The continuing service of the Faqir Brothers as ministers and governors confirms that, even after the death of Ranjit Singh, Sikh rule remained benevolent and fair to the Muslims and minority groups. They always received due respect in the Lahore Durbar. Even the unruly army had great respect for these nobles; indeed, Dhian Singh undertook special measures to strengthen and protect the Muslim contingent. After the demise of Ranjit Singh, there is virtually no significant evidence to prove maltreatment of any Muslim contingent in the Sikh army. Earlier, Maharajah Ranjit Singh had ensured that the army had no role in the state administration. During his lifetime, the British did not dare to confront the Sikhs, and he closely watched the British military developments and engaged European generals to train his army to take on the British. After his death, the civil and military administration deteriorated and the local governors became uncontrollable. They stopped paying revenue and taxes to the Lahore Durbar and hence the state ran short of resources. As a result, it failed to pay the soldiers for their services; some units were not paid for more than two years.

Post-Maharajah Ranjit Singh Period (Contd)

Therefore, the military started looking for other avenues of livelihood to support their families, and the practice of plundering, looting and working for others gradually crept into the army. This turned the army into a tool with which to mollify opponents, making it a powerful force and an important player in struggles for the throne. The non-payment of taxes by various states meant that even the Jagirdari troops were not being paid on a regular basis. During Sher Singh's rule the army set up Panchayats on the pattern of traditional village councils. These Panchayats had direct access to the Maharajah for addressing their concerns. They were also used to penalize officers who were no longer favourites of the Durbar who had lost influence with the army. During this time, recruitment to the army was also politicized. Troops were frequently recruited without the permission of the Durbar during 1839-46. The Dogras, for instance, strengthened Rajput and Muslim contingents, and as a counter-move the anti-Dogra group bolstered contingents of Sikh Jats.15 As a result, the kingdom turned into a military state, something totally unknown during the days of Ranjit Singh. The army had consumed roughly 41 % of the state revenue during the late 1830s when its total strength was around 80,000. However, with the increase in numbers, expenses also increased.16 By 1844 the army was 123,800 strong, consuming two-thirds of the state revenues.17 Ironically, the biggest threat to the state came from none other than its own army, which was supposed to defend it. The rule of Sher Singh was marked by violence and chaos. With the Sandhawalia clan as contenders to the throne, the army became uncontrollable.18 In order to calm them down; Sher Singh raised the soldiers' pay and also allowed them to recruit their relatives to the army. As described earlier, due to this unruly behaviour, Rani Jindan and others decided to bring the Sikh army to face the British forces. Ultimately, the intrigues of the Dogra brothers, vested interests and the inability of the Sikh rulers precipitated the fall of Maharajah Ranjit Singh's Khalsa Sarkar. The result of these devastating developments all across the Punjab was disintegration of the Khalsa state, and establishment of a Hindu state in Multan, a Dogra state in Jammu and an independent trans-Indus frontier with a very small Sikh state in the centre. However, well before the final internal disintegration, war with the British changed the whole scenario in the Punjab. Although completely contained during the rule of Ranjit Singh, the British began planning to take over the Punjab after his death. Incapable Sikh rulers, treacherous Sardars and the weakened Khalsa Sarkar helped the British to accomplish this very easily.

Post-Maharajah Ranjit Singh Period (Contd)

Wider geopolitical developments also played an important role in the downfall of the Sikh government in the Punjab, further helping the British takeover. Although the British failed to install Shah Shuja in Kabul, the Afghans were too engrossed in their internal affairs and were confined to the Khyber Pass. With the takeover of Sindh in 1843, the British found the perfect opportunity to take over the Sikh state and complete their conquest of the subcontinent. The instability of the Lahore Durbar and the anti-British viewpoint of the Khalsa Sarkar provided this opportunity. In 1844, a veteran of the Peninsular Wars against Napoleon, Henry Harding, was appointed Governor General of India. He was known to have a determined personality, although initially he showed some hesitation in taking on the Sikhs. However, after the assassination of Hira Singh, he decided to confront the Sikh state as he believed that it now had no chance of revival. He also connived with Gulab Singh, who promised not to support the Khalsa Sarkar and instead to help the British if needed. Gulab Singh, once a trusted general and ally of Maharajah Ranjit Singh, now stood against the Khalsa state, using the wealth he had looted from Lahore during the anarchy of Sher Singh's rule. While he assured the Lahore Durbar of his full support, he secretly connived with the British for the fall of the Sikh government in the Punjab. He had his own plans to expand his territory to Tibet. The first Anglo-Sikh War opened with the Battle of Mudki in December 1845. The battle revealed that despite the reputed degeneration of the Khalsa, once in battle, they were still formidable, and the British had to fight hard for victory. In subsequent battles at Aliwal (January) and Sabraon (February), the Sikhs lost their critical advantage in artillery, as successive defeats saw most of their cannons fall into British hands. Meanwhile, the British plotting at the Durbar bore fruit. At Sabraon, Tej Singh, who was now secretly corresponding with Harding, was informed of a surprise British attack at dawn. Fleeing his camp, he destroyed the bridge over the Sutlej, leaving his men trapped between the British and the river. In the ensuing battle, 10,000 Sikhs were cut to pieces. Britain and the Company had won the war. The decade from 1839 to 1849 was an eventful period. Many intrigues and conspiracies, alliances and confrontations were made and unmade. However, the picture of the socio-economic, cultural and religious landscape during all these years remains obscure, and information sparse, due largely to preoccupation with the political turmoil. The gazetteers, archives and reports focus on the political and military developments of the Punjab.

Post-Maharajah Ranjit Singh Period (Contd)

However, a broad perspective can be taken from the available evidence. As might be expected, the tumultuous events in the capital had a profound impact on the stability and prosperity of the countryside. After 1839 the authority of the Durbar in the countryside, and particularly at the periphery of the kingdom, underwent a sharp decline. In 1839 minor insurrections broke out in the tributary Rajput states of the lower Himalayas and in the vicinity of Tank on the far side of the Indus. The Kardar took advantage of the political instability throughout the kingdom to extend their own power and wealth. They did this in a number of ways. First, and most obviously, many of them simply fell behind in their revenue remittances and waited until the Durbar threatened them with punishment before sending any instalments to Lahore. As early as August 1843, during the reign of Sher Singh, the annual loss to the state from districts under Durbar-appointed Kardar was reported to be in the vicinity of Rs.20 lakh. In some cases the Kardar bribed members of the Panchayats, the village council, to support his illegal demands from the Zamindars. In other cases he enlisted the support of local notables, religious leaders in particular, by alienating in their favour the greater portion of inams (gifts) that were normally reserved for Zamindars. Generally, the Kardar got away with these illegitimate demands because the central administration's auditing of district accounts had become defective. Most Kardars maintained false records, or no records at all, and patwari (revenue official) establishments were often permitted to run down. In the early 1840s, Diwan Swan Mal, for example, had strengthened his fort and built up his own troops at Multan with a view to declaring his independence from Lahore should a suitable opportunity present itself. With this in mind he had placed a number of his own relatives into administrative offices in and adjacent to Multan. In September 1844, however, a soldier assassinated him. His son, Diwan Mul Raj, took over as nazim. The Durbar demanded of Mul Raj a nazarana of Rs.10 million for the acknowledgement of his succession. At this time the two Sikh battalions stationed at Multan by the Durbar were mutinying, demanding higher pay. Mulraj's followers attacked the mutineers and totally dispersed them. This victory so baffled the Durbar and strengthened Mulraj's position that the new nazim was actually able to negotiate the payment of a much smaller nazarana: after a period of intense bargaining the Durbar accepted Mulraj's offer of Rs.18 lakh, <one-fifth of its original demand. The rise of the Sikh Empire was so quick and dramatic that historians often likened Ranjit Singh to Napoleon due to his extraordinary military astuteness and enigmatic leadership.

Post-Maharajah Ranjit Singh Period (Contd)

However, this comparison does not fully portray his personality. Maharajah Ranjit Singh was a vigilant warrior with a deep insight into martial matters. He would never antagonize an enemy who he thought would be difficult to defeat. He built a great army out of a crowd of undisciplined and unruly Sikh groups. Although he was brutal in battle, he was very peaceful and fair in dealing with and governing his heterogeneous and multi-religious subjects. His successors lacked his prudence and foresight and hence lost everything. They ruined the Khalsa state, which Ranjit Singh had built with great care and hard work. After his death, Sikh rulers were more occupied in conspiring and killing each other than strengthening or consolidating the Sikh Empire. Their energies were drained by their internal disputes and fighting for the throne. Consequently the Sikh state came to an unfortunate and abrupt end at the hands of the British. Nevertheless, Maharajah Ranjit Singh can also be held responsible for this downfall, in not leaving a succession plan and not training potential successors in the art of running the state and army. His failure to do so resulted in incapable rulers and hence the end of Khalsa rules in the Punjab. However, despite all the chaos and anarchy, his successors did maintain the path of fair and benevolent treatment of the non-Sikh communities, including Muslims. Religion and ethnic origin had never set the course of state policies during the days of Ranjit Singh and this continued after his death, throughout the period 1839-49. All the Muslim nobles continued to enjoy their positions and privileges in the Lahore Durbar during this time, and even the unruly army had great regard for most of the Muslim notables, especially the Faqir Brothers.

Faqir Azizuddin

Appendix

The Faqir Family

The role of the Faqir family in the politics of Punjab before the British conquered it is an outstanding example of competence and honesty at its pinnacle. It can be said with considerable surety that since then no family of Punjab has excelled the Faqir family i service to their land. But there is much more to the legend of the three brothers. The three famous Faqir Brothers were Faqir Azizuddin, the foreign minister of the Lahore Durbar, Faqir Nuruddin, the home minister and Faqir Imamuddin, the minister in-charge of the arsenals of the Khalsa Army. Our interest in this piece centres on Faqir Azizuddin, the foreign minister. Faqir Azizuddin was a physician and an outstanding diplomat at the court of Maharajah Ranjit Singh. He was the eldest son of Ghulam Mohyuddin, a leading physician of Lahore who lived in Bazaar Hakeeman – the streets of physicians. His two brothers, Nuruddin controlled the city of Lahore and had been Governor of Gujrat, and Imamuddin was the garrison commander of the Fort of Gobindgarh. The Faqir family claim to be Ansari Arab immigrants from Bukhara, in Central Asia, who settled in Lahore as hakims. The Persian for a mendicant or 'Faqir' was thereafter used by Azizuddin as a mark of humility. In 1799 when Maharajah Ranjit Singh was treated by Azizuddin, he so impressed by his intelligence and skill, that he was appointed personal physician to the Maharajah and assigned a Jagir. Once the Sikh ruler got to see State papers, which were all in Persian, he sought the assistance of Azizuddin. Soon he was also entrusted with drafting official State papers in the Persian language. This brought him still closer to the Maharajah who developed great confidence in him for his ability to correctly interpret his policy. Faqir Azizuddin's first major diplomatic assignment was to look after Charles Metcalfe, the British representative, and to assist in the Maharajah's negotiations with him which culminated in the Treaty of Amritsar (1809). He held negotiations on behalf of the Sikh ruler with David Ochterlony in 1810. Soon the British realised that they were facing a man who could fluently speak seven languages, including English and French. In 1813, he was deputed to settle the dependencies of 'the country of Attock'. With immense skill he negotiated the transfer to the Sikhs of Attock Fort, and in return the Afghan governor Jahan Dad Khan accepted a Jagir. Throughout Maharajah Ranjit Singh's reign, Faqir Azizuddin remained almost solely responsible for the foreign relations of the Sikh kingdom. In 1815, he held tricky negotiations with the rulers of Mandi and Rajouri, and later on with the Nawab of Bahawalpur.

Appendix

The Faqir Family (Contd)

In 1823, he was sent to Peshawar to realise tribute from Yar Muhammad Khan Barakzai. After the death of Raja Sansar Chand of Kangra in 1824, his son, Anirodh Chand, defaulted on payment of 'nazarana' to the Maharajah. It was Azizuddin who went to Nadaun and got him to pay homage to the Maharajah and got his succession recognised. In 1827, he travelled to Simla with a goodwill mission to call on Lord Amherst, the British Governor-General. Again in April 1831, another delegation from the powerful Lahore Durbar met Lord William Bentinck. The team was led by the powerful Sikh general Sardar Hari Singh Nalwa, who had royal instruction to rely on the advice of Azizuddin the 'Faqir'. This meeting led to a meeting between Maharajah Ranjit Singh and Lord William Bentinck in October 1831. Faqir Azizuddin, through Captain Wade, acted as interpreter between the two chiefs. He conducted negotiations that led to the signing of the Tripartite Treaty of 1838 aimed at installing Shah Shuja on the throne of Kabul. Seven years later he again acted as interpreter when the Maharajah met Lord Auckland. Many experts feel that this move by Azizuddin prolonged the life of the Khalsa State. Faqir Azizuddin has been described in British intelligence reports as "the oracle of the Maharajah", and at one place is even termed as "his master's mouthpiece".

The British always met their match when it came to penning legal documents of State. His grasp of Arabic, Persian, English and French made him among the "the most eloquent man of his day". When Maharajah Ranjit Singh died in 1839, the Faqir family withdrew from the frontline of court affairs. However, he continued in the service of the Sikh State. He represented Maharajah Kharrak Singh on a complimentary mission to Lord Auckland at Simla in December 1839, and met Lord Ellenborough at Firozepur in December 1842, under Maharajah Sher Singh's instruction. But by then the affairs of the Sikh State had become very complex and he remained scrupulously aloof from factional intrigues. The turn of events and the death of two of his sons had a dramatic effect on Faqir Azizuddin, who died in Lahore on Dec 3, 1845 at the age of 65.

Today the Faqir family no longer lives in their ancestral house inside Bhati gate. The family has grown in size and spread out. However, their house is now a museum, one every person interested in Lahore should visit. Its exhibits are among the very finest in Lahore and they can be reached through an internet website one member of the family has created. They remain, undoubtedly, among the finest old family of Lahore.

Appendix

Sayad Ghulam Mohyuddin

Ghulam Mohyuddin was born at Rahila on the river Beas. When he was three months old his father Ghulam Shah died, and his widowed mother left in great poverty, came to Lahore to seek help from her husband's friends. Abdullah Ansari a well known physician of Lahore, who had been a Judge in Kashmir early in the reign of Ahmad Shah, took pity upon her and supported both her and her son. He gave Ghulam Mohyuddin a good education; and when the boy had grown up, married his niece, daughter of his brother Khuda Baksh. Ghulam Mohyuddin became a physician and bookseller and pursuit of his trade travelled over a large portion of the Punjab. He became a disciple of Faqir Amanat Shah Kadri, and himself assumed the title Faqir. Faqir Ghulam Mohyuddin left three sons, Azizuddin, Imamuddin, and Nuruddin. Of these Azizuddin the eldest son, was placed him in attendance on Maharajah Ranjit Singh, when soon after capture of Lahore in 1799, was suffering from a severe affection of the eyes. The skill and attention of the young doctor won the Maharajah's regard, and him his own physician.

Faqir Azizuddin

Faqir, Persian for a mendicant or dervish, was adopted by Azizuddin as a mark of simplicity and humility. Faqir Azizuddin, who was as gifted a linguist and scribe as he was a skilled hakim. He had learned his alchemy as a pupil of the Lala Hakim Rai of Lahore and through his mentor came to the attention of the ruler of Lahore whose precious single eye he was able to cure of a threatening infection. Gradually, the dependence of the Sikh ruler on his Muslim physician deepened into trust, and Azizuddin found himself executing assignments on behalf of the Maharajah of increasing complexity and sensitivity. As the Maharajah's 'parrot of sweet sound', Azizuddin not only articulated the opinions of the ruler of Lahore but within the privacy of the court helped significantly, through his sagacious and reasoned advice, to calibrate the fledgling state's foreign policy, ensuring a pragmatic balance between the Maharajah's instinctive urges to expand the frontiers of his growing kingdom and the ambitions of his covetous neighbours. In the year 1808, when Mr. Charles Metcalfe, the British Envoy, was sent to Lahore to draw up an agreement by which Maharajah Ranjit Singh should to be confined to the north of the Satluj, and in 1809, when the British troops moved up to that river, Maharajah Ranjit Singh, supported by his Sardars, had almost determined on the war with the British; but Faqir Azizuddin strongly dissuaded him from such a course, and his wiser consuls at last prevailed. Consequently it led to the Anglo-Sikh treaty of 1809.

Appendix

Faqir Azizuddin (Contd)

Maharajah Ranjit Singh, appreciating the far-sightedness and wisdom of Faqir Azizuddin consulted him on all occasions; and from this time to the end of his reign never undertook any important operation against his advice. In all matters connected with the Europeans and the English government, Faqir Azizuddin was especially employed; and to the Faqir Azizuddin's enlightened and liberal counsels it may be attributed that throughout his long reign the Maharajah maintained such a close friendship with the British government. Faqir Azizuddin's main contribution to Maharajah Ranjit Singh's success as an independent sovereign of the Punjab lay in the consummate skill with which he conducted negotiations with potential adversaries, more particularly the British, in the east across the Sutlej, who envied the Maharajah's glittering court as much as they coveted his rich and extensive kingdom. The measure of Faqir Azizuddin's success in protecting and promoting the interests of the Kingdom of Lahore must be the durability of the various treaties he was able to secure through his negotiating skill.

Trusting implicitly his good faith, he would set out with his whole army on distant expeditions, leaving only the Faqir with few orderlies for the protection of Lahore. Faqir Azizuddin was employed on several occasions on military service. In 1810, he was sent to annex Gujrat the country of Sahib Singh Bhangi. In 1819 he was sent as Envoy to the Bahawalpur Court, and was received there with great honour. He accompanied the expedition against Kangra; and in 1816, when Diwan Kirpa Ram fell into disgrace, Faqir Azizuddin was sent to receive from him the Fort of Phillour, of which he took charge, till it was placed under Sardar Desa Singh Majithia; and shortly before this he had assumed charge of Kapurthala, Jandiala, Hoshiarpur and the Trans- Satluj estate of Sardar Fateh Singh Ahluwalia, who had fled across the Satluj for British protection. In 1831, when Jahan Dad Khan had given up Attock to the Maharajah, he was sent with Sardar Mota Singh, to reinforce the garrison and to settle the district. In April 1831, Faqir Azizuddin in company of General Hari Singh Nalwa was sent to Simla on a complimentary visit to Lord William Bentinck. The envoys was received with great honour, and arrangement were made or a meeting between the Maharajah and the Governor-General, which took place at Rupar in October of the same year. In May 1835, he was present at Peshawar Valley when Amir Dost Mohammad Khan with a large army arrived from Kabul with the intention of recovering Peshawar from Maharajah Ranjit Singh.

Appendix

Faqir Azizuddin (Contd)

Faqir Azizuddin was sent as the principal envoy to the Afghan camp, and contrived to delude the Amir so completely that the Afghan army was almost surrounded by the Lahore army, during the progress of the negotiations, and had to retire to Kabul with all speed. The Maharajah was so pleased with the adroitness of the Faqir on this occasion that on his return to camp a general salute was ordered in his honour. In November 1838, when the British forces were being assembled for the Kabul campaign, the Maharajah visited Lord Auckland, the Governor- General, at Ferozepore, where the splendour of the scene even surpassed that the meeting at Rupar in 1831, which had been called the 'Meeting of the field of gold'. Shortly afterwards Lord Auckland paid the Maharajah a return visit at Lahore and Amritsar; and on both these occasions the Faqir had been foremost in his attentions, during the honours in the most graceful manner for his master, whose health was fast giving way. On the 27TH June 1839, Maharajah Ranjit Singh died. To the last Faqir Azizuddin, the most faithful of his servants, the most devoted of his friends, had remained by him; administering the medicine with his own hand, and telling him news from the various quarters which the Maharajah was anxious to hear. On the accession of Maharajah Kharak Singh, Faqir Azizuddin and Sardar Lehna Singh Majithia was sent to Simla to renew the engagements which had been entered into by Maharajah Ranjit Singh with the British Government. While at Simla, news arrived of the murder of Sardar Chet Singh, the Minister and favourite of Maharajah Kharak Singh, and the assumption power by Prince Nau Nihal Singh. The news caused some hesitation at Simla; but the treaty was eventually renewed, and the envoys returned to Lahore. The influence of the Faqir at the Court did not perceptibly decline during the reign Maharajah Kharak Singh. In May 1840, he was deputed by the Durbar to visit Mr. Clerk at Ferozepore, and he made arrangements for the visit which that officer paid the Maharajah at Lahore in the same month. In September of the same year, he was again sent on a confidential mission to Mr. Clerk to discuss the treatment of the Ghilzai and Barakzai chiefs, and the interpretation of the first article of the Tripartite Treaty of 1838, which had been somewhat infringed by the action taken Lahore forces in Yusafzai and Swat. In the intrigues which succeeded the deaths of Maharajah Kharak Singh and Prince Nau Nihal Singh, the Faqir did not take an active part. Raja Dian Singh indeed always to consult him; and they were both parties to the arrangement by which Mai Chand Kaur was appointed Regent during the pregnancy of Sahib Kaur, widow of Prince Nau Nihal Singh.

Appendix

Faqir Azizuddin (Contd)

Faqir Azizuddin was well aware that this arrangement could not be a successful one, and his sympathies were all with Prince Sher Singh; but his great influence in the Foreign Department, and regarding home politics he at this time rarely ventured an opinion in Durbar. When Sher Singh obtained the throne, he treated Faqir Azizuddin with greatest of kindness; and in March 1841 he sent him to Ludhiana to sound Mr. Clerk, the Agent of Governor- General, as to the willingness of the British Government to aid him in reducing his troops to obedience. Mr. Clerk was not averse to this idea. The Sikhs, before the experience of the Satluj campaign, were not considered formidable in the field, and Mr. Clerk thought that with the twelve thousand troops it was possible to reduce the Lahore army to obedience throughout the plain country of the Punjab; in case of resistance, to disperse and to establish Sher Singh firmly on the throne. The terms of such assistance would be rendered were the cession to the British Government of the Lahore territory south of the Satluj and the payment of forty lacks of rupees for the expense of the expedition. Faqir Azizuddin, with his colleague Munshi Din Mohammad, had no authority to conclude so important a transaction as this; and asked permission, as the matter could not be trusted to paper, to go to Lahore to consult the Maharajah Sher Singh, promising to return in eight days. He never returned. The Maharajah, inspite the revolt of the troops in Mandi, wrote to the Agent to say that he had suppressed all mutiny, and that the Lahore army, obedient and loyal. Sher Singh feared the British army, and once having occupied Lahore, would never again leave it. Faqir Azizuddin, who knew better the policy of the English Government, professed himself still anxious for its interference, and directed his son Shah Din, the Lahore agent at Ludhiana, to urge Mr. Clerk to renew the overtures made, and to send for Sardar Bawa Mahan Singh, a confidential servant of the Maharajah, to conduct the negotiations. But Mr. Clerk did not find it politic again to take the initiative and the scheme was wisely abandoned. About this time an accident befell Faqir Azizuddin, which it was feared would end fatally. He was seated in Durbar, at Shah Bilwal, next to Diwan Bishan Singh, whose sword, as he rose from his seat, wounded the Faqir severely in the leg. He fainted from loss of blood, and it was though that the lockjaw would come on. Gradually he recovered and this accident afforded him an excuse to attend the Durbar less frequently; for he had with the other Ministers, feared the abuse and excesses of the soldiery. In February 1842, Faqir Azizuddin was sent by the Maharajah to Makhu, on the south side of the Satluj to meet Mr. Clerk, who was proceeding to Lahore.

Appendix

Faqir Azizuddin (Contd)

He was on a mission of congratulation on the Maharajah's accession, and condolence on the death of Maharajah Kharak Singh. In December 1842, Sardar Lehna Singh Majithia was deputed by the Lahore Court to wait on Lord Ellenborough, who was present with the British army at Ferozepore. Through some misunderstanding, the Sardar expecting the Agent of the Governor-General to conduct him to the British camp remained in his tent, and the interview failed altogether to come off. Lord Ellenborough thinking the slight intentional demanded explanation. Faqir Azizuddin accordingly proceeded to Ferozepore, where a grand Durbar and review of both Sikh and the British army's were held; he accordingly proceeded to Ferozepore where a grand Durbar and review of both Sikh and the British army's were held. Faqir Azizuddin explained away the apparent discourtesy, and so pleased the Governor-General that he called in full Durbar 'the protector of the friendship of both States,' and taking from his pocket a gold watch presented it to him. Linked as he was so closely to the person of the Maharajah, it was perhaps inevitable that following the death of his patron, Faqir Azizuddin's own relevance and utility would diminish. Even though he was deputed by Maharajah Sher Singh to placate Lord Ellenborough after a diplomatic faux pas at Firozepur in 1842, and succeeded, it was clear that he could not repeat the scale of his earlier triumphs during the meetings he attended between Maharajah Ranjit Singh and Lord Bentinck (then Governor General) at Rupar in 1831 and Lord Auckland at Amritsar and later at Lahore in December 1838.. Azizuddin died on 3RD December 1845, unable to restrain the hot headed elements within the Lahore Durbar from a confrontation with the British. The words of a British administrator – Henry Lawrence – who arrived in the Punjab a year after Azizuddin's death could serve though as a fair epitaph to Azizuddin as a man and a diplomat: 'Step by step he retired from public service. Blind though he was, his other senses were little impaired and it was only because his advice was disregarded that he abandoned his post. His last act was to implore the return of the invading army. I can believe all this; it is in keeping with Faqir Azizuddin's character. He was the most honest and perhaps, the ablest of Ranjit Singh's advisers and was a well-wisher of both states.

Appendix

Faqir Shahdin

Faqir Shahdin, son of Faqir Azizuddin,, was the Lahore court's envoy with the British political agent at Ludhiana and later at Firozepur. Successive British political agents, C.M. Wade, Dr. Murray and George Russell Clerk, spoke of highly for his skill and wisdom. At Firozepur, he acted as the Maharajah's envoy and supply officer. He enjoyed the trust of both the Durbar and the British. In 1839, he was deputed to Mitthankot to supervise the Indus navigation trade on behalf of the Lahore government. Later he accompanied Major Mackeson to Amritsar to exhibit to the British agent the silk manufactures of the Lahore kingdom with a view to promoting export. All speaks highly of the discretion shown by Faqir Shahdin in public Life. The Lahore Durbar rewarded his services and he and his brother. Shahdin died at Lahore in 1842.

Faqir Chiraghdin

Faqir Chiraghdin son of Faqir Azizuddin was governor of Jasrota, a small principality in the Sivalik hills. Shortly afterwards he was placed in attendance on Prince Kharak Singh. In 1842, he succeeded his brother, Shahdin, as the Lahore ruler's envoy (vakil) at Firozepur and continued in the same position with the Council of Regency formed after the First Anglo-Sikh war under the treaty of Lahore of 16TH December 1846.. Chiraghdin died at Lahore in 1851.

Faqir Imamuddin

Faqir Imamuddin was the second son of Ghulam Muhiyddin. In 1808, the fort at Amritsar was rebuilt under the supervision of Faqir Imamuddin. The Maharajah gave it the name of Gobindgarh. Faqir Imamuddin was appointed Qiladar or garrison commander of the Fort. Capable and scholarly Faqir Imamuddin was entrusted with multifarious duties by the Maharajah. He virtually acted as the chief treasurer of the kingdom, authorizing payments on behalf of the Durbar and carrying out commercial transactions through cash and for the purchase of grain. The fort was made the repository of the Maharajah's treasures. With this, Faqir Imamuddin had charge of the magazine, arsenals and royal stables. Gobindgarh fort functioned both as a treasury as well as a jail. It was surrounded by big wall of unburnt bricks containing 8 towers and 2 big porches. A ditch, deep and wide, built of burnt bricks and lime ran around it. It had 20 guns of large calibre mounted on its ramparts. Eventually about 2,000 soldiers guarded it. He was also responsible for the maintenance of the fortifications of Amritsar city, and wellbeing of the people.

Appendix

Faqir Imamuddin (Contd)

Maharajah also allowed him to perform much service in the field; in one or two other campaigns, with a command of 500 horses. He also performed protocol duties on behalf of the Slate when foreign dignitaries arrived for visits. During the tortuous negotiations with Sir Charles Metcalfe that led up to the Anglo-Sikh Treaty of April 1809, both brothers Azizuddin and Imamuddin were omnipresent. In April 1827, he accompanied Diwan Moti Ram to Simla to wait on Lord Amherst with a mission sent by Maharajah Ranjit Singh. In March 1828, on behalf of the Maharajah, he called upon Lord Combermcre, the British Commander-in-Chief at Ludhiana. Contemporary chronicles describe Faqir Imamuddin as a devout Muslim and a learned man of his time. A person of proven integrity and political wisdom, he was one of the most devoted and loyal servants of the Sikh Durbar. Faqir Imamuddin died at Lahore on 5TH December 1847.

Faqir Tajuddin

When Faqir Tajuddin reached maturity, he helped his father, Faqir Imamuddin, to the command of Gobindgarh Fort. On 12TH December 1838, Faqir Imamuddin, accompanied by Faqir Tajuddin, to showed off the Gobindgarh Fort to Lord Auckland. It was a distinct honour, as Maharajah Ranjit Singh would never allow anybody not connected to him, to enter the fort. The Maharajah must have been pleased with the state of readiness at the fort, for on returning to Lahore, he sent Rs 500 as a mark of appreciation to Faqir Imamuddin and his son Tajuddin. The Maharajah breathed his last on the 27TH June 1839. Maharajah Kharak Singh succeeded to the throne of the Sikh Empire. As Maharajah Kharak Singh left for Lahore, Prince Nau Nihal Singh stayed behind to visit the Gobindgarh fort. He ordered Sardar Lehna Singh Majithia to take charge of the stores, and repairs of the fort, and all the papers relating to them, from Faqir Imamuddin and Faqir Tajuddin. Faqir Tajuddin was ordered to ascertain if anything had been embezzled. Misr Beli Ram was arrested brought before Nau Nihal Singh and asked to account for a valuable string of pearls and some daggers. Faqir Tajuddin was ordered to keep him in chains. Finally Beli Ram was released and restored to his old position. After the annexation of the kingdom in 1849, Lord Dalhousie, the Governor General, took keen personnel interest in taking possession of the jewels and relics in the Toshakhana. The Toshakhana were either taken over by the British officials in India or auctioned to public. On 19TH July 1840, Faqir Tajuddin was instructed to remove the marble from the pavilion at Rambagh near Amritsar.

Appendix

Faqir Tajuddin (Contd)

At the death of Maharajah Kharak Singh, on 5TH November 1840 and Prince Nau Nihal Singh on 6TH November 1840, there was a tussle between the widow of Prince Nau Nihal Singh and Sher Singh for the throne. By the 19TH, the battle was over and Maharajah Sher Singh succeeded to the throne. The next few days witnessed a descent into carnage and chaos, as Sher Singh's troops went on rampage and precipitated a collapse of order in the city. The unrest at Lahore ignited a mutiny in Gobindgarh Fort. The troops in the fort rebelled, killed their officers, and then sealed the gate. Faqir Tajuddin happened to be in Lahore and therefore escaped. Eventually Faqir Imamuddin became blind and retired in Amritsar. He was represented at the Lahore court by his son Faqir Tajuddin.

Faqir Nuruddin

Faqir Nuruddin the youngest brother of Faqir Azizuddin was one of the prominent Muslim courtiers serving the Sikh sovereign Maharajah Ranjit Singh and his successors. In 1801, when Ranjit Singh assumed the title of Maharajah, Faqir Nuruddin was appointed hakim or physician to the court and put in charge of dispensaries in the city of Lahore. He also performed protocol duties on behalf of the State. Foreign travellers such as Moor craft, Jacquemont, Burnes, Wolff, Hugel and Fane, whom he received on behalf of the Maharajah or whom he otherwise met on State occasions, have paid tributes to his outstanding abilities. Hugel, for instance, described him as "an upright yet versatile courtier, who has acquired the respect of the natives and the strangers." Nuruddin was indeed a versatile man who was entrusted by Maharajah Ranjit Singh with diverse responsibilities such as the administration of the capital, superintendence of artillery stores, and commissariat arrangements for visiting dignitaries. He was at times also assigned to important administrative responsibilities outside the capital. In June 1810, he took Wazirabad and was soon after appointed governor of Gujrat. In the beginning of 1817, he was sent to settle the Ramgarhia territories seized by Ranjit Singh towards the end of 1816. In 1827, he went to Kapurthala on a mission to restore normal relations after a temporary estrangement between Ranjit Singh and the local chief, Fateh Singh Ahluwalia. Even after the death of Maharajah Ranjit Singh, Faqir Nuruddin retained his position of eminence at the court. At the conclusion of the first Anglo-Sikh war, he was one of the signatories to the Treaty of Lahore, 9 March 1846, and to the Articles of Agreement, 11 March 1846.

Appendix

Faqir Nuruddin (Contd)

He was appointed a member of the Council of Regency formed, under the treaty of 16 December 1846, to conduct the administration of the country during the minority of Maharajah Duleep Singh. The Council ceased to exist with the annexation of the Punjab to the British dominions on 29 March 1849. Nuruddin's jagirs were confirmed to him by the British. Nuruddin died at Lahore on 26TH March 1852.

Shaikh Ghulam Muhiyddin

Shaikh Ghulam Muhiyddin, who rose to be governor of Kashmir in Sikh times, was the son of Shaikh Ujala, a munshi or accountant in the service of Sardar Bhup Singh of Hoshiarpur. At a young age, Shaikh Ghulam Muhiyddin took up service under Diwan Moti Ram, the governor of Kashmir, later shifting to Lahore. He exhibited great diplomatic skill when in 1823, under Maharajah Ranjit Singh's instructions, he persuaded Sardar Muhammad `Azim Khan of Kabul, who had marched upon Peshawar, to retire without firing a shot. In 1827, Kirpa Ram, Diwan Moti Ram's son, took him to Kashmir upon his appointment as governor of the province. After four years, however, Kirpa Ram was recalled, and Shaikh Ghulam Muhiyddin returned with him to Lahore where, according to some sources, he was subjected to punishment for his cruel treatment of the people of Kashmir. But within a year he returned to Kashmir as a deputy to Prince Sher Singh who had been sent as the new governor of that territory. Again the Shaikh was reported to have followed a repressive policy which, coupled with the outbreak of famine, made the lot of the people extremely miserable. The Maharajah recalled Shaikh Ghulam Mohyuddin, and inflicted a heavy fine upon him besides confiscating all of his property and the hidden wealth which he had amassed at Hoshiarpur. The Shaikh remained out of favour with the Durbar for some time but eventually found a patron in Bhai Ram Singh who helped him to secure service with Prince Nau Nihal Singh. Nau Nihal Singh took him to Peshawar, and entrusted to him the management of his financial affairs. In 1839, he was appointed governor of the Jalandhar Doab and in April 1841, after Sher Singh's accession to the throne, governor of Kashmir. In February 1845, Ghulam Mohyuddin made overtures to the British government with a view to transferring his allegiance to them, but died soon afterwards and was buried in the Khanaqah of Shaikh Hamza Makkhum, Hari Parbat, Srinagar

Appendix

Shaikh Imamuddin Khan

Shaikh Imamuddin Khan succeeded his father, Shaikh Ghulam Mohyuddin, as governor of the Sikh province of Kashmir in 1845, had earlier served under Kanwar Nau Nihal Singh in the Derajat and had in 1840 assisted his father in the campaign against Mandi. In April 1841, when a mutiny occurred in Kashmir, Maharajah Sher Singh ordered his father, Sheikh Ghulam Mohyuddin, and then governor of the Jalandhar Doab, to proceed to Kashmir to take charge of the province and restore order. Shaikh Imamuddin was then appointed governor of the Jalandhar Doab. When in September 1843, Wazir Hira Singh had Bhai Gurmukh Singh and Misr Belt Ram arrested, he handed them over to Shaikh Imamuddin Khan for custody. Shaikh Imamuddin Khan kept them in the stables near his house in Lahore. Within a week of their confinement, both of them were put to death at Hira Singh's orders. Shaikh Imamuddin was also involved by Hira Singh in the plot to destroy the Derah of Baba Bir Singh of Naurarigabad which fell within his jurisdiction. During the insurrection in Kashmir in 1844 when Shaikh Ghulam Mohyuddin asked for reinforcements from the Lahore Durbar, Shaikh Imamuddin Khan was sent with a contingent to help him. On the death of his father, Imamuddin took over as governor of Kashmir, with the title of Aminul Mulk Jarig Bahadur. His fortune, however, declined with the conclusion of the Anglo Sikh treaty of 16TH March 1846, according to which Kashmir was to be handed over to Gulab Singh. The arrangement was resented by Raja Lal Singh, minister to the Lahore Durbar, who in a private communication instructed Shaikh Imamuddin Khan to obstruct it. Shaikh Imamuddin Khan was ultimately overcome by the intervention of the British under Major Henry Lawrence to whom he surrendered. He was tried at Lahore by a commission comprising Major General Littler, Lt Colonel Lawrence, Lt Colonel Goldie, Mr Currie and Mr Lawrence, but was exonerated when he produced original letters written by Raja Lal Singh. His property in Lahore, which was earlier confiscated, was restored to him. In June 1848, Shaikh Imamuddin Khan went at the head of 2,000 troops to assist Herbert Edwards in the reduction of Multan, and succeeded in arresting Narain Singh, commander of Diwan Mul Raj. He was later rewaded with the title of Nawab and Bahadur, together with a pension of Rs 11,600 and confirmation of his jagir of Rs 8,400. Again in 1857, he helped the British raise two contingents of cavalry to fight on their behalf in Delhi. He died in March 1859 at the early age of 40 and was buried in the vicinity of the tomb of the famous saint, Data Ganj Bakhsh, at Lahore.

Appendix

Shamasuddin Khan

Kasur was conquered and taken possession of by Maharajah Ranjit Singh in 1807. Shamasuddin Khan was also for many years a servant of the Mamdot Chief, and attendant Lahore Court as his vakil; and for some fault he was summarily dismissed, and became afterwards the confidential agent of Raja Lal Singh. The position he held at the time of the Satluj Campaign, and was the medium of communication between Raja Lal Singh and the British officers. On the 12TH December 1845, when the Lahore army was crossing the Satluj, Raja Lal Singh sent Shamasuddin Khan to Captain Nicholson at Ferozepore to assure him that both he and the Maharani were the friends of the British, and desired nothing more than the Lahore army might be destroyed; that he would keep his force back two days from joining the regulars; and he had marched that day back to Asal, and the next day would march to Harike. To this Nicholson that he would report the matter; that whether Lal Singh's horse joined the regular army or not, was matter of indifference, as the British could thrash one or both with equal case. The next day Raja Lal Singh proposed delaying the army under the pretence of making a bridge at Har ke and discovering fords. On 16TH December, Nicholson, hearing that the Governor-General and Commander-in- Chief were approaching by way of Mudki, sent for Shamasuddin Khan, who stated as before, that his master was well disposed towards the British, that he had influence with certain brigades which he would march, with all his own cavalry, to attack the Governor-General, if the British Force at Ferozepore would attack the remainder. Nicholson said if the Raja had the influence he asserted he would act and not talk, and that his good intentions would be seen his marching as he proposed. On the 18TH Shamasuddin Khan came and reported that the Raja had marched to Ferozeshah, and Nicholson gave him a letter to Major Broadfoot, which it is believed, was delivered to that officer as the troops were going into action at Ferozeshah on the afternoon of 21ST, as it was found in his pocket when his body was brought it in on the 22ND. On the 19TH December, the day after the battle of Mudki, Raja Lal Singh sent a messenger to Major Broadfoot to express his desire to be of any service; but the Major considered that the only object of the Raja was to ascertain the effect of the action of the previous day, and sent him with the guard beyond pickets. Nothing more was heard of the Raja Lal Singh till two days before the battle of Sabraon.

Appendix

Shamasuddin Khan (Contd)

Raja Lal Singh had been hidden in a dry ditch during the battle of Ferozeshah, but gave on that he was wounded, and retired to Amritsar, where according to popular report; he concealed himself in an oven from the fury of the soldiers who swore to murder him. But through the remonstrations of the Maharani he joined the army about the middle of January; and on the 8TH February he sends Shamasuddin Khan to Major H. Lawrence with the plan of the entrenchments and a detailed account of the number and disposition of the Lahore troops. After the first Anglo-Sikh war when Major Lawrence was appointed Resident at Lahore, Shamasuddin Khan was made agent of the Durbar, to communicate its wishes and sentiments to the Resident. In 1848 he did good service, and a donation was granted to him and after the Second Anglo-Sikh war. At the annexation of the Punjab to British India, his Jagir was resumed, he received a life pension. He lived at Kasur and died in 1868.

Nawab Ghulam Ali Khan

On the death of Ghulam Muhiddin in 1841, the cheifship reverted to Nawab Ghulam Ali Khan. In 1843, the Nawab furnished a party of 50 Sowars in suppressing the disturbances at Kaithal. The men of his contingent remained at the disposition of Sir Henry Lawrence for two months, and their services were duly acknowledged in a letter of thanks to the Nawab. He was again forward in assisting during the First Anglo-Sikh war with carriage and supplies. Nawab Ghulam Ali Khan died in 1849.

Commander Sultan Mahmud Khan

Sultan Mahmud Khan, son of General Ghaus Khan, was a commander of a section of heavy artillery during the regime of Maharajah Ranjit Singh. After the death of General Ghaus Khan in 1814, although the chief command of the artillery was entrusted to Misr Divan Chand, the battery under the former's command was placed in the charge of Sultan Mahmud. Sultan Mahmud accompanied Maharajah Ranjit Singh on his expeditions against Multan and Kashmir. After the reorganization of the Sikh army into Brigades in 1835, when a horse battery was attached to each brigade, the heavy siege train continued to be commanded by General Sultan Mahmud as a separate corps. The Topkhanai Sultan Mahmud was present on (lie historic occasion of the Ranjit Singh William Bentinck meeting at Ropar in October 1831. Sultan Mahmud was of exceedingly intemperate habits, and his drunkenness brought him more than once into trouble with his master, but he was a useful officer and was generally treated with favour.

Appendix

Commander Sultan Mahmud Khan (Contd)
When Nau Nihal Singh secured power, Sultan Mahmud lost his command and was sent in charge of a troop of artillery, under General Ventura, to Mandi in the hills, but on the accession of Maharajah Sher Singh he was reinstated and his son Sultan Ahmad Ali Khan was made a Colonel. In 1843, both father and son were engaged in the assault on the Fort of Lahore which had been taken possession of by the Sandhanvalia after the murder of Sher Singh; and, for their services on this occasion, they received additional jagirs from the Dogra Raja Hira Singh. Sultan Mahmud was then sent in command of the artillery to Hazara where he remained until 1848 when both he and his son were moved to the Derajat. At the outbreak of the second Anglo Sikh war, Sultan Mahmud as well as his son, Sultan Ahmad `Ali Khan, joined the rebel Sikh forces at Ramnagar and fought against the English throughout the war. After the annexation of the Punjab, Jagirs of Sultan Mahmud were resumed but he received a life pension of Rs 600 which he held until his death in 1859, at Bharoval, his ancestral village in Amritsar district.

General Ilahi Baksh 1848
He was present at many of the battles during the First Anglo-Sikh War and Second Anglo-Sikh War. He played a key role at the Battle of Chillianwalla, one of the bloodiest British battles fought in India. Three days after the battle, Ilahi Bakhsh defected to the British. Ilahi Baksh gave the British valuable information about the Sikh army. The defection of Bakhsh dealt a major blow to the Sikhs, and they capitulated to the British the following month at Gujrat.

Commander Sikander Khan 1848
Commander Sikander Khan succeeded his father, General Ilahi Baksh, as Chief of the Artillery in the Lahore Army, and later inherited substantial properties in Lahore.

Ali Yar Khan 1848
Ali Yar Khan made useful to Edwards before the outbreak of the Second Anglo-Sikh war. He placed his son Muzaffar Khnn under Edward's orders in command of a body of horse of his own raising .Muzaffar Khan afterwards held the inner Bannu Fort with Malik Fateh Khan Tiwana whom Edwards loft in charge of the district when obliged to proceed in all haste to Multan. Fateh Khan was killed in trying to cut through the Sikh soldiers who hemmed him; but Muzaffar Khan surrendered and was carried prisoner to the main army at Gujrat, where he was allowed to purchase his liberty

Appendix

Lahore Army

The Lahore Army's overdependence on artillery became apparent as the battles unfolded. All the battles were planned and fought in the defensive positions under the cover of guns. It was at Gujrat that for the first time the Lahore Army was outgunned because their General Illahi Baksh and the leading officers went over to the British

The Artillery

The reader may note that many wholly Punjabi Muslim batteries of the Baksh's and Fazal Ali's troops of Horse Artillery of the Khalsa of the old Sikh Durbar, which was re-designated as No.2 Battery raised on 18 May 1849..Similarly the No. 3 Battery raised at Dera Ghazi Khan by Lieutenant Mc Neill of the Bengal Artillery was also largely composed of ex Punjabi Muslim and some Sikh Horse artillery men from the old Khalsa Sikh artillery. Thus the Pakistani artillery which traces its origins to these batteries carries the fine Khalsa traditions.

Sikh Infantryman

Sources

B Robina Shoeb, Anum Iftikhar and Muhammad Hameed Post-Maharajah Ranjit Singh Period an Essay
Beachey, Ray. (1990) The Warrior Mullah, The Horn Aflame. Bellow Publishing: London.
Bhagat Singh. (1990) Maharajah Ranjit Singh and His Times Delhi
Caroe, Olaf. (1964) The Pathans. Macmillan and Co. Ltd: London.
Chupia, B.R. (1969) Kingdom of the Punjab, Hoshiarpur, India
Cook, H.C.B. The Sikh War, 1845-49. London: Leo Cooper, 1975
Cunningham, Joseph Davy. (1966)A History of the Sikhs: Delhi: Chand & Co.
Deol, G.S. (1972) Banda Bahadur, Jalandhar.
Fakir S. Aijazuddin (2015) The Resourceful Fakirs; Three Rivers Publishers; Delhi
Fauja Singh Bajwa (1964) Military System of the Sikhs; Motilal Banarsidass; Delhi
Gopal Singh. (1979) A History of the Sikh People; Delhi
Griffin, Lepel. (1909) Chiefs and Families of Note in the Punjab, Lahore
Griffin, Sir Lepel. (1890) The Punjab Chiefs. Lahore.
Gupta, Hari Ram. (1979) History of the Sikhs, vol. III. Delhi.
Gupta, Hari Ram. (1982) History of the Sikhs, vol. IV. Delhi.
Harbans Singh. (1980) Maharajah Ranjit Singh; Delhi
Harbans Singh. (1983) The Heritage of the Sikhs. Delhi.
Harbans Singh. (1995) The Encyclopaedia of Sikhism, Patiala
Herbert, Christopher. (1978) The Great Mutiny. Allan Lane: London
Irvine, W. (1922) Later Mughals; London
J.D. Cunningham. (1849) A History of the Sikhs; John Murray.
Khushwant Singh. (1962) Ranjit Singh: Maharajah of the Punjab 1780-1839. Bombay.
Khushwant Singh. (1963) A History of the Sikhs, vol. I. Princeton.
Latif, Syed Muhammad. (1961) History of the Panjab. Delhi.
Robson, Brian. (1986) The Road To Kabul. Arms and Armour Press: London.
Singh, Amarinder. (2010) The Last Sunset. Roli Books: New Delhi.
Singh, Harbans. (2004) The Encyclopaedia of Sikhs. Punjabi University: Patiala.
Sinha, N.K. (1933) Ranjit Singh. Calcutta.

Index

Abdulla Khwaja 31
Afghanistan 16
Ahluwalia Misl 55
Ahmad Khan 143
Ahmad Yar Khan 109
Ahmed Khan 99
Ahmed Shah Abdali 45
Ahmed Yar Khan Tiwana 130
Ajit Singh Sandhawalia 155
Alauddin 17
Alexander of Macedon 11
Aliani Laghari 113
Allahdad Khan 118
Allahyar Khan 103
Allayar 23
Amritsar 83
Ancestry of Ranjit Singh 62
Anglo-Sikh Relations 85
Anglo-Sikh Treaty of 1809, 93
Anglo-Sikh Treaty of 1832, 137
Anglo-Sikh Treaty of 1840, 153
Anglo-Sikh Treaty of 1806, 87
Army of Indus 145
Army of Maharajah Ranjit Singh 147
Artillery 78
Assad Khan 109
Attar Khan 84
Attock 102
Ayub Shah 128
Baba Sain Mir 2
Babak 30
Bahalpur State 138
Bambas 100
Banda Singh Bahadur 38
Bannu 129
Battle of Aliwal 178
Battle of Attock 104
Battle of Eminabad 43
Battle of Ferozeshah 172
Battle of Hasan Abad 104
Battle of Mudki 166
Battle of Panipat 48
Battle of Sabraon 189
Begum Gul Bahar 137
Bhai Mardana 20
Bhangi Misl 55
Bhera 83
Bhikhan Khan 35
Bhimber 98
British Army in 1845, 162
British at the battle of Mudki 164
Budha Khan 138
Cavalry 77
Chatar Singh Attariwala 200
Chaudhry Qadir Buksh 84
Chhota Ghallughara 44
Chib Chiefs 97
Cis-Satluj States 93
Clara Rosalind Kaur Dhesi 6
Colonel Imam Shah 196
Colonel Shaikh Basawan 143, 146
Commandant Ibadullah 121
Commandant Mian Baksh 196
Commander Fateh Khan 168
Commander Sultan Khan 107, 155
Contents 3
Court factions 152
Dal Khalsa 42
Dallewala Misl 57
Datarpur 95
Death of Guru Arjan Dev 26
Death of Ranjit Singh 145
Dedication 6
Dera Ghazi Khan 116
Derah Ismail Khan 121
Dhund Tribe 142
Emperor Ranjit Singh 6
Equality 51
Faiz Ali Khan 117

Index

Fatah Khan 141
Fateh Khan Tiwana 113
Firozuddin 106
Firozuddin Khan 103
Forces skipped the First Anglo-Sikh War 197
Forward 4
Frontier 195
General Mian Ghouse Khan 107
General Said Beg 34
General Sham Singh Attariwala 194
Genghis Khan 15
Ghani Khan 36
Ghiyasuddin Tughlaq 18
Ghulam Muhammad Khan 130
Gobindgarh Fort 85
Gujrat 95
Gupta Dynasty 14
Guru Amar Das 22
Guru Angad Dev 22
Guru Arjan Dev 24
Guru Gobind Singh 32
Guru Har Krishan 30
Guru Har Rai 30
Guru Hargobind 27
Guru Nanak Dev 19
Guru Ram Das 24
Guru Tegh Bahadur 31
Hafiz Sarbuland Khan 109 121
Hakim Muhammad Ali Khan 94
Hazara 117
Hill States 77
Iltutmish 17
Indo-Bactrian kingdom, 12
Indus Valley Civilization 8
Infantry 77
Introduction 5
Inyat Khan 99
Islamic Invasions 15
Ismail Khan 195

Jagirdari Cavalry 77
Jamaluddin Khan 134
Jammu 78
Jamrud 141
Jamshaid Khan 36
Jan Muhammad Chattha 72
Jasrota 90
Jaswan 108
Jhang 82
John Brown 129
Kakas 100
Kalu & Bara 62
Kangra 94
Kanhaiya Misl 57
Karora Singhia Misl 57
Kashmir 1812, 101
Kashmir 1812, 105
Kashmir 1814, 106
Kashmir 1819, 115
Kasur 78, 89
Kattu Shah 29
Kazi Fazl Ahmad 129
Kazi Ghulam Muhammad 105
Khairuddin Khan 156
Khan Muhammad Khan 84
Khattars 84
Khewra 81
King Porus 10
King Vardhana 14
Kulu 95
Kushan Empire 13
Lahore 48, 72
Lahore army 1809, 94
Lahore Army in 1845, 158
Lahore Army in 1845, 164
Lahore Durbar 151
Lahore Forces at the battle of Mudki 164
Lahore forces in 1799, 75
Lahore Forces in 1821, 122

Index

Lahore Forces in 1831, 132
Lahore forces in 1839, 144
Langar Khan 119
Langar Khan 155
Laurie Michael Singh Dhesi 6
Lieutenant Herbert Edwards 199
Lieutenant General Dhaliwal 4
Lodhi 18
Lund Tribe 116
Maharajah Kharak Singh 153
Maharajah Nau Nihal Singh 154
Maharajah Ranjit Singh 74
Maharajah Sher Singh 155
Maharani Chand Kaur 154
Mahmud of Ghazni 16
Makhe Khan 118
Makkhum Shah Mahmud 112
Malik Baksh Khan 120
Malik Fateh Khan 138
Malik Fateh Khan Tiwana 139
Malik Yar Khan Tiwana 123
Maliks of Kala Bagh 123
Mandi State 100
Mankera 121
Master of the Misl 69
Mazari Tribe 114
Mazhar Ali 108
Mehrgarh Culture 8
Mian Ghouse Khan 89
Mian Jamal 26
Mian Mir 26
Mian Qadir Bakhsh 118
Mir Mannu 47
Mirza Ghulam Murtaza 111, 156
Misldars 43
Mitha Khan 195
Mitha Tiwana 101
Mohammad Ghori 17
Moran Sarkar 79
Moran Tawaif Masjid 80

Multan 1803, 84
Multan 1807, 89
Multan 1810, 97
Multan 1810, 99
Multan 1818, 111
Multan 1848, 199
Mumtaz 35
Muslim Nawabs 76
Nakai Misl 58
Nawab Ghulam Ali Khan 196
Nawab Kapur Singh 41
Nawab Khan 106
Nawab Sher Muhammad Khan 39
Nihang Khan 35
Nishananvali Misl 58
Nowshera 124
Occupation of Lahore 51
Occupation of Sarhind 51
Painda Khan 28,128
Parthian Empire 13
Peshawar 112
Phulkian Misl 60
Pir Bhikham Shah 33
Pir Budhu Shah 33
Punch 116
Punjab 7
Qazi Ruknuddin 21
Rai Bular 21
Rai Muhammad Khan 131
Raja Ali Khan 108
Raja Azimullah Khan 156
Raja Muhammad Akbar Khan Chib 96
Raja Raheem Ullah Khan 102, 195
Raja Sansar Chand 81
Ramgharia Misl 59
Ramnagar 68
Rao Holkar 87
Saadat Khan 82
Sadik Muhammad Khan 131

Index

Sahiwal 98
Saifullah Khan 111
Sansar Chand 85
Sarbat Khalsa 40
Sardar Budha Singh 62
Sardar Charhat Singh 63
Sardar Jassa Singh Ahluwalia 42
Sardar Kaura Khan 115
Sardar Mahan Singh 65
Sardar Mitha Khan 117
Sardar Naudh Singh 63
Sardar Ranjit Singh 68
Sarkar-i-Khalsa 74
Sayyid Ahmad Khan 135
Sayyid Imamuddin Hussaini 72
Scythian 13
Shah Husain 23
Shah Mahmud 100
Shah Shuja 97
Shah Zaman 98
Shah Zaman's first invasion 69
Shah Zaman's second Invasion 69
Shah Zaman's third invasion 70
Shah Zaman's fourth invasion 71
Shahid Misl 58
Shaikh Farid 31
Shaikh Ghulam Muhiyddin 118
Shamasuddin Khan 165
Shamir Khan 108
Sher Singh Attariwala 200
Sikh Gurus 19
Sikh Jathas 40
Sikh Misls 55
 Sikh Misls 76
Sikhs and Afghans 54
Sikhs and Mughals 52
Sindh 15
Singhpuria Misl 55
Sir Harry Smiths 165

This Book

After the success of his previous books dealing with Sikh Soldier, Mr Dhesi turns his attention to the broad sweep of conflicts into which the Punjabi fighter has thrown himself. From the rise of the first Punjabi people, through Mughal and Afghan tyranny, the flowering of Sikh independence under Maharajahh Ranjit Singh. On his death in 1839, Maharajah Ranjit Singh passed on to his successors a prosperous, peaceful and tolerant Punjab. For 40 years he had ruled the Punjab with a balance of ambition and patience. His ambition expanded the Khalsa Empire from Dera Ghazi Khan to Peshawar and Kashmir and his patience won him the support of the Punjabi warriors. His foresight kept the British away from the Punjab and his fair conduct earned him the allegiance and loyalty of the Muslim majority in the Punjab. Despite the intricate socio-political history of the two communities, he skilfully handled the relationship between Sikhs and Muslims. The Faqir Brothers and other Muslims held portfolios of foreign and internal affairs, medicine, science and the army under the Sarkar Khalsa. The Faqir Brothers were the most prominent among them. They continued their service to the Lahore Durbar as advisors on various matters, especially foreign affairs and medicine and so did the gallant Muslim soldiers. Yet within a few years of his death, all the hard-earned and cherished victories of the 'Lion of the Punjab' were wasted by his unscrupulous successors, and subsequently the Sikh kingdom fell to the British. Many a Muslim soldiers made the supreme sacrifice in the defence of their homeland. Mr Dhesi mixes the big picture with the small detail to create another compelling portrait of the valour of the fighting men from the Punjab.

Narindar Singh Dhesi

Narindar Singh Dhesi was born in 1940 at Eldoret in Kenya, where his father had migrated from the Punjab. He moved to England in 1957 and joined the British Army. After leaving the armed forces in 1964, he worked in the building and construction industry. He is married with four children and living in retirement at Southend on Sea, England. He is the author of numerous books on Sikh Soldier i.e. *Sikh Soldier: Battle Honours (ISBN 978184574891) Sikh Soldier: Gallantry Awards (ISBN 9781845749057)Sikh Soldier: Policing the Empire (ISBN 9781781519851)Sikh Soldier: Warriors and Generals (ISBN 978783310234)Sikh Soldier: At War.(9788183312351) Sikh Soldier: Forgotten Regiments. (9781783313525)Sikh Soldier: The Officer Corps. (9781783314638) Pakistan Armed Forces Gallantry Awards and Muslims and Sarkar-i-Khalsa.* They are available from the Naval and Military Press.

Muslim Artilleryman of Sarkar-i-Khalsa